EASTERN PHILOSOPHY: KEY READINGS

Oliver Leaman

ROUTLEDGE
Taylor & Francis Group

London and New York

First published 2000
by Routledge
11 New Fetter Lane, London EC4P 4EE

Simultaneously published in the USA and Canada
by Routledge
29 West 35th Street, New York, NY 10001

Routledge is an imprint of the Taylor & Francis Group

© 2000 Oliver Leaman

Typeset in Bembo by Keystroke, Jacaranda Lodge,
Wolverhampton
Printed and bound in Great Britain by
T J International Ltd, Padstow, Cornwall

British Library Cataloguing in Publication Data
A catalogue record for this book is available from the British Library

Library of Congress Cataloging in Publication Data
A catalogue record for this book has been requested

ISBN 0–415–17357–4 (hbk)
ISBN 0–415–17358–2 (pbk)

In fond memory of Catherine Tanner

CONTENTS

PREFACE

The whole concept of 'Eastern' philosophy is rather an artificial one, since there are difficult issues in defining where 'East' starts and ends. Some of the thinkers included here operated pretty far in the 'West' (ibn Rushd, for example, spent his life in Spain and North Africa). I decided to include Islamic philosophy since much of it took place and continues to be important in what is clearly the Asian world. On the other hand, a good deal of 'Western' philosophy is an important part of the philosophical curriculum in much of Asia today, and it could then be argued that this should also be classified as Eastern philosophy. I certainly would not want to argue that there is anything specifically different about Eastern as compared with Western philosophy, although there have been arguments which have gone in this direction. The cultural context in which different philosophical traditions arose clearly mark them in an important way, but many of the issues which different traditions discuss are remarkably similar to each other. I have taken Eastern philosophy to include Islamic, Zoroastrian, Chinese, Japanese, Tibetan, Korean and Indian philosophies, and I have selected here a sample from all these traditions.

Eastern philosophy, however that is defined, is a very substantial group of systems of thought, and we have only skimmed the surface here of its richness and diversity. Each of the terms which is given an entry is in itself a highly developed concept within a particular type of philosophy, or philosophies, and there are shelves in libraries on each such term. There is no way that this book could be anything more than indicative at best. I have had to exclude a lot of important terms because I wanted to allow those terms which do appear to have sufficient length to demonstrate a flavour of what they can do.

The point of this book is to make available a sample of interesting arguments and claims by a variety of philosophical traditions which will be relatively unfamiliar to many readers. The book will not have achieved its aim if readers stop here, but the hope is that it will whet the appetite for more detailed discussion of at least some of the issues raised here. It could be usefully read together with my *Key Concepts of Eastern Philosophy*, which explains the leading ideas which occur in these key texts. I hope that readers will experience at least to a degree the excitement and fascination with Eastern philosophy which I feel. The days of parochialism in philosophy have surely now come to an end and we should open ourselves to some understanding of the vast scope of philosophy throughout the world. Of course one cannot specialize in everything but one does not have to specialize all the time either. Whatever area of philosophy is our primary interest can only be enriched by being aware of the wider context in which world philosophy itself takes place.

Readers will notice that there are a variety of different styles of transliteration for the foreign terms, and I did consider initially changing all such terms to a single style for the entire text. I decided in the end not to do this, since readers who continue to explore this area of thought will find a variety of styles of transliteration and they will have to cope with this and not be put off by it in their study of relevant translations and commentaries. I have added at the end of the book a glossary of terms and persons, giving the variety of styles in which each term has been presented in our passages and the approximate pronunciation in simplified form. For the latter I have used the same system as the Routledge *Key Concepts in Eastern Philosophy*. Readers should be aware that there are a variety of ways of representing the languages which are represented in this book, and these are all represented here. The glossary is designed to resolve difficulties which might arise in the mind of the reader, and also provides some brief information about the key figures who are mentioned.

Some of the passages I have selected are easier to understand than others. I considered whether all the passages should be on the same sort of level of difficulty, and initially I thought they should. After all, this is very much an introductory text for non-specialists, designed to introduce the topic to those without much background in the area. On reflection this seemed too restrictive, since it fell into the danger of representing Eastern philosophy as being rather unsophisticated, and nothing could be further from the truth. So some of the passages here are harder than others, and some also present fairly basic information about aspects of the relevant religions. I have introduced many of the extracts, where some initial discussion might be helpful.

This is not a guide to Eastern religions, but it is important that some basic information is supplied on the religious basis of many of the philosophies since otherwise many of the arguments will remain mysterious. I do not want to assume that readers have any background in philosophy or religious studies, and have selected passages accordingly. On the other hand, many of the concepts which are discussed are complex, and readers are invited to follow these up further if, like me, they are intrigued and perplexed by them.

Readers will notice that under each heading there are only a few extracts, or in some cases just one. They should not assume that the absence of any extracts from one of the Eastern philosophical traditions means that they had nothing to say on that topic. Quite the reverse is always the case. Yet choices had to be made and much has had to be excluded. I have often selected commentaries on thinkers and ideas rather than presenting the original texts in translation, and this is because the original texts are often not easy to understand without knowing a great deal about the context. Where possible I have included original texts in translation, and the secondary literature which I have used bring out some of the controversies which exist within Eastern philosophy and its interpretation.

Cross references are indicated where appropriate after each text. Some terms are so ubiquitous (e.g. Mahayana, God) that they do not generally occur in the cross references. Other terms are so much part and parcel of Eastern philosophy itself (e.g. Buddhism, Hinduism) that they do not have separate entries of their own, but occur throughout most of the entries in the book.

I should like to thank those, in particular my students and friends, who have helped me sift through different passages to be included and who have listened to me worrying about what should go in and what left out. The publisher's reader made some very helpful comments also. I must also thank the publishers and authors for permitting me to use their work. Compiling a collection of passages is a rather strange activity. One is neither an author nor an editor. When one starts it seems like a rather simple task, just a matter of adapting to a particular purpose the hard work and scholarship of many thinkers and their translators. But life as a parasite is not as easy as it might seem, since there are so many difficult decisions to be taken, and it seems wrong to select one passage as compared with another. But choices had to be made, and I hope that readers will generally concur with the choices which were made.

Oliver Leaman
Liverpool, November 1998

ACKNOWLEDGEMENTS

I should like to thank the following publishers and/or authors for giving permission for the use of the passages included in the volume. I have made every effort to contact the holders of rights, but if there is anyone who has been missed I do apologize and suggest that they contact the publishers.

Abe, M. (1985) *Zen and Western Thought*, Basingstoke: Macmillan

R. Allinson (ed), *Understanding the Chinese Mind*, Hong Kong: Oxford University Press, 1989

Aurobindo (1987) *The Essential Aurobindo*, ed. R. McDermott, New York: Lindisfarne. Used by permission of Lindisfarne Books, Hudson, NY 12534 USA.

Averroes (1976) *On the Harmony of Religion and Philosophy*, trans. G. Hourani, by permission of Luzac Oriental

Basham, A. (1951) *History and Doctrines of the Ajivikas: A Vanished Indian Religion* Delhi: Motilal Banarsidass

Biderman, S. (1982) 'A "constitutive" God – an Indian suggestion', *Philosophy East and West 32*: 425–37 copyright University of Hawaii Press

Carr, D. (1997) 'Sankaracarya' in *Companion Encyclopedia of Asian Philosophy*, ed. I. Mahalingam and B. Carr, London: Routledge, 189–210: 198–9

Chan Wing-tsit (1963) *A Sourcebook in Chinese Philosophy* Princeton: Princeton University Press. Copyright © 1963 renewed by 1991 Princeton University Press, reprinted by permission of Princeton University Press

Cheng, Chung-Ying (1989) 'Chinese Metaphysics as Non-Metaphysics: Confucian and Daoist Insights into the Nature of Reality', in Allinson *op. cit.* 167–208

Chin, A-P and Freeman, M. *Tai Chen on Mencius: Explorations in Words and Meaning*, London: Yale University Press

Chuang Tzu (1968) *The Complete Works of Chuang Tzu*, trans. B. Watson. From *The Complete Works of Chuang Tzu* tr. B. Watson © 1968, Columbia University Press. Reprinted with the permission of the publisher

Collins, S. (1982) *Selfless Persons: Imagery and Thought in Theravada Buddhism*, Cambridge: Cambridge University Press

Confucius (1993) *The Analects* translated with an introduction and notes by R. Dawson, Oxford: World's Classics, Oxford University Press. Reprinted by permission of Oxford University Press

Conze, E. (1976) *Buddhist Scriptures*, London: Penguin Classics

Dainian, F. and Cohen, R. (eds) (1996) *History and Philosophy of Science and Technology*, Dordrecht: Kluwer

Conze, E. (1980) *A Short History of Buddhism*, © author

Dasgupta, S. (1932) *A History of Indian Philosophy*, II, Cambridge: Cambridge University Press

—— (1940) *A History of Indian Philosophy*, III, Cambridge: Cambridge University Press

Dasgupta, S.B. (1974) *An Introduction to Tantric Buddhism*, Berkeley: Shambhala

de Bary, W. (1991) *The Trouble with Confucianism*, Cambridge, MA: Harvard University Press. Reprinted by permission of the publisher from THE TROUBLE WITH CONFUCIANISM by W.T. de Bary, Cambridge, Mass.: Harvard University Press, Copyright © 1991 by the President and Fellows of Harvard College

—— (ed) 1958 *Sources of Japanese Tradition*, New York: Columbia University Press. From *Sources of Japanese Tradition* ed. Wm. Theodore de Bary © 1958, Columbia University Press. Reprinted with permission of the publisher.

Dreyfus, G. (1997) *Recognizing Reality: Dharmakirti's Philosophy and its Tibetan Interpretations*, Albany: State University of New York Press

Fackenheim, E. (1945) 'A Treatise on Love' *Medieval Studies* 7, 208–28. Reprinted by permission of the Pontifical Institute of Mediaeval Studies, Toronto

Farabi (1961) *The fusul al-madani of al-Farabi*, ed. and trans. D. Dunlop, Cambridge University Press

—— (1974) 'Book of Letters', trans. D. Berman, *Israel Oriental Studies*

Al-Ghazali, *Incoherence of the Philosophers*, in Averroes, *Tahafut al-tahafut*

Gombrich, R. (1972) *Modern Asian Studies* VI. Reprinted by permission of Cambridge University Press

Gregory, P. (ed) 1987 *Sudden and Gradual: Approaches to Enlightenment in Chinese Thought*, Honolulu: University of Hawaii Press

Guenther, H. and Trungpa, C. (1975) *The Dawn of Tantra* ed. M. Kohn, Berkeley: Shambhala

Ha'iri Yazdi, M. (1992) *The Principles of Epistemology in Islamic Philosophy: Knowledge by presence*, Albany: State University of New York Press

Han Yong-woon, tr. Y. Mu-woong, in Shin-Yong, C. (ed) (1974) *Buddhist Culture in Korea*, Seoul: International Cultural Foundation

Han Fei Tzu (1964) *Han Fei Tzu: Basic Writings*, trans. B. Watson, New York: Columbia University Press

Hansen, C. (1989) 'Language in the Heart-Mind' in Allinson op. cit. 75–124

Hoshino (1997) *Japanese and Western Bioethics*, Dordrecht: Kluwer Academic Publishers. With kind permission from Kluwer Academic Publishers

Kalupahana, D. (1996) *Buddhist Philosophy: A Historical Analysis*, Honolulu: University of Hawaii Press

Krishna, D. (1991) *Indian Philosophy*, Delhi: Oxford University Press

Kukai, *Kukai: Major Works* trans. by Y. Hakeda © 1972, Columbia University Press. Reprinted with the permission of the publisher

Lai, Whalen (1996) "Friendship in Confucian China", in O. Leaman (ed.) *Friendship East and West: Philosophical Perspectives*, Richmond: Curzon

Lao Tzu (1989) trans. R. Henricks *Te Tao Ching*, New York: Random House. Reprinted by permission of Ballantine Books, a Division of Random House Inc.

—— (1997) '"Power and Paradox" – Selections from a New Translation of the *Tao Te Ching*', Parabola Summer 1997 trans. U.K. Le Guin

Leaman, O. (1985) *An Introduction to Medieval Islamic Philosophy*, Cambridge: Cambridge University Press

—— (ed.) 1996 *Friendship East and West: Philosophical Perspectives*, Richmond: Curzon

—— (1997) *Averroes and his Philosophy*, Richmond: Curzon

Lipner, J. (1986) *The Face of Truth: A Study of Meaning and Metaphysics in the Vedantic Theology of Ramanuja*, Basingstoke: Macmillan

Lishi, F. and Youyuan, Z. (1996) 'Concepts of Space and Time in Ancient China and in Modern Cosmology', in Dainian and Cohen op. cit. 55–60

Mahalingam, I. (1996) in O. Leaman (ed) *Friendship East and West: Philosophical Perspectives*, Richmond: Curzon

Matilal, B. (1986) *Perception: An Essay on Classical Indian Theories of Knowledge*, Oxford: Clarendon Press. Reprinted by permission of Oxford University Press

Mohanty, J. (1992) *Reason and Tradition in Indian Thought: An Essay on the Nature of Indian Philosophical Thinking*, Oxford: Clarendon Press. Reprinted by permission of Oxford University Press

Murti, T. (1995) *The Central Philosophy of Buddhism*, London: HarperCollins

Nasr, S. (1993) *The Need for a Sacred Science*, Albany: State University of New York Press

Neville, R. (1989) 'The Chinese Case in a Philosophy of World Religions', in Allinson *op. cit.* 48–74

Nichiren, from *Selected Writings of Nichiren*, ed. Phillip Yampolsky © 1990, Nichiren Shoshu International Center. Reprinted with permission of the publisher.

Parrinder, G. *Avatar and Incarnation*, Oxford: Oneworld

Potter, K (1972) *Presuppositions of India's Philosophies*, Westport, Conn.: Greenwood Press

Rahman, F. (1958) *Prophecy in Islam* © author

Sen, A. (1997) 'Indian Traditions and the Western Imagination' reprinted by permission of *Daedalus*, Journal of the American Academy of Arts and Sciences, from the issue entitled "Human Diversity" Spring 1997, Vol. 126, No. 2

Sen, K. (1973) *Hinduism*, Harmondsworth: Pelican, 1961: Reproduced by permission of Penguin Books Ltd. copyright © the Estate of K.M. Sen, 1961

Simmer-Brown, J. (1997) "Inviting the Demon" reprinted from PARABOLA, The Magazine of Myth and Tradition, vol. XXII, No. 2

Stafford Betty, L. 'Nagarjuna's masterpiece – logical, mystical, both, or neither?', *Philosophy East and West 33*: 123–38 copyright University of Hawaii Press

Suzuki, D. 1973 *Zen and Japanese Culture*, Princeton: Princeton University Press. Copyright © 1973 by Princeton University Press, Eleventh Printing for Myths Series, reprinted by permission of Princeton University Press

—— (1956) *Zen Buddhism* ed. W. Barrett, New York: Doubleday

Sze-Kwang, L. (1989) 'On Understanding Chinese Philosophy: An Inquiry and a Proposal' in Allinson *op. cit.* 265–93

Thurman, R. *The Tibetan Book of the Dead*, London: HarperCollins

Tsunoda, R. et al. (1964) *Sources of Japanese Tradition*, New York: Columbia University Press

Tu Wei-Ming (1988) *Centrality and Commonality: An Essay on Confucian Religiousness*, Albany: State University of New York Press

Yu-Lan, F. (1952) *A History of Chinese Philosophy*. Princeton:

Princeton University Press. Copyright © 1952 by Princeton University Press. Reprinted by permission of Princeton University Press

—— (1948) *A Short History of Chinese Philosophy*, New York: Free Press. Reprinted with the permission of The Free Press, a Division of Simon & Schuster, from A SHORT HISTORY OF CHINESE PHILOSOPHY by Fung Yu-Lan. Edited by Derek Bodde. Copyright © 1948 by The Macmillan Company; copyright renewed 1976 by Chung Liao Fung and Derek Bodde

Zaehner, R (1958) *At Sundry Times: An Essay in the Comparison of Religions*, London: Faber and Faber

—— (1955) *Zurvan: A Zoroastrian Dilemma*, New York: Biblio and Tanven

LIST OF ENTRIES

LIST OF ENTRIES AND THEIR
SOURCES

ABHIDHARMA

Sanskrit term for the body of literature and doctrines from around 400–300 BCE in India (Abhidhamma in Pali), referring to a systematic organization of the *dharmas*, the basic teachings and ideas of Buddhism

Pervading the Buddhist teaching were several notions about the nature of existence and the meaning of spiritual insight. One of the most important of these notions was the assertion that a human being has no permanent essence (*ātman*) and is only a changing conglomerate of material, mental, and psychic factors (*dharmas*). These factors interact to form the experienced world as we are aware of it in everyday living, and all objects of perception or ideas are seen to be without independent bases of existence. The "arising of existence," which generally is also the arising of turmoil, comes about through interdependent and reciprocal forces of the factors (*dharmas*) – forces which find their roots in man's ignorant clinging to the objects that "he" unwittingly is fabricating! For "the arising of existence" to cease, the fabricating ignorance must cease; and the quelling of ignorance requires spiritual insight (*prajñā*). When fabricating ignorance is overcome and the residue of the fabricating force has dissipated, then there is *nirvāṇa* – the "dying out" of the flame of desire for illusory objects.

During the seven centuries between the life of the Buddha and the Buddhist adept Nāgārjuna, this doctrine was elaborated and explained in different ways. In the *Abhidharma* the many factors of existence (*dharmas*) were defined, analyzed, and catalogued for a more perfect understanding by those who sought wisdom. Together with intellectual comprehension went

1

the meditational practices, each providing a reciprocal thrust into new possibilities of insight. About three hundred years before Nāgārjuna, a body of literature began to develop which emphasized the perfection of wisdom (*Prajñāpāramitā* literature) whereby one understood how phenomena arose, the inter-dependent nature of all factors of existence, and the release from fabricated attachment that was achieved as understanding deepened. At its highest point the perfection of wisdom led to the awareness that all things are "empty." It was in this intellectual and religious milieu that Nāgārjuna systematized his understanding of the Buddhist Middle Way (*Mādhyamika*). . . .

The term *"Abhidharma"* applies both to a method of under-standing and to the treatises formulating the understanding which became the third section of the Buddhist canonical writings. Though there was a concern to clarify and classify different aspects of the teaching (*dharma*) very early in the life of the Buddhist community, the development and formulation of the *Abhidharma* texts which are available to us now took place primarily between the time of Aśoka (third century B.C.) and Kaniṣka (first century A.D.). This period was a time for consolidating doctrines, for expressing new conceptions, and for grouping into "schools." While there developed more than one recension of the *Abhidharma*, all the schools recognized the four trends of logical analysis (*catu-paṭisam-bhida*). These were (1) the analysis of the meaning (*attha*) of words and sentences, (2) analysis of the teaching (*dharma*), which means analysis of causes, (3) analysis of *nirutti*, which may mean here grammar and definitions, and (4) analysis of knowing (*paṭibhāṇa*) from a psycho-epistemological standpoint.

The purpose for the elaborate classification of elements in the *Abhidharma* was not to add to the Buddha's teaching. Rather, it was to help the faithful community eliminate false assumptions about man and existence that supported clinging to illusion. The intent was soteriological, not speculative. Originally the *Abhidharma* literature systematized the tenets found scattered in different sermons by the Buddha as an aid for instruction, and in time it developed a technique of its own in which the nature of reality and the cause of suffering were analyzed topically. The techniques include: (1) a strict treatment of experience in terms of momentary cognizable states and definition of these states, (2) creation of a "schedule" consisting of a double and triple classification for sorting these states, and (3) enumeration of twenty-four kinds of conditioning relations.

Streng, F. (1967) *Emptiness: A Study in Religious Meaning*, Nashville: Abingdon Press, pp. 30–1

See also MADHYAMAKA

ACTION

Lao Tzu (Laozi) presents a Taoist (Daoist) analysis of the nature of action. **1**
The references are to parts of the book *Lao-tzu* or *Dao dejing*:

> ... to be content safeguards one from going too far, and therefore from reaching the extreme. Lao Tzu says: "To know how to be content is to avoid humiliation; to know where to stop is to avoid injury." (Ch. 45.) Again: "The sage, therefore, discards the excessive, the extravagant, the extreme." (Ch. 29.)
>
> All these theories are deducible from the general theory that "reversing is the movement of the *Tao.*" The well-known Taoist theory of *wu-wei* is also deducible from this general theory. *Wu-wei* can be translated literally as "having-no-activity" or "non-action." But using this translation, one should remember that the term does not actually mean complete absence of activity, or doing nothing. What it does mean is lesser activity or doing less. It also means acting without artificiality and arbitrariness.
>
> Activities are like many other things. If one has too much of them, they become harmful rather than good. Furthermore, the purpose of doing something is to have something done. But if there is over-doing, this results in something being over-done, which may be worse than not having the thing done at all. A well-known Chinese story describes how two men were once competing in drawing a snake; the one who would finish his drawing first would win. One of them, having indeed finished his drawing, saw that the other man was still far behind, so decided to improve it by adding feet to his snake. Thereupon the other man said: "You have lost the competition, for a snake has no feet." This is an illustration of over-doing which defeats its own purpose. In the *Lao-tzu* we read: "Conquering the world is invariably due to doing nothing; by doing something

one cannot conquer the world." (Ch. 48.) The term "doing nothing" here really means "not over-doing."

Fung Yu-Lan (1948) *A Short History of Chinese Philosophy*, New York: Free Press, p. 100

See also DAOISM

2   A section from the *Dao dejing* (*Tao Te Ching*) in which the point is made that what looks weak may well be strong, and so what looks like not acting may turn out to be very effective action:

> The softest, most pliable thing in the world runs roughshod over the firmest thing in the world.
> That which has no substance gets into that which has no spaces or cracks.
> I therefore know that there is benefit in taking no action.
> The worldless teaching, the benefit of taking no action –
> Few in the world can realize these!

Laozi, trans. R. Henricks (1989) *Lao-Tzu: Te Tao Ching*, New York, Ballantine, Ch. 43 p. 12

See also DAOISM

3   An account of action in the *Bhagavad Gita* which questions how far our actions are really our own:

> The *Gītā* seems to hold that everywhere actions are always being performed by the *guṇas* or characteristic qualities of *prakṛti*, the primal matter. It is through ignorance and false pride that one thinks himself to be the agent. In another place it is said that for the occurrence of an action there are five causes, viz. the body, the agent, the various sense-organs, the various life-functions and biomotor activities, and the unknown objective causal elements or the all-controlling power of God (*daiva*). All actions being due to the combined operation of these five elements, it would be wrong to think the self or the agent to be the only performer of actions. Thus it is said that, this being so, he who thinks the self alone to be the agent of actions, this wicked-minded person through his misapplied intelligence does not see

things properly. Whatever actions are performed, right or wrong, whether in body, speech or mind, have these five factors as their causes. The philosophy that underlies the ethical position of the *Gītā* consists in the fact that, in reality, actions are made to happen primarily through the movement of the characteristic qualities of *prakṛti*, and secondarily, through the collocation of the five factors mentioned, among which the self is but one factor only. It is, therefore, sheer egoism to think that one can, at his own sweet will, undertake a work or cease from doing works. For the *prakṛti*, or primal matter, through its later evolutes, the collocation of causes, would of itself move us to act, and even in spite of the opposition of our will we are led to perform the very action which we did not want to perform. So Kṛṣṇa says to Arjuna that the egoism through which you would say that you would not fight is mere false vanity, since the *prakṛti* is bound to lead you to action. A man is bound by the active tendencies or actions which necessarily follow directly from his own nature, and there is no escape. He has to work in spite of the opposition of his will. *Prakṛti*, or the collocation of the five factors, moves us to work. That being so, no one can renounce all actions. If renouncing actions is an impossibility, and if one is bound to act, it is but proper that one should perform one's normal duties. There are no duties and no actions which are absolutely faultless, absolutely above all criticism; so the proper way in which a man should purify his actions is by purging his mind of all imperfections and impurities of desires and attachment. But a question may arise how, if all actions follow necessarily as the product of the five-fold collocation, a person can determine his actions? The general implication of the *Gītā* seems to be that, though the action follows necessarily as the product of the fivefold collocation, yet the self can give a direction to these actions; if a man wishes to dissociate himself from all attachments and desires by dedicating the fruits of all his actions to God and clings to God with such a purpose, God helps him to attain his noble aim.

Dasgupta, S. (1932) *A History of Indian Philosophy*, II Cambridge: Cambridge University Press, pp. 515–16

See also BHAGAVAD GITA, GUNAS, NYAYA-VAISHESHIKA, PRAKRITI

ADVAITA/ADVAITA VEDANTA

Advaita is the school of Vedanta which literally means 'not two' and whose major thinker was Shankara. It emphasizes the view that reality is one and undifferentiated.

1 In this passage we see the gist of the Advaita conception of what is real in terms of *brahman*, what does not change. The ordinary things in the world are not unreal, but they are far from unchanging, and so cannot strictly speaking be counted as real either:

> Falsity must have a status above negation but below reality. It is not real (*sat*) like Brahman, but it isn't unreal (*asat*) like nonsense either. It is *sadasadvilakṣaṇa*, "other than real or unreal."
>
> But, asks the ultra-realist such as the Nyāya-Vaiśeṣika or Rāmānuja, why *isn't* the piece of silver real like Brahman? One might think immediately of answering that inasmuch as it at best has an inadequacy about it one may say that it is unreal since it is only a *part* of reality. But this would surely be an odd use of "real." If something is, in ordinary usage, said to be real, a part of it would be admitted to be real too, though partial. So the question now becomes: what is the point of introducing a technical, un-common-sensical use of "real" at this juncture? The Advaitin has more in mind by calling something "unreal" than merely that it is part of Brahman. Everything is part of Brahman (or nothing is, depending on the meaning of "part"), it being a ticklish but perhaps inconsequential point whether Brahman is part of itself.
>
> Specifically, the "real" is defined frequently in Advaita as *trikālābādhya*, "unsublated through the three times (past, present and future)." That is to say, the real is that which we don't ever entertain and subsequently reject. Better, the real is that which we couldn't possibly ever entertain and subsequently reject. It is, by definition, eternal. The unreal is, therefore, the non-eternal. It is that which comes into and goes out of existence, while the real – Brahman – is not subject to change at all.

Potter, K. (1972) *Presuppositions of India's Philosophies*, Westport, Conn.: Greenwood Press, pp. 221–2

See also BRAHMAN, NYAYA-VAISHESHIKA

Vivekananda explains how from the perspective of the Advaita the nature of   2
the self must be eternal:

ACCORDING to the Advaita philosophy, there is only one
thing real in the universe, which it calls Brahman; everything
else is unreal, manifested and manufactured out of Brahman
by the power of Mâyâ. To reach back to that Brahman is our
goal. We are, each one of us, that Brahman, that Reality, plus
this Maya. If we can get rid of this Maya or ignorance, then we
become what we really are. According to this philosophy, each
man consists of three parts – the body, the internal organ or the
mind, and behind that, what is called the Atman, the Self. The
body is the external coating and the mind is the internal coating
of the Atman who is the real perceiver, the real enjoyer, the
being in the body who is working the body by means of the
internal organ or the mind.

The Atman is the only existence in the human body which is
immaterial. Because it is immaterial, it cannot be a compound,
and because it is not a compound, it does not obey the law of
cause and effect, and so it is immortal. That which is immortal
can have no beginning, because everything with a beginning
must have an end. It also follows that it must be formless; there
cannot be any form without matter. Everything that has form
must have a beginning and an end. We have none of us seen a
form which had not a beginning and will not have an end. A
form comes out of a combination of force and matter. This chair
has a peculiar form, that is to say a certain quantity of matter
is acted upon by a certain amount of force and made to assume
a particular shape. The shape is the result of a combination of
matter and force. The combination cannot be eternal; there
must come to every combination a time when it will dissolve. So
all forms have a beginning and an end. We know our body will
perish; it had a beginning and it will have an end. But the Self
having no form, cannot be bound by the law of beginning and
end. It is existing from infinite time; just as time is eternal, so is
the Self of man eternal. Secondly, it must be all-pervading. It is
only form that is conditioned and limited by space; that which
is formless cannot be confined in space. So, according to Advaita
Vedanta, the Self, the Atman, in you, in me, in every one, is
omnipresent.

Vivekananda, S. (1961) *Jnana-Yoga*, Calcutta: Advaita Ashrama, pp. 317–19

See also ATMAN, BRAHMAN, MAYA, TIME

AFTERLIFE

1   A modern version of the traditional Hindu view of the wider context within which human life takes place:

> All the known circumstances and results of birth presuppose an unknown before, and there is a suggestion of universality, a will of persistence of life, and inconclusiveness in death which seem to point to an unknown hereafter. What were we before birth and what are we after death, are the questions, the answer of the one depending upon that of the other, which the intellect of man has put to itself from the beginning without even now resting in any final solution. The intellect indeed can hardly give the final answer: for that must in its very nature lie beyond the data of the physical consciousness and memory, whether of the race or the individual, yet these are the sole data which the intellect is in the habit of consulting with something like confidence. In this poverty of materials and this incertitude it wheels from one hypothesis to another and calls each in turn a conclusion. Moreover, the solution depends upon the nature, source and object of the cosmic movement, and as we determine these, so we shall have to conclude about birth and life and death, the before and the hereafter.

Aurobindo (1987) *The Essential Aurobindo*, ed. R. McDermott, Great Barrington, MA: Lindisfarne Press, pp. 92–3. Used by permission of Lindisfarne Books, Hudson, NY 12534 USA.

See also DEATH

---

2   We see that Nature develops from stage to stage and in each stage takes up its past and transforms it into stuff of its new development. We see too that human nature is of the same make; all the earth-past is there in it. It has an element of matter taken up by life, an element of life taken up by mind, an element of mind which is being taken up by spirit: the animal is still present in its humanity; the very nature of the human being presupposes a material and a vital stage which prepared his emergence into mind and an animal past which moulded a first

element of his complex humanity. And let us not say that this is because material Nature developed by evolution his life and his body and his animal mind, and only afterwards did a soul descend into the form so created: there is a certain truth behind this idea, but not the truth which that formula would suggest. For that supposes a gulf between soul and body, between soul and life, between soul and mind, which does not exist; there is no body without soul, no body that is not itself a form of soul: Matter itself is substance and power of spirit and could not exist if it were anything else, for nothing can exist which is not substance and power of Brahman; and if Matter, then still more clearly and certainly Life and Mind must be that and ensouled by the presence of the Spirit. If Matter and Life had not already been ensouled, man could not have appeared or only as an intervention or an accident, not as a part of the evolutionary order.

We arrive then necessarily at this conclusion that human birth is a term at which the soul must arrive in a long succession of rebirths and that it has had for its previous and preparatory terms in the succession the lower forms of life upon earth; it has passed through the whole chain that life has strung in the physical universe on the basis of the body, the physical principle. Then the farther question arises whether, humanity once attained, this succession of rebirths still continues and, if so, how, by what series or by what alternations. And, first, we have to ask whether the soul, having once arrived at humanity, can go back to the animal life and body, a retrogression which the old popular theories of transmigration have supposed to be an ordinary movement. It seems impossible that it should so go back with any entirety, and for this reason that the transit from animal to human life means a decisive conversion of consciousness, quite as decisive as the conversion of the vital consciousness of the plant into the mental consciousness of the animal. It is surely impossible that a conversion so decisive made by Nature should be reversed by the soul and the decision of the spirit within her come, as it were, to naught. It could only be possible for human souls, supposing such to exist, in whom the conversion was not decisive, souls that had developed far enough to make, occupy or assume a human body, but not enough to ensure the safety of this assumption, not enough to remain secure in its achievement and faithful to the human type of consciousness. Or at most there might be, supposing certain animal propensities to be vehement enough to demand a separate satisfaction quite of their own kind, a sort of partial rebirth, a loose holding of an animal form by a human soul, with an immediate subsequent reversion to its normal progression. The movement of Nature is always sufficiently complex for us not to deny dogmatically such a possibility, and, if it be a fact, then there may exist this modicum of truth behind the exaggerated popular belief which assumes an animal rebirth of the soul once lodged in man to be quite as normal and possible as a human reincarnation. But whether the animal reversion is possible or not, the normal law must be the recurrence of birth in new human forms for a soul that has once become capable of humanity.

Ibid., pp. 111–12

See also BRAHMAN, CAUSATION, *PRAKRITI, SAMSARA*

3 Another modern Hindu view, by Vivekananda, in which the infinity of space and time is used as an argument for the eternal repetition of the way nature is organized:

The question of immortality is not yet settled. We have seen that everything in this universe is indestructible. There is nothing new; there will be nothing new. The same series of manifestations are presenting themselves alternately like a wheel, coming up and going down. All motion in this universe is in the form of waves, successively rising and falling. Systems after systems are coming out of fine forms, evolving themselves, and taking grosser forms, again melting down, as it were, and going back to the fine forms. Again they rise out of that, evolving for a certain period and slowly going back to the cause. So will all life. Each manifestation of life is coming up and then going back again. What goes down? The form. The form breaks to pieces, but it comes up again. In one sense bodies and forms even are eternal. How? Suppose we take a number of dice and thrown them, and they fall in this ratio 6–5–3–4. We take the dice up and throw them again and again; there must be a time when the same numbers will come again; the same combination must come. Now each particle, each atom, that is in this universe, I take for such a die, and these are being thrown out and combined again and again. All these forms before you are one combination. Here are the forms of a glass, a table, a pitcher of water, and so forth. This is one combination; in time, it will all break. But there must come a time when exactly the same combination comes again, when you will be here, and this form will be here, this subject will be talked, and this pitcher will be here. An infinite number of times this has been, and an infinite number of times this will be repeated. Thus far with the physical forms. What do we find? That even the combination of physical forms is eternally repeated.

Vivekananda, S. (1961) *Jnana-Yoga*, Calcutta: Advaita Ashrama, pp. 278–9

See also CAUSATION

Averroes (ibn Rushd) presents his response to how Islamic philosophy can **4** avoid appearing to criticize the religious view of the afterlife. The literal understanding of the Qur'an implies that some will experience an afterlife in a physical form, which philosophers had difficulties accepting:

All religions, as we have said, agree on the fact that souls experience states of happiness or misery after death, but they disagree in the manner of symbolizing these states and explaining their existence to men. And it seems that the [kind of] symbolization which is found in this religion of ours is the most perfect means of explanation to the majority of men, and provides the greatest stimulus to their souls to [pursue the goals of] the life beyond; and the primary concern of religions is with the majority. Spiritual symbolization, on the other hand, seems to provide less stimulus to the souls of the masses towards [the goals of] the life beyond, and the masses have less desire and fear of it than they do of corporeal symbolization. Therefore it seems that corporeal symbolization provides a stronger stimulus to [the goals of] the life beyond than spiritual; the spiritual [kind] is more acceptable to the class of debating theologians, but they are the minority.

[There are three interpretations of the symbols by Muslims. (1) The life beyond is the same in kind as this one, but it is permanent, not limited in duration. (2) It differs in kind: (a) The life beyond is spiritual, and is only symbolized by sensible images for the purpose of exposition. (b) It is corporeal, but the bodies are other, immortal ones not these perishable ones. This opinion is suitable for the élite.

15

It avoids the absurdity of (I), arising from the fact that our bodies here provide material for other earthly bodies and so cannot at the same time exist in the other world. But every opinion is permissible except total rejection of another life.]

For this reason we find the people of Islam divided into three sects with regard to the understanding of the symbolization which is used in [the texts of] our religion referring to the states of the future life. One sect holds that that existence is identical with this existence here with respect to bliss and pleasure, i.e. they hold that it is of the same sort and that the two existences differ only in respect of permanence and limit of duration, i.e. the former is permanent and the latter of limited duration. Another group holds that there is a difference in the kind of existence. This [group] is divided into two subdivisions. One [sub-] group holds that the existence symbolized by these sensible images is spiritual, and that it has been symbolized thus only for the purpose of exposition; these people are supported by many well-known arguments from Scripture, but there would be no point in enumerating them. Another [sub-] group thinks that it is corporeal, but believes that that corporeality existing in the life beyond differs from the corporeality of this life in that the latter is perishable while the former is immortal. They too are supported by arguments from Scripture, and it seems that Ibn 'Abbās was one of those who held this opinion, for he is reported to have said, 'There is nothing in this lower world like the next world except the names.'

It seems that this opinion is more suitable for the élite; for the admissibility of this opinion is founded on facts which are not discussed in front of everyone. One is that the soul is immortal. The second is that the return of the soul to other bodies does not involve the same absurdity as <its> return <to> those same [earthly] bodies. This is because it is apparent that the materials of the bodies that exist here are successively transferred from one body to another: i.e. one and the same material exists in many persons at different times. Bodies like these cannot possibly all exist actually [at the same time], because their material is one: for instance, a man dies, his body is transformed into dust, that dust is transformed into a plant, another man feeds on that plant; then semen proceeds from him, from which another man is born. But if other bodies are supposed, this state of affairs does not follow as a consequence.

The truth in this question is that every man's duty is [to believe] whatever his study of it leads him to [conclude], provided that it is not such a study as would cause him to reject the principle altogether, by denying the existence [of the future life] altogether; for this manner of belief obliges us to call its holder an unbeliever, because the existence of this [future] state for man is made known to people through their Scriptures and their intellects.

Note: square brackets refer to George Hourani's additions to the original text which he has here translated.

Averroes (1976) *On the Harmony of Religion and Philosophy* trans. G. Hourani, London: Luzac, pp. 78–9

See also DEATH

A Zoroastrian account: 5

(4–5) Zardusht asked Ohrmazd: 'From where shall the body be reassembled which the wind has blown away, and the water carried off? And how shall the resurrection take place?' Ohrmazd answered: 'When I created the sky without pillars . . . ; and when I created the earth which bears all physical life . . . ; and when I set in motion the sun and moon and stars . . . ; and when I created corn, that it might be scattered in the earth and grow again, giving back increase . . . ; and when I created and protected the child in the mother's womb . . . ; and when I created the cloud, which bears water for the world and rains it down where it chooses; and when I created the wind . . . which blows as it pleases – then the creation of each one of these was more difficult for me than the raising of the dead. For . . . consider, if I made that which was not, why cannot I make again that which was?'

From the 'Greater Bundahishn', ch. 34, p. 52. Concerning the resurrection. Boyce, M. (1984) *Textual Sources for the Study of Zoroastrianism*, ed. and trans. M. Boyce, Manchester: Manchester University Press

AHIMSA

Literally 'non-violence', an important notion in many of the philosophies which originated in India. It is of crucial significance in Jainism.

1 The defenders of *ahimsa* were constantly being challenged with examples of where refusing to injure anything at all would result in greater subsequent injury to others. Gandhi presents here an answer to the dilemma:

There can be no two opinions on the fact that Hinduism regards killing a living being as sinful. I think all religions are agreed on the principle. There is generally no difficulty in determining a principle. The difficulty comes in when one proceeds to put it into practice. A principle is the expression of a perfection, and as imperfect beings like us cannot practise perfection, we devise every moment limits of its compromise in practice. So Hinduism has laid down that killing for sacrifice is no *himsa* (violence). This is only a half-truth. Violence will be violence for all time, and all violence is sinful. But what is inevitable is not *regarded* as a sin, so much so that the science of daily practice has not only declared the inevitable violence involved in killing for sacrifice as permissible but even regarded it as meritorious.

But unavoidable violence cannot be defined. For it changes with time, place, and person. What is regarded as excusable at one time may be inexcusable at another. The violence involved in burning fuel or coal in the depth of winter to keep the body warm may be unavoidable and therefore a duty, for a weak-bodied man, but fire unnecessarily lit in midsummer is clearly violence.

We recognize the duty of killing microbes by the use of disinfectants. It is violence and yet a duty. But why go even as far as that? The air in a dark closed room is full of little microbes, and the introduction of light and air into it by opening it is destruction indeed. But it is ever a duty to use that finest of disinfectants – pure air.

These instances can be multiplied. The principle that applies in the instances cited applies in the matter of killing rabid dogs. To destroy a rabid dog is to commit the minimum amount of violence. A recluse, who is living in a forest and is compassion incarnate, may not destroy a rabid dog. For in his compassion he has the virtue of making it whole. But a city-dweller who is responsible for the protection of lives under his care and who does not possess the virtues of the recluse, but is capable of destroying a rabid dog, is faced with a conflict of duties. If he kills the dog he commits a sin. If he does not kill it, he commits a graver sin. So he prefers to commit the lesser one and save himself from the graver.

I believe myself to be saturated with *ahimsa* – non-violence. *Ahimsa* and truth are as my two lungs. I cannot live without them. But I see every moment with more and more clearness, the immense power of *ahimsa* and the littleness of man. Even the forest-dweller cannot be entirely free from violence, in spite of his limitless compassion. With every breath he commits a certain amount of violence. The body itself is a house of slaughter and therefore *Moksha* and Eternal Bliss consist in perfect deliverance from the body, and therefore all pleasure, save the joy of *Moksha*, is evanescent, imperfect.

That being the case, we have to drink, in daily life, many a bitter draught of violence.

Gandhi, M. (1958) *Hindu Dharma*, Ahmedabad: Navajivan Publishing House, pp. 172–3

See also JAINISM, *MOKSHA*

An account of the spiritual significance of *ahimsa*, which links it more with worship and less with activity:

2

In the list of the qualities conducive to purity, as given by Ramanuja, there are enumerated, Satya, truthfulness; Ârjava, sincerity; Dayâ, doing good to others without any gain to one's self; Ahimsâ, not injuring others by thought, word, or deed; Anabhidhyâ, not coveting others' goods, not thinking vain thoughts, and not brooding over injuries received from another. In this list, the one idea that deserves special notice is Ahimsâ, non-injury to others. This duty of non-injury is, so to speak, obligatory on us in relation to all beings; as with some, it does not simply mean the non-injuring of human beings and merci-lessness towards the lower animals; nor, as with some others, does it mean the protecting of cats and dogs and the feeding of ants with sugar, with liberty to injure brother-man in every horrible way. It is remarkable that almost every good idea in this world can be carried to a disgusting extreme. A good practice carried to an extreme and worked in accordance with the letter of the law becomes a positive evil. The stinking monks of certain religious sects, who do not bathe lest the vermin on their bodies should be killed, never think of the discomfort and disease they bring to their fellow human beings. They do not, however, belong to the religion of the Vedas!

The test of Ahimsâ is absence of jealousy. Any man may do a good deed or make a good gift on the spur of the moment, or under the pressure of some superstition or priestcraft; but the real lover of mankind is he who is jealous of none. The so-called great men of the world may all be seen to become jealous of each other for a small name, for a little fame, and for a few bits of gold. So long as this jealousy exists in a heart, it is far away from the perfection of Ahimsâ. The cow does not eat meat, nor does the sheep. Are they great Yogis, great non-injurers (Ahimsakas)? Any fool may abstain from eating this or that; surely that gives him no more distinction than to herbivorous animals. The man who will mercilessly cheat widows and orphans, and do the vilest deeds for money, is worse than any brute, even if he lives entirely on grass. The man whose heart never cherishes even the thought of injury to any one, who rejoices at the prosperity of even his greatest enemy, that man is the Bhakta, he is the Yogi, he is the Guru of all, even though he lives every day of his life on the flesh of swine. Therefore we must always remember that external practices have value only as helps to develop internal purity. It is better to have internal purity alone, when minute attention to external observances is not practicable.

Vivekananda, S. (1959) *Bhakti-Yoga*, Calcutta: Advaita Ashrama, pp. 60–62

See also BHAKTI

AMIDA

Japanese for boundless light, referring to the pure land where the seeker after salvation can go after sincerely calling on the Buddha's name.

1   A good example of the role of the Buddha in salvation according to the Pure Land school, and the overwhelming significance of faith:

How can we find true salvation? How can we solve this problem (the problem of human passions)? Man, whose knowledge is limited, cannot produce a satisfactory answer to this problem. We can never discover by pure intellectual knowledge a way to wipe out all afflictions. Of course, in ordinary daily life money, medicine, or good deeds may solve immediate problems. But the fundamental suffering and anxiety of human existence cannot be eliminated by our feeble activities. Man is quite helpless and incapable of resolving the problems of existence through his own power. Man is filled with passions and desires which becloud his insight and restrain his efforts. Only in the power of the Buddha which transcends man is there to be found salvation. . . . Just as a babe must be tended by its mother, so we too gain salvation through the compassion of the Buddha of Infinite Mercy. Because the Buddha presents eternal life to us, his compassion is the foundation upon which we can build a noble life. . . . This power [scil. the power of the Main Vow of Amida] which transcends all relative and limited things is eternal and unlimited, and because by it all limited things are saved, it is called salvation by a power outside of them. . . . The faith which looks up to the benevolence of the Buddha becomes a foun-tainhead of power for living the good life. Though we live in an existence filled with suffering and passion, yet in the power of our faith that we live in Buddha's mercy and compassion, we find hope, strength and encouragement.

Otani, K. (1957) *Sermons on Shin Buddhism*, pp. 14–15

See also ENLIGHTENMENT, *LOTUS SUTRA*

ANALYSIS

All philosophies discuss the appropriate criteria for argument. Motse (Mozi) **1**
points to the links between those criteria, Chinese culture and pragmatic considerations:

> Motse said: To make any statement or to publish any doctrine, there must first be established some standard of judgment. To discuss without a standard is like determining the directions of sunrise and sunset on a revolving potter's wheel. Even skilful artisans could not get accurate results in that way. Now that the

truth and error (of a doctrine) in the world is hard to tell, there must be three tests. What are the three tests? They are the test of its basis, the test of its verifiability, and the test of its applicability. To test the basis of a doctrine we shall examine the will of Heaven and spirits and the deeds of the sage-kings. To test its verifiability we shall go to the books of the early kings. As to its applicability it is to be tested by its use in the administration of justice and government. These then are the three tests of a doctrine.

Mozi (1974) *The Ethical and Political Works of Motse*, trans. Yi-Pao Mei, Taipai: Ch'eng Wen Publishing Company, p. 189

See also HEAVEN

2   Al-Farabi outlines different kinds of analysis, with rigorous or demonstrative reasoning being later in time than more popular but weaker forms of reasoning. This is a traditional account in Islamic philosophy, where all types of argument are accorded some degree of certitude, and where religion and theology are regarded as different ways of arguing logically which make allowances for the capacities of audiences to understand what they are told:

> Dialectical and sophistical powers, together with philosophy grounded on opinion, or philosophy based on sophistical thinking, should have preceded in time certain, i.e. demonstrative, philosophy. And religion, regarded as a human matter, is later in time than philosophy in general, since it is aimed at teaching the multitude theoretical and practical things which were deduced from philosophy in ways which facilitate the multitude's understanding of them, either through persuasion or representation, or through them both together. The arts of theology and jurisprudence are later in time than religion and are subordinate to it. And if the religion is subordinate to an ancient philosophy, either based on opinion, or on sophistical thinking, then the theology and the jurisprudence which are subordinate to it accord with either of them, but are below either of them.

Farabi, 'Book of Letters', trans. L. Berman, 'Maimonides, the disciple of Alfarabi', *Israel Oriental Studies* 4 (1974), p. 156

See also POLITICS AND POWER

ANATMAN/ANATTA

Anatman (s) and *anatta* (p) mean 'not-self', and stand in opposition to the idea that there exists a persisting and eternal self. The critique of the idea of a permanent self represents one of the main theses of Buddhism. The first two views presented here come from the Theravada tradition.

Malalasekera identifies the Buddhist refusal to accept the permanent nature of the self as its defining statement:

> This is the one doctrine which separates Buddhism from all other religions, creeds, and systems of philosophy and which makes it unique in the world's history. All its other teachings . . . are found, more or less in similar forms, in one or other of the schools of thought or religions which have attempted to guide men through life and explain to them the unsatisfactoriness of the world. But in its denial of any real permanent Soul or Self, Buddhism stands alone. This teaching presents the utmost difficulty to many people and often provokes even violent antagonism towards the whole religion. Yet this doctrine of No-soul or *Anattā* is the bedrock of Buddhism and all the other Teachings of the Buddha are intimately connected with it . . . Now, what is this 'Soul' the existence of which the Buddha denies? Briefly stated, the soul is the abiding, separate, constantly existing and indestructible entity which is generally believed to be found in man . . . it is [regarded as] the thinker of all his thoughts, the doer of his deeds and the director of the organism generally. It is the lord not only of the body but also of the mind; it gathers its knowledge through the gateways of the senses . . . Buddhism denies all this and asserts that this belief in a permanent and a divine soul is the most dangerous and pernicious of all errors, the most deceitful of illusions, that it will inevitably mislead its victim into the deepest pit of sorrow and suffering.

Malalaseekara, G. (1957) *The Buddha and his teachings*, The Buddhist Council of Ceylon, pp. 33–4

See also ATMAN, MAYA

2   Nyanatiloka suggests that the doctrine of no-self is closely linked with the
     Buddhist notion of liberation:

> There are three teachers in the world. The first teacher teaches
> the existence of an eternal ego-entity outlasting death: that is
> the Eternalist, as for example the Christian. The second teacher
> teaches a temporary ego-entity which becomes annihilated at
> death: that is the annihilationist, or materialist. The third teacher
> teaches neither an eternal nor a temporary ego-entity: that is the
> Buddha. The Buddha teaches that what we call ego, self, soul,
> personality, etc., are merely conventional terms not referring
> to any real independent entity. And he teaches that there is only
> to be found this psychophysical process of existence changing
> from moment to moment . . . This doctrine of egolessness of
> existence forms the essence of the Buddha's doctrine of eman-
> cipation. Thus with this doctrine of egolessness, or *anattā*, stands
> or falls the entire Buddhist structure.

Nyanatiloka, M. (1973) *Impermanence*, Buddhist Publication Society, Wheel
no. 186–7, Ceylon, pp. 2–3

See also ATMAN

3   From a Mahayana perspective Abe links the doctrine of no-self with the
     concept of emptiness:

> Buddhist ideas of *anātman* or absence of an eternal self, the
> impermanence of all things, and dependent origination, all
> imply the negation of being, existence, and substantiality. It is
> Nāgārjuna who established the idea of *Śūnyatā* or Emptiness by
> clearly realizing the implication of the basic ideas transmitted
> by the earlier Buddhist tradition. It must be emphasized that
> Nāgārjuna's idea of Emptiness is not nihilistic. Emptiness which
> is completely without form is freed from both being and
> non-being because 'non-being' is still a form as distinguished
> from 'being'. In fact, Nāgārjuna not only rejected what came to
> be called the 'eternalist' view, which proclaimed the reality of
> phenomena as the manifestation of one eternal and unchange-
> able substance, but additionally denounced its exact counterpart,
> the so-called 'nihilistic' view, which insisted that true reality is
> empty and non-existent. He thus opened up a new vista liber-
> ated from every illusory point of view concerning affirmation or

negation, being or non-being, as the standpoint of Mahayana Emptiness, which he called the Middle Path. Accordingly, Nāgārjuna's idea of the Middle Path does not indicate a midpoint between the two extremes as the Aristotelian idea of *to meson* might suggest. Instead, it refers to the Way which transcends every possible duality including that of being and non-being, affirmation and negation. Therefore, his idea of Emptiness is not a mere emptiness as opposed to fullness. Emptiness as *Śūnyatā* transcends and embraces both emptiness and fullness. It is really formless in the sense that it is liberated from both 'form' and 'formlessness'. Thus, in *Śūnyatā*, Emptiness as it is is Fullness and Fullness as it is is Emptiness; formlessness as it is is form and form as it is is formless. This is why, for Nāgārjuna, true Emptiness is wondrous Being.

Abe, M. (1985) *Zen and Western Thought*, Basingstoke: Macmillan, pp. 126–7

See also EMPTINESS, MADHYAMAKA

An account of how the analysis of no-self leads to further analysis of the nature of experience itself which reveals the lack of real things behind that experience: 4

Q: What would you say is the basic point in the Buddhist view?
G: One basic thing that must be learned is what is meant by the I or the ego. We must understand this because the ego is the great stumbling block, a kind of frozenness in our being, which hinders us from any authentic being. Traditionally, the Buddhists ask what such an entity could consist of. Is it what we would call our physical aspect? Our feelings, motivations, our thought processes? These are the things we try to identify as ourselves, as "I." But there are many things that can be pointed out with regard to each one of these identifications to show that it is spurious.

The word "I" has very special peculiarities. We generally assume that this word is like any other; but actually it is unique in that the noise "I" can only issue in a way that makes sense from a person who uses it signifying himself. It has a peculiar groundless quality. "I" cannot apply to anything other than this act of signifying. There is no ontological object which corresponds to it. Nevertheless, philosophies, Oriental as well as Western, have continually fallen into the trap of assuming there is something corresponding to it, just as there is to the word "table." But the word "I" is quite different from other nouns and pronouns. It can never refer to anyone but the subject. It is actually a shortcut term which refers to a complicated system of interlocking forces, which can be identified and separated, but which we should not identify with.

To undermine the naive persistence of the ego notion is one of the first steps in Buddhism, a prerequisite for all further study. Furthermore, we have to see that the various aspects of ourselves that we tend to identify with from moment to moment as "I" – the mind, the heart, the body – are only abstractions from a unitary process. Getting this back into perspective is also a basic step. Once these steps have been taken, a foundation is laid; although in fact for a very long time we must continue to fall back into spurious identification.

This identification also has its objective pole. When we perceive something, we automatically believe that there is something real corresponding to the perception. But if we analyze what is going on when we perceive something, we learn that the actual case is quite different. What is actually given in the perceptual situation are constitutive elements of an object. For example, we perceive a certain colored patch and we say we have a tablecloth. This tablecloth is what is called the epistemological object. But automatically we believe that we have not only an epistemological object, an object for our knowledge, but also an ontological object corresponding to it, which we believe to be an actual constitutive element of being.

But then, on the other hand, we have certain other perceptions, and we say, "Oh, well, there is certainly nothing like this." If some one has delirium tremens and he sees pink rats, we certainly say there are no pink rats. But here he goes ahead anyhow and tries to catch them – and he behaves towards them as we do towards ordinary objects. In a certain sense, from the Buddhist point of view, we are constantly chasing about trying to catch pink rats. So here the question arises: if one perception is adjudged delusive and the other veridical, what could be the criterion used to make the distinction? All that can be said is that any object before the mind is an object in the mind. Any belief in ontologically authentic objects is based on an assumption which cannot withstand critical analysis.

What we have, then is a phenomenon which appears as having some reference beyond itself. But our analysis has shown us that this reference is only an apparent one on which we cannot rely as valid. Now this analysis is extremely valuable because it brings us back to our immediate experience, before it is split into subjective and objective poles. There is a strong tendency at this point to objectify this immediate experience and say that this fundamental and unassailable thing we have got back to is the mind. But there is absolutely no reason to posit such an entity as the mind; moreover, postulating this entity again shifts the attention out of the immediacy of experience back onto a hypothetical level. It puts us back into the same old concatenation of fictions that we were trying to get away from.

So there is a constant analysis, a constant observation that must go on, applied to all phases of our experience, to bring us back to this complete immediacy. This immediacy is the most potent creative field that can exist. The creative potential of this field is referred to in the tantric texts as *bindu*, or in Tibetan, *thig-le*.

Guenther, H. and Trungpa, C. (1975) *The Dawn of Tantra*, ed. G. Eddy (The Clear Light Series) Shambhala: Berkeley, pp. 71–3

See also ANALYSIS, CONSCIOUSNESS, *PRAJNA, TANTRA*

ASCETICISM

Zhuang zi (Chuang Tzu) presents a defence of the simple life.

Shun tried to cede the empire to Shan Ch'üan, but Shan Ch'üan said, "I stand in the midst of space and time. Winter days I dress in skins and furs, summer days, in vine-cloth and hemp. In spring I plow and plant – this gives my body the labor and exercise it needs; in fall I harvest and store away – this gives my form the leisure and sustenance it needs.

When the sun comes up, I work; when the sun goes down, I rest. I wander free and easy between heaven and earth, and my mind has found all that it could wish for. What use would I have for the empire? What a pity that you don't understand me!' In the end he would not accept, but went away, entering deep into the mountains, and no one ever knew where he had gone.

Chuang Tzu (1968) *The Complete Works of Chuang Tzu*, Tr. B. Watson, New York: Columbia University Press, pp. 309–10. Reprinted with the permission of the publisher.

See also HEAVEN

ATMAN

1 Nagarjuna's account of the central principles of Madhyamaka Buddhist thought on the nature of the self. It brings out the way in which the notion of the self is linked with the other key philosophical concepts, and argues that Buddhism defends a middle position on what is real and what is unreal:

> An Analysis of the Individual Self (*ātma*)
> 1. If the individual self (*ātma*) were [identical to] the "groups" (*skandha*), then it would partake of origination and destruction.
>   If [the individual self] were different from the "groups," then it would be without the characteristics of the "groups."
> 2. If the individual self does not exist, how then will there be something which is "my own"?
>   There is lack of possessiveness and no ego on account of the cessation of self and that which is "my own."
> 3. He who is without possessiveness and who has no ego – He, also, does not exist.
>   Whoever sees "he who is without possessiveness" or "he who has no ego" [really] does not see.
> 4. When "I" and "mine" have stopped, then also there is not an outside nor an inner self.
>   The "acquiring" [of *karma*] (*upādāna*) is stopped; on account of that destruction, there is destruction of very existence.
> 5. On account of the destruction of the pains (*kleśa*) of action there is release; for pains of action exist for him who constructs them.
>   These pains result from phenomenal extension (*prapañca*); but this phenomenal extension comes to a stop by emptiness.
> 6. There is the teaching of "individual self" (*ātma*), and the teaching of "non-individual self" (*anātma*);
>   But neither "individual self" nor "non-individual self" whatever has been taught by the Buddhas.

7. When the domain of thought has been dissipated, "that which can be stated" is dissipated.
   Those things which are unoriginated and not terminated, like *nirvāṇa*, constitute the Truth (*dharmatā*).
8. Everything is "actual" (*tathyam*) or "not-actual," or both "actual-and-not-actual,"
   Or "neither-actual-nor-not-actual": This is the teaching of the Buddha.
9. "Not caused by something else," "peaceful," "not elaborated by discursive thought,"
   "Indeterminate," "undifferentiated": such are the characteristics of true reality (*tattva*).
10. Whatever exists, being dependent [on something else], is certainly not identical to that [other thing],
    Nor is a thing different from that; therefore, it is neither destroyed nor eternal.

Streng, F. (1967) *Emptiness: A Study in Religious Meaning*, Nashville: Abingdon Press, pp. 204

See also ANATMAN, CAUSATION, *KARMA*

Ramanuja presents an opposing Dvaita view. According to him, there is something real behind our notion of the self, namely, brahman or the principle of reality itself:

Where the support is the finite *ātman* and the thing supported its material body, the ontological (modal) dependence of latter on former is not absolute. It is true, of course, as Rāmānuja points out, that the body cannot subsist as an organic entity independently of the existential support of its *ātman*; that at death, i.e. at the separation of body and *ātman*, the body ceases to be a body in the proper sense and disintegrates. Nevertheless the finite *ātman* is not the bestower of being to its body in the absolute sense: it has no intrinsic power to originate its prakṛtic body (which is thrust upon it by the outworking of *karma*) or to stave off biological death permanently. However, in the case of Brahman as ontological support and the world/its individual substantial entities as thing supported, Brahman is, absolutely speaking, the bestower and mainstay of being. Finite being totally depends on Brahman's existential support.

Lipner, J. (1986) *The Face of Truth: A Study of Meaning and Metaphysics in the Vedantic Theology of Ramanuja*, Basingstoke: Macmillan, p. 125

See also *BRAHMAN, KARMA, PRAKRITI*

3   Buddhism sets itself firmly against the idea of *brahman* sustaining our world of experience as defended by various philosophical schools in Hinduism:

The Buddhist doctrine that there is no such thing as self is usually taken for granted. That this represents the real view of the Buddha is certainly true if by 'self' we understand the empirical ego only. How does it stand with the *ātman*, the 'second self' or eternal soul? The Sāṁkhya and Jains, of course, believed in the separate existence of an infinite number of individual souls: neither believed in the existence of a God or Absolute. How do things stand with primitive Buddhism?

There is, of course, no doubt that Buddhism denies both God and Absolute. This seems clear enough from the *Tevijja Sutta*[1] where the Buddha refutes representatives of various Brahmanical schools all of whom claim that the teaching of their own sect 'is the straight path . . . the direct way which makes for salvation, and leads him, who acts according to it, into the state of union with Brahmā (*brahmasahavyatāya*)'.[2] Now, though the grammatical form of Brahmā is here masculine, it is fairly clear, as T. W. Rhys Davids points out,[3] that the Buddha is here referring to all that the Brāhmans meant by the neuter Brahman as well as the masculine Brahmā. In fact 'union with Brahmā' must mean union with the Absolute as understood in the Upanishads, that is to say, as the eternal ground of the universe. The Brāhmans in question further maintain that all their teachings in fact culminate in this same union with Brahmā, which, since they are Brāhmans, must be the Brahman-Ātman synthesis. For them the teachings of all sects must lead to this same goal. 'Just . . . as near a village or a town,' they argue, 'there are many and various paths, yet they all meet together in the village, just in that way are all the various paths taught by various Brāhmans.'[4] They are all 'saving paths', and they all lead to 'a state of union with Brahmā'.

The Buddha will have none of all this. For him union with Brahmā could not be the goal of religion, for none of these Brāhmans had ever met or heard of anyone who had seen

Brahmā, knew him by experience, or knew his where, whence, or whither.

1 *Dīgha Nikāya, Sutta* 13.
2 *Tevijja Sutta,* § 4 ff.
3 *Buddhist Suttas* in *Sacred Books of the East*, vol. xi, p. 168, n. 2.
4 Ibid., § 10.

Zaehner, R. (1958) *At Sundry Times: An Essay in the Comparison of Religions*, London: Faber, pp. 96–7

See also *ANATMAN, BRAHMAN*, GOD, JAINISM, SANKHYA-YOGA, *UPANISHADS*

An explanation of the links between the notion of *atman* and wider 4 metaphysical theories.

Often enough, especially in his commentary on the *Bhagavadgītā*, Rāmānuja expresses sentiments in accord with the experience and language of monotheists throughout the world – that God is everything and we are nothing; that he must become greater and greater in all things, while we become less and less. The problem here is that, if such talk is taken to its logical extreme, finite persons cease to have any intrinsic value and become mere means, not only in their relationships with God but in their dealings with each other as well. Rāmānuja rejects this extreme. The individual *ātman* is assured that it is an end-in-itself, a value-bestower in its own right, through its relationship with its material body i.e. its body. This assurance comes not only from scripture but from personal experience in the human individual's dealings with God and with other persons. Rāmānuja's analysis of self-consciousness, complemented by his reading of scripture, is adduced to show that by having a (conscious and blissful) nature essentially similar to Brahman's, we reflect in our own right as persons the intrinsic value that characterises Brahman as an end-in-himself. Not even Brahman, as a respecter of his own nature, can violate the essential person-hood of our beings.

Lipner, J. (1986) *The Face of Truth: A Study of Meaning and Metaphysics in the Vedantic Theology of Ramanuja*, Basingstoke: Macmillan, p. 139

See also BHAGAVAD GITA, BRAHMAN, GOD

ATOMISM

1 A thoroughgoing materialist philosophy such as that defended by the Ajivikas held a different account of atomism from other Indian theories:

> If we compare Ājīvika atomism with other Indian atomic theories we find significant agreements and differences. With the Jainas the atom (*paramâṇu*) is not differentiated according to elements; it is permanent and unchanging in its substance, but liable to change in its qualities. Atoms are susceptible to taste, smell, colour, and touch, and combine into aggregates or molecules (*skandha*). The atom is the minutest separable portion of the ultimate undifferentiated matter (*pudgala*), of which the universe is formed, and its classification by elements is not fundamental. While differing from Ājīvika atomism in this very important respect, Jaina theory agrees in its tendency to conceive categories as material which by other sects are thought of as abstract or spiritual. Thus both *dharma* and *karma* are looked on by the Jainas as atomic. But with the Jainas *jīva*, the soul, is not *paudgalika*, or material, and thus Ājīvikism goes further than Jainism in its materialism.

Basham, A. (1951) *History and Doctrines of the Ajivikas: A Vanished Indian Religion*, Delhi: Motilal Banarsidass, pp. 267–9

See also JAINISM, MATERIALISM

2 The contrast between the unity of reality and the variety of experience has always been a potent source of philosophical reflection in Indian thought, and frequently came to be analyzed by some form of atomism:

> Actions in Nyāya-Vaiśeṣika are explicitly said to be only movements of objects in space. They lead to the displacement of bodies. They are however 'momentary' in the sense that in each moment the so-called moving bodies 'inch forward' (i.e. get a new spatial location) with a *new* motion or action, which dies to make room, under suitable circumstances, for another *new* motion. The motions are therefore momentary motion-particulars. There is thus not just a single action or motion in a

ball that moves for two minutes but a series of momentary motion-particulars. Such an 'atomic' notion of motion is supposed to answer some pertinent objection and paradoxes that Nāgārjuna pointed out while criticizing the general conception of motion in *Madhyamakaśāstra*.

The view of Bhartṛhari says that the ultimate reality is one unbreakable, unanalysable, unstructured whole, which is the ultimate reference of all linguistic expressions and all thoughts. In our thoughts and speech, however, we are in the habit of cutting bits and pieces out of the whole reality and assigning to each of them a 'metaphorical' existence. We mentally sever them from the whole (indivisible) reality, and reify them as reals. The system is monistic in the sense that there is only one existent entity. It refutes pluralism of any sort. The plurality of universals, particulars, relations etc. would be considered as part of the realm of 'metaphorical' existence – the realm that is essentially language-generated and mind-dependent. They are the products of *vikalpa* (= the imaginative and analytic faculty of the human mind). Our thought reifies such entities, and there cannot be any end to it. . . .

The attempt of the Yogācāra (Buddhist) idealists has been to show that our knowledge of the external world is not consistent, i.e. it does not yield a consistent theory of the external realities. Vasubandhu wanted to prove the paradoxicality of our notion of the external object in perception in his Yogācāra text *Viṃśikā* (*Vijñaptimātratāsiddhi*) in the following way. Some (i.e. the Nyāya-Vaiśeṣikas) hold that the object perceived is one (single) 'whole' (*eka*, an *avayavin*), e.g. a chair or a tree. Others (the Vaibhāṣika Buddhists) believe that it is a multitude of atoms (*aneka*, e.g. many colour-atoms) that we perceive. Still others (perhaps the Sautrāntika Buddhists) believe that we see a multitude of atoms formed in a conglomerate. All these views can be faulted easily. Hence, Vasubandhu says, the so-called external perception arises without there being any external object to regulate or control it just as it happens in dreams etc.

In fact each of the three views depends on some form of atomism, either on the *material* atoms constituting the material bodies, the wholes such as a tree, or on the *phenomenalistic* atoms which constitute each perceived phenomenon and are therefore ultimately real according to the *Abhidharmakośa*, verse VI.4. The first view is easily rejected by pointing out that we never realize the 'whole' in perception as a separate entity over and above its parts, constituents, or atoms. The difficulties of proving the distinctness of the whole from its parts are well known. Besides, atomism in general suffers from insuperable objections. The concept of an impartite and indivisible atom (which coming together with many others must constitute the material body or gross form) is, in short, paradoxical. For, Vasubandhu says, if six atoms came from six different directions to combine and 'touch' the atom in the middle, then it would have at least six parts, and if they came to occupy the same spatial location, the gross body would never be constituted by them. For there would not be the required increase in size of the constituted form since the atoms in this case would 'swallow' one another! . . .

Vasubandhu, however, in his non-Yogācāra text (*Abhidharmakośa-bhāṣya*) defended atomism, i.e. the notion of atoms constituting the perceived phenomena. Although these atoms are not 'physical' in the sense of constituting the physical bodies of the Nyāya-Vaiśeṣika school, still the question of their 'extension' in space remains open. The atoms are by definition indivisble and partless. This nature would be contradicted if they had 'extension', i.e. 'touched' one another to form a continuous spatial stretch. The Vaibhāṣikas argue that they do not 'touch' for they have intervening space between them (cf. *sāntara*), but a gathering of atoms can touch another similar gathering, for such a gathering is no longer impartite or indivisible. Hence we can say, 'a stone sticks to another stone' and 'one palm hits the other palm'. The other view maintains that there could be no gap between atoms (*nirantara*) when a conglomerate is perceived. Quoting an authority, Bhadanta, Vasubandhu says that although the atoms do not *touch*, when they are situated in the closest, gapless proximity we can say in words, 'they touched'. This avoids the quandary of the previous view, for if there were gaps between atoms a third atom could move in and therefore the resistance that a cluster of atoms creates for another cluster would be difficult for us to explain.

Matilal, B. (1986) *Perception: An Essay on Classical Indian Theories of Knowledge*, Oxford: Clarendon Press, pp. 359–61

See also NYAYA-VAISHESHIKA, YOGACHARA

3 A problem arose in Buddhist theories which did not wish to acknowledge the reality of the external world nor the reality of atoms themselves:

Apparently the Buddhist atomists argued against their Yogācāra opponents that to account for what is called the *ālambana-pratyaya* in Buddhist terminology, the causal and objective foundation of our perceptions, we have to refer to the external world, the atoms in space, and hence the external realities exist beside the *citta*, awareness or consciousness. Diṅnāga's strategy against this realism is this: the causal-objective foundation or *ālambana* by definition must fulfil two conditions: (i) it must cause the perception-episode, and (ii) it must also be apprehended in that cognition. The atoms, if they exist, may cause perceptions in the way the sense-organs do, but we can never apprehend individual atoms in such perceptions. The gross form which we apprehend in perception can never cause perceptions to arise for all the atomists presumably maintain that the gross form is only a phenomenal or nominal object which lacks causal power. Hence neither the atoms nor the (external) gross forms can be the objective-causal support of our perceptions.

Ibid., pp. 362–3

See also KNOWLEDGE, *PRAJNA*, YOGACHARA

Buddhists atomists presented different accounts of how the atoms combined **4** to make up our familiar world of experience:

Buddhist atomism reduces the spatial extension of external realities to atoms, the infinitesimals. The Buddhist 'flux' doctrine reduces the temporal extension, i.e. the temporal continuity of objects, to moments (the infinitesimals again). Modern examples are found in the techniques of photography and the movie. In photography, when discrete dots on a plate are put together without (perceptible) gaps, they create the picture of an extended object, the picture of a table. In a movie show, a sequence of frames showing the movements of a horse running are projected before our eyes fast enough (without perceptible time-gaps) to generate the illusion of a continuous motion-picture of a horse running. Although quite unaware of these examples, the Buddhist atomists and those Buddhists who upheld the flux doctrine but refuted atomism debated among themselves to find out the relative advantage of one position over the other.

Ibid., pp. 367–8

5 Discussion of atoms came to be understood in terms of analysis of the reality of relations:

There are, we may note, usually two extreme views regarding the ontological status of relation. One is presented by the Buddhist and explicitly advocated by Dharmakīrti. It may be stated as follows: If a universe consists of unique and independent (self-sufficient) atomic simples, no ontology of relation is necessary.

To summarize roughly Dharmakīrti's argument; a real relation may imply either dependence of one item upon another or a sort of mutual dependence (parāpekṣā). If an entity is already existent (has obtained its being) it cannot depend upon anything else. And if it is yet to come into existence, it can have no need to depend upon anything, for how can an absent (a non-existent) entity really depend on anything? Mutual dependence also cannot apply to two entities that are already existent, self-sustained, and distinct. And non-existent entities would be only like a pair of rabbit's horns. A real relation may also mean, according to some Buddhists, mingling, actual 'touching' of atoms that generate coloured shapes (rūpaśleṣa). But as we have already seen, partless atoms cannot really 'touch' each other. And if the atoms cannot touch, they cannot create gross visible forms. Therefore, if the world is a world of simple, atomic, self-sustained particulars, there can be no place for any real relation or connector. All so-called connectors would only be our subjective attribution.

Dharmakīrti further argues that if we seriously entertain the notion of a real connector we arrive at the following paradox: 'if two (entities) are related by virtue of there being a connection/relation between them, then what relates that relation to either of the two relata? It leads to infinite regress. Therefore, there is no *real* relation that we may come to know between the (first) two.'

Ibid., p. 412

See also CAUSATION, ONTOLOGY

AVATAR

1 Avatars are created by God and sent down to our world to help us find salvation:

Rāmānuja gives full treatment to the Epic teaching on Avatars, and adds ideas from his own theology. The theism which he struggled at length and with great subtlety to maintain, is well illustrated in the beautiful passage which concludes his commentary on the Vedānta Sūtra, and which other theists can appreciate:

'We know from Scripture that there is a Supreme Person whose nature is absolute bliss and goodness; who is fundamentally antagonistic to all evil; who is the cause of the origination, sustenation and dissolution of the world; who differs in nature from all other beings, who is all-knowing, who by his mere thought and will accomplishes all his purposes; who is an ocean of kindness as it were for all who depend on him; who is all-merciful; who is immeasurably raised above all possibility of any one being equal or superior to him; whose name is the Highest Brahman.

'And with equal certainty we know from Scripture that this Supreme Lord, when pleased by the faithful worship of his devotees . . . frees them from the influence of Nescience which consists of *karma* . . . and allows them to attain to that supreme bliss which consists in the direct intuition of his own true nature . . .

'We need not fear that the Supreme Lord, when once having taken to himself the devotee whom he greatly loves, will turn him back to *saṁsāra* (transmigration). For he himself has said, "To the wise man I am very dear, and he is dear to me".'

Parrinder, G. (1997) *Avatar and Incarnation*, Oxford: Oneworld, p. 57

See also KARMA

BHAGAVAD-GITA

Shankara presents an Advaita Vedanta understanding of the *Gita*: 1

THE *Gītā* is regarded by almost all sections of the Hindus as one of the most sacred religious works, and a large number of commentaries have been written on it by the adherents of different schools of thought, each of which explained the *Gītā* in its own favour. . . .

Saṅkara in his interpretation of the *Gītā* seeks principally to emphasize the dogma that right knowledge can never be combined with Vedic duties or the duties recommended by the legal scriptures. If through ignorance, or through attachment, a man continues to perform the Vedic duties, and if, as a result of sacrifice, gifts and *tapas* (religious austerities), his mind becomes pure and he acquires the right knowledge regarding the nature of the ultimate reality – that the passive Brahman is the all – and then, when all reasons for the performance of actions have ceased for him, still continues to perform the prescribed duties just like common men and to encourage others to behave in a similar manner, then such actions are inconsistent with right knowledge. When a man performs actions without desire or motive, they cannot be considered as *karma* at all. He alone may be said to be performing *karma*, or duties, who has any interest in them. But the wise man, who has no interest in his *karma*, cannot be said to be performing *karma* in the proper sense of the term, though to all outward appearances he may be acting exactly like an ordinary man. Therefore the main thesis of the *Gītā*, according to Śaṅkara, is that liberation can come only through right knowledge and not through knowledge combined with the performance of duties. Śaṅkara maintains that all duties hold good for us only in the stage of ignorance and not in the stage of wisdom. When once the right knowledge of identity with Brahman dawns and ignorance ceases, all notions of duality, which are presupposed by the performance of actions and responsibility for them, cease.

Dasgupta, S. (1932) *A History of Indian Philosophy*, II, Cambridge: Cambridge University Press, pp. 437–8

See also ACTION, ADVAITA, *BRAHMAN, KARMA*

2 The discussion between Krishna and Arjuna deals with the clash between individual ethical demands on the one hand and responsibilities to the community on the other. This was developed into complex philosophical theories:

Kṛṣṇa offers a number of reasons ranging from the metaphysical to the moral and social to persuade Arjuna that he must fight this lawful war (war of righteousness) regardless of the relationship that Arjuna has with the members of [the] opposing army. The moral reason offered by Kṛṣṇa is closely connected to the intrinsic nature of an individual and the social organisation of the community into the different *varṇas* (castes) – *brāhmin, kṣatriya, vaiśya* and *śūdra*. The right thing to do for Arjuna, according to Kṛṣṇa is to perform his duty. This is derived from the intrinsic nature and station of the individual. Accordingly, a *brāhmin's* duties are serenity, self-control, austerity, purity, forbearance and uprightness, wisdom, knowledge, and faith in religion. Heroism, vigour, steadiness, resourcefulness, not fleeing even in a battle, generosity, and leadership are the duties of the *kṣatriya*. Agriculture, tending cattle and trade are the duties of a *vaiśya* and work of the character of service is the duty of a *śūdra*. A perfect or happy life consists of doing that which is ordained by one's intrinsic nature (*svadharma*). It is important that one follows one's *svadharma* however imperfectly it may be done rather than following the *dharma* of another for which one is intrinsically unfit. As Kṛṣṇa says:

> Devoted each to his own duty man attains perfection . . .
> Better is one's own law though imperfectly carried out
> than the law of another carried out perfectly. One does not
> incur sin when one does the duty ordained by one's own
> nature. One should not give up the work suited to one's
> nature . . . though it may be defective, for all enterprises are
> clouded by defects as fire by smoke.

So, as a *kṣatriya* it is Arjuna's duty to fight the lawful war and not lay down his arms and leave the battle field or renounce the world as he suggests. But what of his feelings of attachment to his uncles, cousins, friends and companions? How should he rate his duty as a *kṣatriya* against his personal feelings? Is his duty as a *kṣatriya* such that he is to disregard his sentiments and kill even those he loves and respects? In response, Kṛṣṇa tells Arjuna that he must perform his duty, his social obligations as a *kṣatriya*, without any thought about the results of his action. His duty should not be viewed as a means to an end, as a means to attaining the kingdom, but as the end in itself. In other words, Arjuna must do his duty for duty's sake. Arjuna must not renounce the world but must renounce the fruits (*phala*) of his action (*karma*) – that is, his actions must be done in a dispassionate and detached manner. He should not think about the personal benefits or personal detriments – i.e. the consequences – that his actions may bring about for to do so would only result in pain and more sorrow. Perfection or freedom from human misery is achieved only by acting in a detached manner.

On the basis of the brief account of the discourse involving moral and social reasons between Kṛṣṇa and Arjuna the following observations of a general nature can be made:

1 Even though the *Gītā* addresses Arjuna's particular predicament its focus is on community directed social obligations.
2 The nature of an individual's social obligations is such that there is no room to accommodate an individual's needs and desires.
3 An individual must perform his duty for duty's sake, and not for the consequences that may flow from the performance of the duty.
4 Freedom from human misery can be achieved only by living in the midst of society and doing one's duty in the right frame of mind and not by living outside of it.

Mahalingam, I. (1996) "Friendship in Indian Philosophy" in *Friendship East and West: Philosophical Perspectives*, ed. O. Leaman, Richmond: Curzon, pp. 266–7

See also ACTION, CASTE, *KARMA*

---

3 Aurobindo argues that the *Gita* outlines a spiritual development from the idea of doing one's duty to something much higher:

The Gita intervenes with a restatement of the truth of the Spirit, of the Self, of God and of the world and Nature. It extends and remoulds the truth evolved by a later thought from the ancient Upanishads and ventures with assured steps on an endeavour to apply its solving power to the problem of life and action. The solution offered by the Gita does not disentangle all the problem as it offers itself to modern mankind; as stated here to a more ancient mentality, it does not meet the insistent pressure of the present mind of man for a collective advance, does not respond to its cry for a collective life that will at last embody a greater rational and ethical and, if possible, even a dynamic spiritual ideal. Its call is to the individual who has become capable of a complete spiritual existence; but for the rest of the race it prescribes only a gradual advance, to be wisely effected by following out faithfully with more and more of intelligence and moral purpose and with a final turn to spirituality the law of their nature. Its message touches the other smaller solutions but, even when it accepts them partly, it is to point them beyond themselves to a higher and more integral secret into which as yet only the few individuals have shown themselves fit to enter.

The Gita's message to the mind that follows after the vital and material life is that all life is indeed a manifestation of the universal Power in the individual, a derivation from the Self, a ray from the Divine, but actually it figures the Self and the Divine veiled in a disguising Maya, and to pursue the lower life for its own sake is to persist in a stumbling path and to enthrone our nature's obscure ignorance and not at all to find the true truth and complete law of existence. A gospel of the will to live, the will to power, of the satisfaction of desire, of the glorification of mere force and strength, of the worship of the ego and its vehement acquisitive self-will and tireless self-regarding intellect is the gospel of the Asura and it can lead only to some gigantic ruin and perdition. The vital and material man must accept for his government a religious and social and ideal Dharma by which, while satisfying desire and interest under right restrictions, he can train and subdue his lower personality and scrupulously attune it to a higher law both of the personal and the communal life.

The Gita's message to the mind occupied with the pursuit of intellectual, ethical and social standards, the mind that insists on salvation by the observance of established Dharmas, the moral law, social duty and function or the solutions of the liberated intelligence, is that this is indeed a very necessary stage, the Dharma has indeed to be observed and, rightly observed, can raise the stature of the spirit and prepare and serve the spiritual life, but still it is not the complete and last truth of existence. The soul of man has to go beyond to some more absolute Dharma of man's spiritual and immortal nature. And this can only be done if we repress and get rid of the ignorant formulations of the lower mental elements and the falsehood of egoistic personality, impersonalise the action of the intelligence and will, live in the identity of the one self in all, break out of all ego-moulds into the impersonal spirit. The mind moves under the limiting compulsion of the triple lower nature, it erects its standards in obedience to the tamasic, rajasic or at highest the sattwic qualities; but the destiny of the soul is a divine perfection and liberation and that can only be based in the freedom of our highest self, can only be found by passing through its vast impersonality and universality beyond mind into the integral light of the immeasurable Godhead and supreme Infinite who is beyond all Dharmas.

The Gita's message to those, absolutist seekers of the Infinite, who carry impersonality to an exclusive extreme, entertain an intolerant passion for the extinction of life and action and would have as the one ultimate aim and ideal an endeavour to cease from all individual being in the pure silence of the ineffable Spirit, is that this is indeed one path of journey and entry into the Infinite, but the most difficult, the ideal of inaction a dangerous thing to hold up by precept or example before the world, this way, though great, yet not the best way for man and this knowledge, though true, yet not the integral knowledge. The Supreme, the all-conscious Self, the Godhead, the Infinite is not solely a spiritual existence remote and ineffable; he is here in the universe at once hidden and expressed through man and the gods and through all beings and in all that is. And it is by finding him not only in some immutable silence but in the world and its beings and in all self and in all Nature, it is by raising to an integral as well as to a highest union with him all the activities of the intelligence, the heart, the will, the life that man can solve at once his inner riddle of Self and God and the outer problem of his active human existence. Made Godlike, God-becoming, he can enjoy the infinite breadth of a supreme spiritual consciousness that is reached through works no less than through love and knowledge. Immortal and free, he can continue his human action from that highest level and transmute it into a supreme and all-embracing divine activity, – that indeed is the ultimate crown and significance here of all works and living and sacrifice and the world's endeavour.

Aurobindo (1987) *The Essential Aurobindo*, ed. R. McDermott, Great Barrington, MA: Lindisfarne Press, pp. 137–9

See also BRAHMAN, DHARMA, GUNAS, MAYA, UPANISHADS

4 An argument that the *Gita* emphasizes the unity between spirituality and practice, between the transcendental and the material:

The central interest of the Gita's philosophy and Yoga is its attempt, the idea with which it sets out, continues and closes, to reconcile and even effect a kind of unity between the inner spiritual truth in its most absolute and integral realisation and the outer actualities of man's life and action. A compromise between the two is common enough, but that can never be a final and satisfactory solution. An ethical rendering of spirituality is also common and has its value as a law of conduct; but that is a mental solution which does not amount to a complete practical reconciliation of the whole truth of spirit with the whole truth of life and it raises as many problems as it solves. One of these is indeed the starting-point of the Gita; it sets out with an ethical problem raised by a conflict in which we have on one side the Dharma of the man of action, a prince and warrior and leader of men, the protagonist of a great crisis, of a struggle on the physical plane, the plane of actual life, between the powers of right and justice and the powers of wrong and injustice, the demand of the destiny of the race upon him that he shall resist and give battle and establish, even though through a terrible physical struggle and a giant slaughter, a new era and reign of truth and right and justice, and on the other side the ethical sense which condemns the means and the action as a sin, recoils from the price of individual suffering and social strife, unsettling and disturbance and regards abstention from violence and battle as the only way and the one right moral attitude. A spiritualised ethics insists on Ahinsa, on non-injuring and non-killing, as the highest law of spiritual conduct. The battle, if it is to be fought out at all, must be fought on the spiritual plane and by some kind of non-resistance or refusal of participation or only by soul resistance, and if this does not succeed on the external plane, if the force of injustice conquers, the individual will still have preserved his virtue and vindicated by his example the highest ideal. On the other hand, a more insistent extreme of the inner spiritual direction, passing beyond this struggle between social duty and an absolutist ethical ideal, is apt to take the ascetic turn and to point away from life and all its aims and standards of action towards another and celestial or supracosmic state in which alone beyond the perplexed vanity and illusion of man's birth and life and death there can be a pure spiritual existence. The Gita rejects none of these things in their place, – for it insists on the performance of the social duty, the following of the Dharma for the man who has to take his share in the common action, accepts Ahinsa as part of the highest spiritual-ethical ideal and recognises the ascetic renunciation as a way of spiritual salvation. And yet it goes boldly beyond all these conflicting positions; greatly daring, it justifies all life to the spirit as a significant manifestation of the one Divine Being and asserts the compatibility of a complete human action and a complete spiritual life lived in union with the Infinite, consonant with the highest Self, expressive of the perfect Godhead.

Aurobindo (1987) *The Essential Aurobindo*, ed. R. McDermott, Great Barrington, MA: Lindisfarne Press, pp. 132–3

See also *AHIMSA, DHARMA,* YOGA

5   A description of part of the discussion between Krishna and Arjuna in which many of the key concepts of the *Gita* emerge. These came to be much discussed in subsequent Hindu philosophies:

The first argument urged by Kṛṣṇa to persuade Arjuna to fight was that the self was immortal and that it was the body only that could be injured or killed, and that therefore Arjuna need not feel troubled because he was going to kill his kinsmen in the battle of Kurukṣetra. Upon the death of one body the self only changed to another, in which it was reborn, just as a man changed his old clothes for new ones. The body is always changing, and even in youth, middle age and old age, does not remain the same. The change at death is also a change of body, and so there is no intrinsic difference between the changes of the body at different stages of life and the ultimate change that is effected at death, when the old body is forsaken by the spirit and a new body is accepted. Our bodies are always changing, and, though the different stages in this growth in childhood, youth and old age represent comparatively small degrees of change, yet these ought to prepare our minds to realize the fact that death is also a similar change of body only and cannot, therefore, affect the unperturbed nature of the self, which, in spite of all changes of body at successive births and rebirths, remains unchanged in itself. When one is born one must die, and when one dies one must be reborn. Birth necessarily implies death, and death necessarily implies rebirth. There is no escape from this continually revolving cycle of birth and death. From Brahmā down to all living creatures there is a continuous rotation of birth, death and rebirth. In reply to Arjuna's questions as to what becomes of the man who, after proceeding a long way on the path of *yoga*, is somehow through his failings dislodged from it and dies, Krsna replies that no good work can be lost and a man who has been once on the path of right cannot suffer; so, when a man who was proceeding on the path of *yoga* is snatched away by the hand of death, he is born again in a family of pure and prosperous people or in a family of wise *yogins*; and in this new birth he is associated with his achievements in his last birth and begins anew his onward course of advancement, and the old practice of the previous birth carries him onward, without any effort on his part, in his new line of progress. By his continual efforts through many lives and the cumulative effects of the right endeavours of each life the *yogin* attains his final realization. Ordinarily the life of a man in each new birth depends upon the desires and ideas that he fixes upon at the time of his death. But those that think of God, the oldest instructor, the seer, the smallest of the small, the upholder of all, shining like the sun beyond all darkness, and fix their life-forces between their eyebrows, and control all the gates of their senses and their mind in their hearts, ultimately attain their highest realization in God.

Dasgupta, S. (1932) *A History of Indian Philosophy*, II, Cambridge: Cambridge University Press, pp. 518–19

See also DEATH, GOD, *SAMSARA*, YOGA

BHAKTI

Bhakti is worship, and *bhakti yoga* is following the path to enlightenment through worship

An account of the *Gita* as a discussion of the relationship between worship **1** and practice:

The first six chapters of the Gita form a sort of preliminary block of the teaching; all the rest, all the other twelve chapters are the working out of certain unfinished figures in this block which here are seen only as hints behind the large-size execution of the main motives, yet are in themselves of capital importance and are therefore reserved for a yet larger treatment on the other two faces of the work. If the Gita were not a great written Scripture which must be carried to its end, if it were actually a discourse by a living teacher to a disciple which could be resumed in good time, when the disciple was ready for farther truth, one could conceive of his stopping here at the end of the sixth chapter and saying, "Work this out first, there is plenty for you to do to realise it and you have the largest possible basis; as difficulties arise, they will solve themselves or I will solve them for you. But at present live out what I have told you; work in this spirit." True, there are many things here which cannot be properly understood except in the light thrown on them by what is to come after. . . .

Arjuna, himself, if the Teacher were to break off his discourse here, might well object: "You have spoken much of the destruction of desire and attachment, of equality, of the conquest of the senses and the stilling of the mind, of passionless and impersonal action, of the sacrifice of works, of the inner as preferable to the outer renunciation, and these things I understand intellectually, however difficult they may appear to me in practice. But you have also spoken of rising above the Gunas, while yet one remains in action, and you have not told me how the Gunas work, and unless I know that, it will be difficult for me to detect and rise above them. Besides, you have spoken of Bhakti as the greatest element in Yoga, yet you have talked much of works and knowledge, but very little or nothing of Bhakti. And to whom is Bhakti, this greatest thing, to be offered? Not to the still impersonal Self, certainly, but to you, the Lord. Tell me, then, what you are, who, as Bhakti is greater even than this self-knowledge, are greater than the immutable Self, which is yet itself greater than mutable Nature and the world of action, even as knowledge is greater than works. What is the relation between these three things? between works and knowledge and divine love? between the soul in Nature and the immutable Self and that which is at once the changeless Self of all and the Master of knowledge and love and works, the supreme Divinity who is here with me in this great battle and massacre my charioteer in the chariot of this fierce and terrible action?" It is to answer these questions that the rest of the Gita is written, and in a complete intellectual solution they have indeed to be taken up without delay and resolved. But in actual *sādhanā* one has to advance from stage to stage, leaving many things, indeed the greatest things to arise subsequently and solve themselves fully by the light of the advance we have made in spiritual experience. The Gita follows to a certain extent this curve of experience and puts first a sort of large preliminary basis of works and knowledge which contains an element leading up to Bhakti and to a greater knowledge, but not yet fully arriving. The six chapters present us with that basis.

Aurobindo (1987) *The Essential Aurobindo*, ed. R. McDermott, Great Barrington, MA: Lindisfarne Press, pp. 120–1

See also BHAGAVAD GITA, YOGA

A defence of worship as a route to God, as compared with the route of   2
jnana yoga, the use of knowledge to achieve that end:

Bhakti-Yoga is a real, genuine search after the Lord, a search beginning, continuing, and ending in Love. One single moment of the madness of extreme love to God brings us eternal freedom. "Bhakti," says Nârada in his explanation of the Bhakti-aphorisms, "is intense love to God." – "When a man gets it, he loves all, hates none; he becomes satisfied for ever." – "This love cannot be reduced to any earthly benefit," because so long as worldly desires last, that kind of love does not come. "Bhakti is greater than Karma, greater than Yoga, because these are intended for an object in view, while Bhakti is its own fruition, its own means, and its own end." . . .

There is not really so much difference between Knowledge (Jnana) and Love (Bhakti) as people sometimes imagine. We shall see as we go on, that in the end they converge and meet at the same point. . . .

The one great advantage of Bhakti is that it is the easiest, and the most natural way to reach the great divine end in view; its great disadvantage is that in its lower forms it oftentimes degenerates into hideous fanaticism. . . . That singleness of attachment (Nishthâ) to a loved object, without which no genuine love can grow, is very often also the cause of the denunciation of everything else. All the weak and undeveloped minds in every religion or country have only one way of loving their own ideal, i.e. by hating every other ideal. Herein is the explanation of why the same man who is so lovingly attached to his own ideal of God, so devoted to his own ideal of religion, becomes a howling fanatic as soon as he sees or hears anything of any other ideal.

This kind of love is somewhat like the canine instinct of guarding the master's property from intrusion; only, the instinct of the dog is better than the reason of man, for the dog never mistakes its master for an enemy in whatever dress he may come before it. Again, the fanatic loses all power of judgement. Personal considerations are in his case of such absorbing interest that to him it is no question at all what a man says – whether it is right or wrong; but the one thing he is always particularly careful to know is, who says it. The same man who is kind, good, honest, and loving to people of his own opinion, will not hesitate to do the vilest deeds, when they are directed against persons beyond the pale of his own religious brotherhood.

But this danger exists only in that stage of Bhakti which is called the *preparatory*. When Bhakti has become ripe and has passed into that form which is called the *supreme*, no more is there any fear of these hideous manifestations of fanaticism; that soul which is over-powered by this higher form of Bhakti is too near the God of Love to become an instrument for the diffusion of hatred.

It is not given to all of us to be harmonious in the building up of our characters in this life: yet we know that that character is of the noblest type in which all these three – knowledge and love and Yoga – are harmoniously fused. Three things are necessary for a bird to fly – the two wings and the tail as a rudder for steering. Jnana (knowledge) is the one wing, Bhakti (love) is the other, and Yoga is the tail that keeps up the balance. For those who cannot pursue all these three forms of worship together in harmony, and take up, therefore, Bhakti alone as their way, it is necessary always to remember that forms and ceremonials, though absolutely necessary for the progressive soul, have no other value than taking us on to that state in which we feel the most intense love to God.

Vivekananda, S. (1959) *Bhakti-Yoga*, Calcutta: Advaita Ashrama, p. 3, pp. 4–6

See also KARMA, KNOWLEDGE, LOVE, YOGA

BODHI

1   A description of how achieving enlightenment in Hua Yan Buddhism is seeing things in the right way:

"Bodhi" means in Chinese the Way or enlightenment. It means that when we look at the lion, we see right away that all dharmas produced through causes, even before disintegration, are from the very beginning quiescent and extinct. By being free from attachment or renunciation one will flow right along this way into the sea of perfect knowledge. Therefore it is called the Way. One understands right away that from time immemorial all afflictions resulting from passions originally have no reality. This is called enlightenment. The ultimate possession of the wisdom that knows all is called the achievement of perfect wisdom.

Chan, Wing-tsit (1972) *A Source Book in Chinese Philosophy*, Princeton: Princeton University Press, p. 413

See also ENLIGHTENMENT, HUA YAN

These very famous verses bring out the idea that achieving enlightenment 2 can be seen as like brushing the dust off a mirror and allowing the pure light of reality into the mind:

> The body is the tree of perfect wisdom (*bodhi*)
> The mind is the stand of a bright mirror.
> At all times diligently wipe it.
> Do not allow it to become dusty.

7. . . . The Fifth Patriarch said, "The verse you wrote shows some but not complete understanding. You have arrived at the front door but you have not yet entered it. Ordinary people, by practicing in accordance with your verse, will not fail. But it is futile to seek the supreme perfect wisdom while holding to such a view. One must enter the door and see his own nature. Go away and come back after thinking a day or two. Write another verse and present it to me. If then you have entered the door and have seen your own nature, I will give you the robe and the Law." Head Monk Shen-hsiu went away and for several days could not produce another verse.

8. . . . I (Hui-neng) also composed a verse. . . . My verse says:

> Fundamentally perfect wisdom has no tree.
> Nor has the bright mirror any stand.
> Buddha–nature is forever clear and pure.
> Where is there any dust?

Another verse, which says:

> The mind is the tree of perfect wisdom.
> The body is the stand of a bright mirror.
> The bright mirror is originally clear and pure.
> Where has it been defiled by any dust?

Ibid., p. 431–2

See also ZEN

BODHICHITTA

The enlightened or awakened mind is the aim of Buddhism.

1   A description of the links between the *bodhichitta*, on the one hand, and compassion and emptiness on the other. The enlightened mind, on the tantric view, is when it is most open:

> When, through prajna, the point is reached where shunyata and karuna are indivisible, there emerges *bodhicitta* (the bodhi-mind). Bodhicitta is that in which all that has been a limit has fallen away and all the positive qualities of mind have become active. This active aspect of the bodhicitta is what is meant by karuna. On this level, karuna is compassion in the true sense of that word – *con-passio*, "to feel with." This means to feel with what is real. It goes with the recognition of what is real and valuable in itself, not by virtue of some assigned or projected value which is basically subjective in character.
>
> We have such a strong tendency to approach our experience only as a possible confirmation of the conceptions we already have. If we are able to open, we grow. If we seek to relate everything to our preconceptions, then we are narrowing ourselves, narrowing being and we become lifeless. If we fail to see the vividness of life and try to pigeonhole it, we ourselves become pigeonholed, trapped. We must attempt to relate to this innate capacity for openness that is there, this self-existing freedom. If we are aware in this way, we will act accordingly. If we see things as valuable in themselves, then we will act productively so that value is retained and augmented rather than destroyed and reduced.
>
> If we constantly relate to and defend our preconceived ideas, everything is automatically reduced to what is known as *vikalpa*,

concept, which means something that is cut off from the whole. Then we have just the fragmentary world in which we are usually involved.

The foundation of the creative approach is openness, shunyata. It is more than the "nothing," by which it is usually translated. According to Buddhist tradition, this openness is the basis on which we can enrich our lives. It is the basis of the various tantric practices.

Guenther, H. and Trungpa, C. (1975) *The Dawn of Tantra*, Berkeley: Shambhala, pp. 32–3

See also COMPASSION, EMPTINESS, IMAGINATION, *TANTRA*

Kukai was the originator of shingon or tantric Buddhism in Japan. Here 2 he describes how the *bodhisattva*, the individual who is on the verge of becoming enlightened, can achieve his or her aim:

"The Buddha said: 'It is one's mind which seeks after enlightenment and all-inclusive wisdom. Why? The original nature of mind is pure and clean: it is neither within nor without; nor is it obtainable between them. O Lord of Mysteries, the perfect enlightenment of the Tathagata is neither blue, yellow, red, white, pink, purple, nor of crystal color; neither is it long, short, round, square, bright, dark; nor is it male, female, or androgynous. O Lord of Mysteries, the mind is identical neither with the nature of the world of desire, nor with that of the world of forms, nor with that of the world of formlessness. . . . It does not rest upon the world of perceptions of the ear, of the tongue, or of the mind. There is in it neither seeing nor seen. Why? The mind whose characteristic is like that of empty space, transcends both individuation and nonindividuation. The reason is that since the nature [of the mind] is identical with that of empty space, the nature is identical with the Mind; since the nature is identical with the Mind, it is identical with enlightenment. Thus, O Lord of Mysteries, these three – the mind, the characteristic of empty space, and enlightenment – are identical. They [the mind and enlightenment] are rooted in the spirit of compassion and are fully endowed with the wisdom of means. O Lord of Mysteries, I preach the doctrines in this way in order to make all bodhisattvas whose *bodhicitta* (enlightened mind) is pure and clean realize their mind. O Lord of Mysteries, if any man or woman wishes to realize it, he should realize his own mind in this way. O Lord of Mysteries, to realize one's own mind is to understand that the mind is unidentifiable in all causally conditioned phenomena, whether it is in colors, form, objects, things, perceptions, conceptions, predispositions, mind, I, mine, subjects of clinging, objects of clinging, pure state, sense organs, sense data, etc. O Lord of Mysteries, this teaching of the pure *bodhicitta* of the bodhisattvas is called the preliminary way of clarifying the Dharma.'"*

* The *Mahāvairocana Sutra.* T18, p. 3b.

trans. Hakeda, Y. (c) (1972) *Kukai: Major Works*, New York, Columbia University Press, pp. 208–9. Reprinted with permission of the publisher.

See also *BODHI, BODHISATTVA, DHARMA,* GENDER, *TANTRA, TATHAGATA*

3   An account of a central Mahayana thesis, that one should only achieve enlightenment for the sake of others, and a description of the stages towards it:

In connection with the idea of the Bodhisattva we should have a clear idea of Bodhicitta and its production (*bodhicitto-tpāda*), which play a very important part in the theological speculations of the Tāntric Buddhists as also in their Sādhanā of sexo-yogic practices. Bodhicitta means a *citta* or mind firmly bent on attaining *bodhi* (enlightenment) and becoming a Buddha thereby; and the production of Bodhicitta means the actual taking of the vow of attaining Buddhahood through the attainment of enlightenment. Ordinarily, a man may feel inclined towards Buddhism by listening to the preachings, or reading the scriptures and discussing them or by observing the activities of the advanced ones; but he will not be a Bodhisattva unless he actually produces the Bodhicitta within him. Again it has to be observed that the final aim of producing this Bodhicitta is to serve all beings by way of rendering all possible help to them in attaining liberation. One is to attain enlightenment and become a Buddha only for the sake of others; it has therefore been said, "Bodhicitta is perfect enlightenment (attained) for the sake of others (*bodhicittaṁ parārthāya samyaksambodhikā matā*)." This Bodhicitta is the immutable support of all the virtues and is the pre-requisite for the march towards Buddhahood through the various stages. . . . As Bodhicitta aims at the welfare of the Beings, there cannot be Bodhicitta without *Karuṇā* (compassion). This, we shall find, led to a new definition of Bodhicitta in the Tāntric Buddhist texts where it is said that Bodhicitta comprises in it two elements, *viz.*, enlightenment of the nature of essencelessness (*śūnyatā*) and universal compassion (*karuṇā*). This definition of Bodhicitta as the perfect commingling of *śūnyatā* and *karuṇā* had far-reaching effects in the transformation of the Mahāyānic ideas into the Tāntric ideas. After the production of Bodhicitta the adept becomes a Bodhisattva and proceeds on in an upward march through ten different stages which are called the *bodhisattva-bhūmis* (i.e., the stages of the Bodhisattva). The first of these is the stage of *Pramuditā* or the stage of delight or joy. Here the Bodhisattva rises from the cold, self-sufficing and nihilistic conception of *Nirvāṇa* to a higher spiritual contemplation. The second is styled as the *Vimalā* or the stage free from all defilement. The third is the *Prabhākarī* or that which brightens; in this stage the Bodhisattva attains a clear insight – an intellectual light about the nature of the dharmas. The fourth stage is the *Arciṣmatī* or 'full of flames', – these flames are the flames of Bodhi which burn to ashes all the passions and ignorance. At this stage the Bodhisattva practises thirty-seven virtues called *bodhi-pākṣikas* which mature the *bodhi* to perfection. The next is the *Sudurjayā* stage or the stage which is almost invincible. This is a stage from which no evil passion or temptation can move the Bodhisattva. The sixth stage is called the *Abhimukhī*, where the Bodhisattva is almost face to face with *prajñā* or the highest knowledge. The seventh is the *Dūraṅgamā* which literally means 'going far away'. In this stage the Bodhisattva attains the knowledge of the expedience which will help him in the attainment of salvation. Though he himself abides here by the principles of void and non-duality and desirelessness, yet his compassion for beings keeps him engaged in the activities for the well-being of all the creatures. The eighth is the stage of *Acalā*, which means 'immovable'. The next is the *Sādhumati* or the 'good will'; when the Bodhisattva reaches such a stage all the sentient beings are benefited by his attainment of the highest perfect knowledge. The tenth or the last is the stage of *Dharma-megha* (literally the 'clouds of dharma'), where the Bodhisattva attains perfect knowledge, great compassion, love and sympathy for all the sentient beings. When this last stage of *Dharma-megha* is reached, the aspirer becomes a perfect Bodhisattva or a Buddha.

This idea of the upward march of the Bodhisattva, after he produces the Bodhicitta within, got associated, all see, with the sexo-yogic process of the upward march of Bodhicitta after it is produced in the plexus of the navel region through the union of the *Prajñā* and *Upāya* – which were transformations of *Śūnyatā* and *Karuṇā*. Bodhicitta attains its perfection in the form of supreme bliss (*mahā-sukha*) after it reaches the highest plexus situated in the cerebrum region – and this realisation of the supreme bliss makes a Bodhisattva the Buddha himself.

Dasgupta, S. B. (1974) *An Introduction to Tantric Buddhism*, Shambhala: Berkeley 1974, pp. 8–10

See also BODHI, BODHISATTVA

BODHISATTVA

The *bodhisattva* is someone who has taken the vow to become a perfect Buddha and who acts appropriately.

1 Although Buddhists do not accept the notion of the self, they do emphasize the significance of acting for the sake of others:

> The Buddhists do not accept the notion of self, but they do accept a relationship between the realized and the unrealized persons, and articulate it in their notion of *karuṇā* or *mahākaruṇā*. Parallel to this is the notion of the *Bodhisattva* who feels his obligation to the suffering humanity to such an extent that he is prepared to forego entering the state of *nirvāṇa* in order to help them. But even though this is a great advance in the articulation of the relationship between those who have attained liberation and those who have not, it is still an asymmetrical relationship. It is the suffering humanity that needs the *Bodhisattva*; the *Bodhisattva* has no need of it. The seemingly similar notion of *avatāra* in Hindu thought is even more asymmetrical, as it is a relationship between God and man. It is only in certain schools of *bhakti* that the relation becomes a little more symmetrical, as God is supposed to need men almost as much as men need God.

But the relation between men . . . becomes basically contingent as it is only as *bhaktas*, that is, as devotees of the Lord, that they can have any real relation with one another.

Krishna, D. (1991) *Indian Philosophy: A Historical Analysis*, Delhi: Oxford University Press, p. 197. Reprinted by permission of Oxford University Press, New Delhi

See also AVATAR, *BHAKTI*, COMPASSION, *NIRVANA*

'BOOK OF CHANGES'

This is variously referred to as the *Zhouyi* or *Chou I* (WG), or *Yijing* or *I Ching* (WG). The former means the 'Changes of Zhou' and the latter 'Book of Changes':

The basic distinction between Chinese and Western metaphysics is that the former is largely concerned with working out the nature of the whole of reality, whereas the latter breaks up that reality in order to understand it. The symbols and their combinations in the 'Book of Changes' represents both the variety of the world, its basic principles and how they can operate together: [1]

> The *Zhouyi* symbolism presents itself as a system of 64 hexagrams which are ready to be used for practical divination. But this practical divination is premised on the fact that the world is a complex of complicated situations which requires a complex representation to the level of 64 hexagrams. Hence the hexagram system is practically, cosmologically, and existentially orientated. Furthermore, it is made relative to human needs and the experiences of human existence so that the hexagram representation makes totalistic and individualistic sense.

Cheng Chung-Ying 'Chinese metaphysics as non-metaphysics: Confucian and Daoist insights into the nature of reality' 167–208, extracts taken from *Understanding the Chinese mind*, ed. R. Allinson, Hong Kong: Oxford University Press, pp. 186–7

See also ONTOLOGY, *YIN* and *YANG*

2   For the present purpose of illustrating the *Yijing* metaphysical thinking as the originating form of Chinese philosophy and Chinese metaphysics, we shall concentrate on explaining the primary unity of the polarities of *yin* and *yang* as the founding experience of existence, life, and reality in Chinese philosophy. The most important characteristic of this way of thinking is that nothing in the experience of reality is left out in understanding reality. In fact, the experience is that of total reality and reality is that of total experience. The basic motif in Chinese metaphysical thinking is to preserve and present this totality of experience of reality and this reality of total experience in a comprehensive system of symbols, language, and undertaking.

The demarcation line in this way of metaphysical thinking is the integration of change and transformation and unchanging order and permanence, and hence the integration of difference and identity, and the integration of cosmic generation and *ontic* being. In short, it is the integration of becoming and being without giving up either becoming or being. It is in this sense that I have labelled the Chinese way of metaphysical thinking as *seeking the way*, in contrast with the Western way of metaphysical thinking as the *quest for being* which amounts to the elimination of becoming from being from the Chinese metaphysical point of view. The *Yijing* symbolic way of thinking precisely inaugurated Chinese metaphysical thinking as seeking the way, and has succeeded in making the integration of being and becoming possible.

The meanings of the primary symbols *yin* and *yang* are derived from the existential situation of man in understanding and relating to the world. The *yin* is the dark, shady side of the hill, whereas the *yang* is the bright and lighted side of the hill. This experience of shade and light is one of nature, but is also one of relevance for life-survival and death. For light can signify the conditions of growth, activity, and life; shade can signify the conditions of decline, rest, and lack of life or cessation of life.

Ibid., p. 187

See also YIN and YANG

---

3   An explanation of how a book of divination became a metaphysical text:

The *I Ching* (Book of Changes) was first of all a book of divination. Its original corpus is made up of the famous eight trigrams (*pa kua*), each consisting of combinations of three broken or unbroken lines, as follows: ☰ ☱ ☲ ☳ ☴ ☵ ☶ ☷. These are traditionally said to have been drawn by the mythological Emperor Fu Hsi. There are also sixty-four hexagrams derived from the original eight trigrams by combining any two of these into diagrams of six lines each, thus making a total of sixty-four different combinations. . . .

It is probable that during the Shang dynasty (1766?–1123? B.C.) the *I Ching's* eight trigrams were not yet in existence, since the Shang people then made divinations not by means of the divining plant (with which the *I Ching's* trigrams were originally associated), but by means of the tortoise shell. The former method was an invention of the Chou people, made either to substitute, or to supplement, the tortoise shell method. The *I Ching's* trigrams and hexagrams thus would seem to have originally been made as pictorial substitutes for the cracks formed in the tortoise shell when this was heated with fire by the diviner; while the explanations in the *I Ching* on each hexagram, and on the individual lines of each hexagram, would seem to correspond to the prognostications made by the Shang diviners when they examined the tortoise shell cracks. After such examination, these diviners would either make prognostications that were entirely new, or would sometimes utilize earlier prognostications. These earlier prognostications would be followed if the new cracks made in the shell were similar in form to cracks that were already known from former occasions; but when no prototypes existed, an entirely new prognostication had to be devised.

The cracks thus formed from the heating of a tortoise shell were numerous and intricate and hence difficult to interpret. Consequently the prognostications based on them were also complicated and difficult to remember. The use of the divining plant in conjunction with the *I Ching's* diagrams, however, put an end to these difficulties. For the diagrams of the *I Ching*, formed of broken and unbroken lines in such a way that they bore a certain resemblance to the cracks appearing in the tortoise shell, were at the same time limited in number to sixty-four combinations, with the result that their prognostications were likewise limited. Thus when divination was made up with the divination plant, a standard prognostication could always be obtained corresponding to whichever hexagram or line in the hexagram happened to be encountered, and the meaning of the prognostication could then be applied to the situation at hand. This was certainly a far easier method than that of the tortoise shell, in which any combination of new cracks might appear. Perhaps this explains the *I Ching's* alternative name of *Chou I*. It was named *Chou* from the fact that it was composed by the people of the Chou dynasty, and *I* because its method of divination was an easy one.

Fung, Yu-Lan (1952) *A History of Chinese Philosophy*, trans. D. Bodde, Princeton, Princeton University Press, pp. 379–80

4   A comparison of the hexagrams or symbols and the variables of logic:

Symbols are similar to what in symbolic logic are called variables. A variable functions as a substitute for a class or a number of classes of concrete objects. An object belonging to a certain class and satisfying certain conditions can fit into a certain formula with a certain variable; that is, it can fit into the comment made on a certain hexagram or a certain line within a hexagram, these hexagrams or lines being taken as symbols. This formula represents the *tao* which the objects of this class ought to obey. From the point of view of divination, if they obey it, they will enjoy good luck, but if not, they will suffer bad fortune. From the point of view of moral teaching, if they obey it, they are right, but if not, they are wrong.

Fung, Yu-Lan (1948) *A Short History of Chinese Philosophy*, New York: Free Press, p. 168

See also ANALYSIS, LOGIC

5   The Appendices of the *Yijing* bring out clearly what relationship is taken to exist between the principles of change and the idea of balance, an idea which was attractive to Confucianists:

One meaning of the name *Yi*, is transformation and change. The "Appendices" emphasize that all things in the universe are ever in a process of change. The comment on the third line of the eleventh hexagram states: "There is no level place without

58

a bank, and no departure without a return." This saying is considered by the "Appendices" as the formula according to which things undergo change. This is the *Tao* of the transformation of all things.

If a thing is to reach its completion and the state of completion is to be maintained, its operation must occur at the right place, in the right way, and at the right time. In the comments of the *Yi*, this rightness is usually indicated by the words *cheng* (correct, proper) and *chung* (the mean, center, middle). As to *cheng*, "Appendix I" states: "The woman has her correct place within, and the man has his correct place without. The correctness of position of man and woman is the great principle of Heaven and Earth. . . . When the father is father, and the son son; when the elder brother is elder brother, and the younger brother younger brother; when husband is husband, and wife wife: then the way of the family is correct. When it is correct, all under Heaven will be established."

Chung means neither too much nor too little. The natural inclination of man is to take too much. Hence both the "Appendices" and the *Lao-tzu* consider excess a great evil.

Ibid., pp. 170–1

See also GOLDEN MEAN, HEAVEN

An explanation of the popularity of the 'Book of Changes' with both Confucianists and Daoists: 6

The *Book of Changes* is one of the basic Confucian Classics. It is also much cherished by the Taoists. It is divided into the texts and commentaries. The texts consist of sixty-four hexagrams and judgments on them. These hexagrams are based on the Eight Trigrams, each of which consists of three lines, divided or undivided, the divided representing the weak, or yin, and the undivided representing the strong, or yang. Each of these eight corresponds to a direction, a natural element, a moral quality, etc. For example, *ch'ien* (Heaven) ☰ is heaven, *k'un* (Earth) ☷ is earth, *chen* (activity) ☳ is thunder, *sun* (bending) ☴ is wind, *k'an* (pit) ☵ is water, *li* (brightness) ☲ is fire, *ken* (to stop) ☶ is mountain, and *tui* (pleasure) ☱ is a collection of water. Each trigram is combined with another, one upon the other, thus making sixty-four hexagrams. These hexagrams symbolize all possible situations. For example, the hexagram with the water trigram over the fire trigram symbolizes conquest, success, etc.

Chan, Wing-tsit (1972) *A Source Book in Chinese Philosophy*, Princeton, Princeton University Press, p. 262

BRAHMAN

1   Shankara's account of the nature of reality, and its links with other key concepts in Indian philosophy:

ŚAṄKARA says that Brahman, as pure intelligence (*cin-mātram*) entirely divested of any kind of forms, is the ultimate reality (*paramārtha*), and that all differences of the knower, the known, and the diverse forms of cognition are all imposed on it and are false. Falsehood with him is an appearance which ceases to exist as soon as the reality is known, and this is caused by the defect (*doṣa*), which hides the true nature of reality and manifests various forms. The defect which produces the false world appearance is ignorance or nescience (*avidyā* or *māyā*), which can neither be said to be existent nor non-existent (*sad-asad-anirvacanīyā*), and this ceases (*nivṛtta*) when the Brahman is known. It is, indeed, true that in our ordinary experience we perceive difference and multiplicity; but this must be considered as faulty, because the faultless scriptures speak of the one truth as Brahman, and, though there are the other parts of the Vedas which impose on us the performance of the Vedic duties and therefore imply the existence of plurality, yet those texts which refer to the nature of Brahman as one must be considered to have greater validity; for they refer to the ultimate, whereas the Vedic injunctions are valid only with reference to the world of appearance or only so long as the ultimate reality is not known. Again, the scriptures describe the Brahman as the reality, the pure consciousness, the infinite (*satyaṃ jñānam anantaṃ brahma*); these are not qualities which belong to Brahman, but they are all identical in meaning, referring to the same differenceless identical entity, absolutely qualityless – the Brahman.

Dasgupta, S. (1940) *A History of Indian Philosophy*, III Cambridge: Cambridge University Press, pp. 165

See also ADVAITA, *BRAHMAN, MAYA*, VEDAS

Ramanuja opposed Shankara's account of reality, making it much more 2
similar to the idea of an ultimate cause:

> Thus Brahman as the world's efficient cause, i.e. as initiating
> and sustaining the action which brings the world into being,
> supports the world in the sense that the world cannot be realised
> as existent apart from him, but at the same time is seen to
> transcend the world through his sovereign (i.e. unnecessitated)
> causual action. . . .
>
> Rāmānuja differed from Śaṃkara. Śaṃkara also accepted that
> Brahman was both the substantial and the efficient cause of the
> world – but only in respect of the conditioned (i.e. the *saguṇa*)
> Brahman: Brahman viewed through the illusory spectacles of
> duality. From the final standpoint there is no ground for polarity-
> discourse, since there is but one reality (the *nirguṇa* Brahman)
> – non-dual, relationless and ineffable. Rāmānuja, by contrast,
> affirmed the permanent value of polarity-discourse in theology,
> and developed it methodologically. In fact, it is distinctive of
> his theological method to identify and to develop, on the basis
> of an equal hermeneutic status given to the different kinds
> of scriptural text (dualist, non-dualist, and so forth) and the
> religious experience grounded on these, a range of polarities, and
> to use their mutually counterbalancing modes of discourse,
> within the general framework of the self–body model, to
> articulate and 'comprehend' the unique sort of identity-in-
> difference he sought to preserve between his God and the world.
> Thus, though describing Brahman simultaneously as the world's
> substantial and efficient causes is not distinctive of Rāmānuja's
> system (Śaṃkara also calls Brahman the substantial and the
> efficient cause of the world, though he says this only of the *saguṇa*
> Brahman), identifying Brahman's originative causality in terms of
> a polarity is distinctive.

Lipner, J. (1986) *The Face of Truth: A Study of Meaning and Metaphysics in the Vedantic Theology of Ramanuja*, Basingstoke: Macmillan, pp. 135–6

See also CAUSATION, GOD

3   An argument based around a text of the *Mundaka Upanishad* to suggest that
the scriptures believe that God is even more basic than *brahman*:

> Brahman is the imperishable, immortal, manifesting itself as
> breathing spirit, speech, and mind. It is the 'beyond', the other
> world; but the Person, that is, the personal God, is beyond both
> this *and* the other world beyond. He is explicitly dissociated
> from both the 'imperishable' Brahman, from the breathing spirit,
> speech, and mind, with which in other Upanishads Brahman
> had been successively identified. He is the Creator Brahman, the
> matrix from which it proceeds.

> 'When the seer sees Him whose colour is gold
> The Creator (*kartāram*), Lord, Person, matrix of Brahman,
> Then, knowing good and evil, he shakes them off;
> Unstained he reaches the highest likeness (*sāmyam*) [to Him].'

> God's superiority and priority to the impersonal Brahman
> is here unambiguously recognized. Brahman corresponds to
> the ideal world of Plato, it is the stuff of soul and all immortal
> substances, but created or rather generated by God.

Zaehner, R. (1958) *At Sundry Times: An Essay in the Comparison of Religions*,
London: Faber, p. 108

See also GOD, *UPANISHADS*

---

4   An account of the links between knowledge, God, the soul and *brahman*:

> Here 'knowledge' is identified with the immortal Brahman,
> 'ignorance' with the perishable. This is the source of the later
> Vedāntin theory of *avidyā* as the cosmic ignorance which inheres
> in Brahman. Brahman, when understood in the sense of both
> the ideal and the phenomenal worlds must thereby remain
> permanently imperfect because permanently subject to change
> in one half of himself. Because, to the theistic conscience this is
> intolerable, God is seen as the Lord of Brahman, other than it,
> the Creator of the imperishable as well as the perishable world of
> matter. He is the Lord who sustains them both.
>   The classical Yoga, as we have already seen, admits a god,
> *īśvara*, who, however, is little more than the one pure soul which
> is eternally exempt from contact with matter, the exemplar,

then, of all souls still bound in matter. In the Śvetāśvatara Upanishad we have the natural development of this idea. Besides the general distinction drawn between the perishable and the imperishable there is also a distinction between imperishable beings or souls as such. On the one hand there is the Lord God who is omniscient and all-powerful, and on the other are all other souls which, through their union with matter, are ignorant and feeble. To *know* God means to be delivered from existence in space and time, to be released from all 'fetters'. Thus the idea of salvation is not substantially different from that of the Sāṁkhya-Yoga, it is not union with God, but realization of God's nature and His ability to assist the human soul out of its temporal existence into the imperishable world of Brahman. It is still *kaivalyam* or 'isolation', but it is an isolation in which an eternal something is recognized as constituting the real self or soul (*ātmasaṁstham*). This 'something' is the eternal soul-stuff, identical with God in that it shares with Him an eternal mode of existence, but not identical with Him as the creative source of both the eternal and the temporal modes of existence. It is possible to say, in the terminology of the Śvetāśvatara Upanishad, that the soul or *ātman* is Brahman because this simply means, as it does in Buddhism, that the soul is eternal or 'imperishable'.

Ibid., p. 110

See also ATMAN, GOD, KNOWLEDGE, SANKHYA-YOGA

Brahman identified with something much more basic at the source of nature 5
in the familiar Advaita Vedanta thesis:

Brahman is defined by Sankara as:

> That omniscient and omnipotent source . . . from which occur the birth, continuance, and dissolution of this universe that is manifested through name and form, that is associated with diverse agents and experiences, that provides the support for actions and results, having well-regulated space, time, and causation, and that defies all thoughts about the real nature of its creation. (BSB p. 14)

Shankara (1972) *Brahmasutrabhasya* (BSB), trans. S. Gamhirananda, Calcutta: Advaita Ashrama, p. 14

See also CAUSATION

6　By contrast with the preceding passage, *brahman* is here identified by Shankara with the individual self in quite a familiar way:

> The Self [*Brahman*] is not absolutely beyond apprehension, because It is apprehended as the content of the concept "I"; and because the Self, opposed to the non-Self, is well known in the world as an immediately perceived (ie. self-revealing) entity. (BSB p. 3)

Ibid., p. 3

See also ATMAN

BUDDHA

1　The Buddha sets out to oppose the methodological principles of Hinduism by seeking to understand the nature of human experience, not the abstract principles which are believed to exist behind it. Although this means making comments which appear to be paradoxical, they are part of the route to ultimate enlightenment:

> The early Upanishads are primarily metaphysical treatises concerned with identifying the Brahman, the ground of the universe. They are not consistent with themselves, nor are they consistent with the Sāṃkhya-Yoga which probably developed at much the same time. Yet wide as is their range, they are never concerned with a personal God in our sense of the word. That was an aspect of the older Vedic religion which they had almost entirely lost sight of. The later Upanishads and above all the Bhagavad-Gītā were to reverse this trend: they were to grope towards a personal, omnipotent, and omniscient God to whom even the neuter Brahman would be subjected. Before this was to happen, however, Buddhism was to intervene.
>
> The essence of early Brahmanism is the search for the Absolute and its natural development is in Vedāntin monism which claims that the soul is identical with the Absolute. We have seen that, in terms of experience, this probably means no more than the realization of the immortality of the soul. This experience was of supreme importance to the Brāhmans: it was

technically referred to as *mokṣa* or *mukti*, meaning 'release' from temporal existence, but in the Upanishads 'release' from temporal existence tends to be supplemented by self-realization as Brahman, or the All, or simply as the 'Self'. The Upanishads, however, remain primarily metaphysical, although the quite irrational elements of nature mysticism and monistic mysticism are certainly present, though always they try to explain these experiences metaphysically. This might be regarded as their greatest weakness. Be that as it may, they are not content to leave things unexplained.

The Buddha started from quite different premises. He is the complete empiricist. Unlike the Hindus he refused to admit (or deny) the existence of the Absolute; he is not even looking for one. He starts rather from the empirical standpoint and affirms that so far as anything is real, this world in which we live is real – and a very unpleasant world it is. Only one thing is empirically verifiable, and that is that all things are in a perpetual state of flux, not staying the same for a single moment. This is not only true of the universe in general; it is even more true of the human being, for the body is an ever-changing organism, never for two minutes the same. This is so obvious that even an ignorant man would conceive an aversion to the body as a loathsome, because a perishable, thing. Only one degree less foolish than the man who is not disgusted with his body is the man who thinks that there is any stability in mind or consciousness; for mind, so far from being more stable than body, is less so. The body may last a hundred years, but the mind 'keeps up an incessant round by day and night of perishing as one thing and springing up as another'.* Since there is no permanence in either body or mind, such a thing as a centre of consciousness in the shape of an ego or self cannot exist. Impermanence is the one basic fact of existence in the physical and mental world, and impermanence can be construed as pain or suffering. All existence is suffering – pain without beginning and without end.

The Buddha knew very well that his conviction that there is no such thing as a self or personality was not likely to be shared by the great majority of his contemporaries. The only way to convince them was by example, by leading a life in which there was never any thought of self but which was, nevertheless, perfectly serene. Only by example could others be made to understand that beatitude lies in the literal loss of self. Because he believed that the very idea of personality which he expressed in the words, 'This is mine; this am I; this is my self', was the source of all evil and was what made the attainment of Nirvāṇa impossible, he preached unselfishness in the most literal sense of that word – 'There is no such thing as the self' – and at the root of the false idea of self lies the basic evil which keeps this dreadful world in being, concupiscence or desire in all its manifestations, the desire to be as much as the desire to have.

*Saṁyutta Nikāya, xii, 62 in H. C. Warren, *Buddhism in Translations*, Cambridge, Mass., 1896, p. 151.

Zaehner, R. (1958) *At Sundry Times: An Essay in the Comparison of Religions*, London: Faber, pp. 94–5

See also ATMAN, BHAGAVAD GITA, BRAHMAN, MOKSHA, NIRVANA, SANKHYA-YOGA, UPANISHADS

---

2   The interesting question arose as to whether those who achieved the status of Buddha are different individuals or just parts of the same person. The answer explored here is that the nature of each Buddha is identical to the nature of every other Buddha, but they can take various forms and different names. This would be done as part of their effort to spread enlightenment around more generally:

The Dharma-body implied the unity of all Buddhas, and so their identity. Therefore *the* Buddha was actually *all* the Buddhas of the past. And on the other hand, according to the Sarvāstivādins, since the Dharmas are identical in all the Buddhas, the faithful does not take refuge in the physical Buddha but in his Dharma. The corporeal life of a Buddha was illusory anyway, for 'it is a rule' that all Bodhisattvas do so and so, and therefore it could be deduced that none of this was done in the flesh.

The Laṅkāvatāra Sūtra ('The Visit to Ceylon', Laṅkā) discusses the affirmation attributed to the Blessed One, 'I am all the Buddhas of the past'. This means that he had not only gone through a hundred thousand mortal births as men and animals, but also that he was previously the Buddhas Kāśyapa and others. The author distinguished four kinds of sameness in Buddhas. They are: (1) the sameness of letters, since his name B-u-d-d-h-a is used also for other Buddhas; (2) the sameness of words, in that he uses the sixty-four sounds of the Brahmin language like others; (3) the sameness of teachings, since all

Tathāgatas know the teachings of thirty-seven branches of enlightenment; and (4) the sameness of body, in that all Tathāgatas are the same in their Dharma-body, with signs and perfections. There is no distinction among them, except that the Tathāgata manifest varieties of forms to different beings.

This means that all Buddhas have the same essence. But, when they wish to do so, they can appear in various forms to many beings. These are acts of grace, or perfection, and it is often stressed that there is no karma which forces a Buddha to be born. Karma, which determines the births of all other creatures, has been destroyed, or never really existed, in such a divine being, and he appears, or appears to appear, by his own choice and will. The one Buddha assumes many names, and these are not only personal designations, but also abstract titles such as No-birth, Emptiness, Suchness, Eternity, Cessation, Nirvāna.

Parrinder, G. (1997) *Avatar and Incarnation*, Oxford: Oneworld, p. 178

See also BODDHISATTVA, DHARMA, KARMA, NIRVANA, TATHAGATA

BUDDHA NATURE

Everything can be seen as sharing the nature of the Buddha, even material things, and this is because anything can be a symbol of something more significant and capable of leading to enlightenment: **1**

There is a Zen saying that even a blade of grass can become a Buddha. How are we to understand this? Usually we consider that a blade of grass simply belongs to the physical world; it is not even a sentient being, since it has no feelings, makes no judgments, has no perceptions. The explanation is that everything is of the nature of Buddha, so grass is also of this nature. It is not that it in some way contains Buddha-nature, that we can nibble away analytically at the various attributes of the blade of grass until there is nothing left but some vague leftover factor that we then pigeonhole as Buddha-nature. Rather, the blade of grass actually constitutes what we call Buddhahood or an ultimate value.

It is in this sense that a blade of grass or any other object can be a symbol of transformation. The whole idea of symbols

of transformation is made possible by the philosophical development of the Yogacaras, who saw that what comes to us in earthly
vessels, as it were, the elements of our ordinary experience, *is* the
fundamental mind, the ultimate value. The ultimate value comes
in forms intelligible to us.

Guenther, H. and Trungpa, C. (1975) *Dawn of Tantra*, ed. G. Eddy (The
Clear Light Series) Berkeley: Shambhala, p. 18

See also YOGACHARA, ZEN

BUDDHI

1   *Buddhi* or intellect is linked to matter and to the notion of the mind and self:

In addition to its perceptual activities, *manas* is held to be
responsible for the cognitive functions of analysis, deliberation
and decision. It is closely allied to *buddhi*, which is somewhat
roughly translated as the faculty of 'intellect' or 'reason.' *Buddhi*
is a subtler and more powerful faculty than *manas*, and is responsible for the higher level intellectual functions, which require
intuition, insight and reflection. The Indian *buddhi* is in some
ways comparable to the Greek *nous*, while *manas* is responsible
for lower level discursive thought and analysis. But *buddhi*
is still regarded as a manifestation of *prakṛti*, albeit the most
subtle and refined form which material substance can assume.
The combination of *manas* and *buddhi* roughly correspond to
what is meant by the objective or 'impersonal' mental faculties
in western philosophical discourse. In addition, Sāṅkhya-Yoga
recognizes a third component of mind, *ahamkāra*, which is
the ego or phenomenal self. *Ahamkāra* appropriates all mental
experiences to itself, and thus 'personalizes' the objective activities of *manas* and *buddhi* by assuming possession of them. The
combination of these three faculties is referred to as *antahkaraṇa*,
the 'inner instrument,' which approximately comprises the
individual mind-self of the western philosophical tradition.

Schweitzer, P. (1993) "Mind/Consciousness Dualism in Sankhya-Yoga
Philosophy", *Philosophy and Phenomenological Research* LIII, 4, 845–59, p. 848

See also MANAS, SANKHYA-YOGA

The nature of intellect is variously understood by different philosophers. 2
Since the intellect is an effect of *brahman*, one might wonder how far it
could understand what caused it, and the *Upanishads* seem to throw doubt
on this possibility. All that is left as a means of understanding is meditation.

When the Upaniṣad says "that art thou," the idea at the back of
it is that the self is not to be identified with any of the elements
of the psychosis – the *buddhi* – or with any of the evolutes of the
prakṛti. The self is part of the pure consciousness – the Brahman.
When a man learns from the Upaniṣad text or one's teacher that
he is a part of Brahman he tries to realize it through a process
of meditation. The difference of the Vedāntic view from that of
Sāṃkhya is that the latter rests with the individual selves as the
ultimate entities whereas the former emphasizes the Brahman
as the ultimate reality, and also the fact that the reality of all other
things, the selves and the matter, depends ultimately on their
participation in it.

Brahma-Experience and Experience.

Cause may be defined as the productivity due to direct and
immediate perception of the material cause. The *buddhi* is
regarded as an effect because, like jugs and other things, it is
produced through some direct and immediate intuition of
its causal material. This naturally implies that the *buddhi* has a
causal material which is directly perceived by some Being and
to which His creative activity is directed and this Being is
God. It is said in the *Brahmasūtras* that Brahman can be known
by the testimony of the scriptures. But this cannot be true,
for the Upaniṣads say that the Brahman cannot be expressed
by words or known by intellect. The reply to this is that the
denial contemplated in such passages refers only to the fact that
Brahman cannot be known in entirety or in its uniqueness by the
scriptural texts, but these passages do not mean that it is not
possible to have a generic knowledge of the nature of Brahman.
It is only when we have such a generic knowledge from the
scriptures that we enter the sphere from which we may proceed
further and further through the processes of Yoga and have
ultimately a direct intuitive apperception of it. The specific
nature of God as devoid of any quality or character only means
that His nature is different from the nature of all other things, and
though such a nature may not be realized by ordinary perception,
inference or other sources of knowledge, there cannot be any

objection to its being apprehended by the intuition of Yoga meditation.

Dasgupta, S. (1940) *A History of Indian Philosophy*, III, Cambridge: Cambridge University Press, pp. 464–5

See also BRAHMAN, CAUSATION, GOD, MEDITATION, *PRAKRITI*, SANKHYA-YOGA, YOGA

BUSHIDO

The way of the samurai or warrior

1 The idea that losing fear of death leads to expertise in fighting is based on the principle that following the way (*do*) is natural provided we allow ourselves to go with the flow:

> To quote one of the stories cited in the *Hagakure*: Yagyū Tajima no kami Munenori was a great swordsman and teacher in the art to the Shogun of the time, Tokugawa Iyemitsu. One of the personal guards of the Shogun one day came to Tajima no kami wishing to be trained in swordplay. The master said, "As I observe, you seem to be a master of the art yourself; pray tell me to what school you belong, before we enter into the relationship of teacher and pupil."
>
> The guardsman said, "I am ashamed to confess that I have never learned the art."
>
> "Are you going to fool me? I am teacher to the honorable Shogun himself, and I know my judging eye never fails."
>
> "I am sorry to defy your honor, but I really know nothing."
>
> This resolute denial on the part of the visitor made the swordsmaster think for a while, and he finally said, "If you say so, that must be so; but still I am sure of your being master of something, though I know not just what."
>
> "Yes, if you insist, I will tell you this. There is one thing of which I can say I am complete master. When I was still a boy, the thought came upon me that as a samurai I ought in no circumstances to be afraid of death, and ever since I have grappled with the problem of death now for some years, and finally the problem has entirely ceased to worry me. May this be what you hint at?"
>
> "Exactly!" exclaimed Tajima no kami. "That is what I mean. I am glad I made no mistake in my judgment. For the ultimate

secrets of swordsmanship also lie in being released from the thought of death. I have trained ever so many hundreds of my pupils along this line, but so far none of them really deserve the final certificate for swordsmanship. You need no technical training, you are already a master."

Suzuki, D. (1973) *Zen and Japanese Culture*, Princeton: Princeton University Press, p. 71

See also DEATH

CASTE

Some have argued that the caste system is based on conduct not birth:　　**1**

The idea of a hereditary caste structure is not accepted in many Hindu documents, which suggest that caste should be determined by conduct not by birth.[1] Yudhisthira, for example, defined Brahmins in terms of their behaviour (truthful, forgiving, kind, and so on) and pointed out that a person should not be considered a Brahmin just because he was born in a Brahmin family, nor need he be a *Śūdra* even though his parents were *Śūdras* (*Mahābhārata, Vana Parva*, 180).

    1. That, at least in theory, caste was looked upon as a matter of character rather than of birth alone, is clearly seen in an interesting story of *Chāndogya Upanishad* (4, 4): 'Satyakāmá, the son of Jabālā, addressed his mother and said: "I wish to become a *Brahmacārin* (religious student), mother. Of what family am I?" She said to him: "I do not know, my child, of what family thou art. In my youth when I had to move about much as a servant (waiting on the guests in my father's house), I conceived thee. I do not know of what family thou art. I am Jābālā by name, thou art Satyakāma. Say that thou art Satyakāma Jābāla." He, going to Gautama Hāridrumata, said to him, "I wish to become a *Brahmacārin* with you, Sir. May I come to you, Sir?" He said to him: "Of what family are you, my friend?" He replied: "I do not know, Sir, of what family I am. I asked my mother, and she answered: 'In my youth when I had to move about much as a servant, I conceived thee. I do not know of what family thou art. I am Jabālā by name, thou art Satyakāma.' I am therefore Satyakāma Jābāla, Sir." He said to him: "No one but a true Brahmin would thus speak out. Go and fetch fuel, friend, I shall initiate you. You have not swerved from the truth"' (English translation by Max Müller from *Hindu Scriptures*. Everyman's Library, 1938, pp. 148–9).

Sen, K. (1973) *Hinduism*, Harmondsworth: Penguin, pp. 30–1

See also ETHICS

CAUSE/CAUSALITY/CAUSATION

1   Al-Ghazali argues that causal relations only seem to be necessary. Really they are just reflections of what God does, and have no inherent necessity at all. The passage from his *Incoherence of the Philosophers*, his attack on philosophy, is reproduced in Averroes' (ibn Rushd's) *Incoherence of the Incoherence*, a defence of philosophy:

> Ghazali demands from the philosophers a proof of sufficient rigour to establish the logical nature of the relationship between cause and effect. He does not in any way challenge the belief that some events in the world bring about other events, and that our experience of such facts provides us with good grounds for believing that we can make sense of what is going on in the world. All he challenges is the thesis that the causal nexus is necessary. Causal relations are only as they are because of God's organization of events in the world. Ghazali uses a number of examples to make his point. One involves a piece of cotton put in touch with a flame. He claims that there is no logical flaw in one's reasoning were one to deny that the cotton *must* catch fire:

> > We regard it as possible that the contact might occur without the burning taking place, and also that the cotton might be changed into ashes without any contact with fire, although the philosophers deny this possibility. The discussion of this matter has three points. The first is that our opponent claims that the agent of the burning is the fire alone; this is a natural, not a voluntary agent, and cannot abstain from what is in its nature when it is brought into contact with a receptive substratum (*TT* 316).

> Averroes is in no doubt concerning the serious implications of Ghazali's view:

> > Denial of cause implies the denial of knowledge, and denial of knowledge implies that nothing in this world can be really known, and that what is supposed to be known is nothing but opinion, that neither proof nor definition exist, and that the essential attributes which compose definitions are void. The man who denies the necessity of any item of knowledge must admit that even this, his own affirmation, is not necessary knowledge (*TT* 319).

> Two claims are made in this passage. The weaker claim is that were Ghazali correct, there could be no such thing as knowledge.

Were we to abandon the search for causes, then all enquiry would come to an end. However, we shall see that Ghazali is not in favour of abandoning the search for causes. The stronger objection is that if Ghazali were right then he refutes himself, since his proposition will have no sense. The connection between a concept of a thing and its causal properties is not just accidental, but it is rather a question of meaning. A concept of a thing has as part of its meaning various causal properties, and denying the necessary nature of this relation is to reject the meaning of the term itself. Indeed, we often only count a particular thing as a member of a certain class of objects if it shares basic causal properties with those other objects. For instance, a pencil with which it is impossible to write because it has no lead might well be denied the name 'pencil' given its lack of the causal power generally associated with pencils.

Leaman, O. (1985) *An Introduction to Medieval Islamic Philosophy*, Cambridge: Cambridge University Press, pp. 76–7

Note: TT reference is to (1978) *Averroes' Tahafut al-Tahafut* (*The Incoherence of the Incoherence*) trans. S. Van Den Bergh, London: Luzac

See also KNOWLEDGE, LANGUAGE

The different accounts of causation which the different theories produce try to answer the question whether a new thing is produced when a cause leads to an effect. Is the effect something which was already there in the cause, or is it something genuinely distinct?   2

One expects a mechanistic theory of nature to rule out emergence of new products and a teleological theory to allow it. But Indian thought belies this expectation. The Nyāya-Vaiśeṣika with its theory of atom-combinations vehemently argues for the thesis that when parts combine to produce a whole, the whole is more than the sum of those parts. The Sāṃkhya, which argues for nature's subservience to the purposes of spirits, yet construes that process of unfolding of nature as becoming-explicit of what is already implicitly there, so that there is no new production. From this contrast one may jump to the conclusion that, in the Indian mind, atomic combination was taken to yield a novel product: some forms of Buddhism show, however, that an atomism (of a sort) need not entail emergence of novelty. It would be instructive to look at these three possibilities as laying down the parameters of Indian thought about nature.

The Nyāya-Vaiśeṣika, Buddhism, and Sāṃkhya may be regarded as pushing to the centre of their thinking three quite different metaphors. The Nyāya-Vaiśeṣika metaphor is that of a potter putting together two parts (of a would-be jar) – that being the way the potter worked – to produce a jar. The Buddhist metaphor is that of a heap of sand (consisting, obviously, of innumerable tiny grains of sand). The Sāṃkhya root metaphor is that of oil-seed being pressed to yield oil that is already in it.

The issue between the Nyāya-Vaiśeṣika and Buddhism may be stated thus: is a whole a *mere* aggregate of parts or is it more than the sum of parts, i.e. a new entity over and above its parts? If the putative whole is nothing but the aggregate of its parts, that would be tantamount to saying that there is, strictly speaking, no genuine whole. The issues then may also be stated thus: are there, besides the elements, also wholes (*avayavin*)?

Mohanty, J. (1992) *Reason and Tradition in Indian Thought: An Essay on the Nature of Indian Philosophical Thinking*, Oxford: Clarendon Press, p. 215

See also ATOMISM, NYAYA-VAISHESHIKA, SANKHYA-YOGA

3 A summary of some of the main views on causation based on the *Gita* and their critics:

The *Gītā* is probably the earliest document where a definite statement is made regarding the imperishable nature of existent things and the impossibility of that which is non-existent coming into being. It says that what is non-existent cannot come into being, and that what exists cannot cease to be. In modern times we hear of the principle of the conversation of energy and also of the principle of the conversation of mass. The principle of the conservation of energy is distinctly referred to in the *Vyāsa-bhāṣya* on *Patañjali-sūtra*, IV. 3, but the idea of the conservation of mass does not seem to have been mentioned definitely anywhere. Both the Vedāntist and the Sāṃkhyist seem to base their philosophies on an ontological principle known as *sat-kārya-vāda*, which holds that the effect is already existent in the cause. The Vedānta holds that the effect as such is a mere appearance and has no true existence; the cause alone is truly existent. The Sāṃkhya, on the other hand, holds that the effect is but a modification of the causal substance, and, as such, is not non-existent, but has no existence separate from the cause; the effect may therefore be said to exist in the cause before the starting of the causal operation (*kāraṇa-vyāpāra*). Both these systems strongly object to the Buddhist and Nyāya view that the effect came into being out of non-existence, a doctrine known as *a-sat-kārya-vāda*.

Dasgupta, S. (1932) *History of Indian Philosophy*, II, Cambridge: Cambridge University Press, p. 517

See also *BHAGAVAD GITA*, NYAYA-VAISHESHIKA, SANKHYA-YOGA

An argument that the effect is really nothing but the cause, albeit in a different form: 4

If it be true that nature is uniform throughout, if it be true, and so far no human experience has contradicted it, that the same method under which a small grain of sand is created, works in creating the gigantic suns and stars and all this universe, if it be true that the whole of this universe is built on exactly the same plan as the atom, if it be true that the same law prevails throughout the universe, then, as it has been said in the Vedas, "Knowing one lump of clay we know the nature of all the clay that is in the universe". Take up a little plant and study its life, and we know the universe as it is. If we know one grain of sand, we understand the secret of the whole universe. Applying this course of reasoning to phenomena, we find, in the first place, that everything is almost similar at the beginning and the end. The mountain comes from the sand, and goes back to the sand, the river comes out of vapour, and goes back to vapour; plant life comes from the seed, and goes back to the seed; human life comes out of human germs, and goes back to human germs. The universe with its stars and planets has come out of a nebulous state and must go back to it. What do we learn from this? That the manifested or the grosser state is the effect, and the finer state the cause. Thousands of years ago, it was demonstrated by Kapila, the great father of all philosophy, that destruction means going back to the cause. If this table here is destroyed, it will go back to its cause, to those fine forms and particles which, combined, made this form which we call a table. If a man dies, he will go back to the elements which gave him his body; if this earth dies, it will go back to the elements which gave it form. This is what is called destruction, going back to the cause. Therefore we learn that the effect is the same as the cause, not different. It is only in another form. This glass is an effect, and it had its cause, and this cause is present in this form. A certain amount of the material called glass plus the form in the hands of the manufacturer, are the causes, the instrumental and the material, which, combined, produced this form called a glass. The force which was in the hands of the manufacturer is present in the glass as the power of adhesion, without which the particles would fall apart; and the glass material is also present. The glass is only a manifestation of these fine causes in a new shape, and if it be broken to pieces, the force which was present in the form of adhesion will go back and join its own element, and the particles of glass will remain the same until they take new forms.

Thus we find that the effect is never different from the cause. It is only that this effect is a reproduction of the cause in a grosser form. Next, we learn that all these particular forms which we call plants, animals, or men are being repeated *ad infinitum*, rising and falling. The seed produces the tree. The tree produces the seed which again comes up as another tree, and so on and on; there is no end to it. Waterdrops roll down the mountains into the ocean, and rise again as vapour, go back to the mountains and again come down to the ocean. So, rising and falling, the cycle goes on. So with all lives, so with all existence that we can see, feel, hear, or imagine. Everything that is within the bounds of our knowledge is proceeding in the same way, like breathing in and breathing out in the human body. Everything in creation goes on in this form, one wave rising, another falling, rising again, falling again. Each wave has its hollow, each hollow has its wave. The same law must apply to the universe taken as a whole, because of its uniformity. This universe must be resolved into its causes; the sun, moon, stars, and earth, the body and mind, and everything in this universe must return to their finer causes, disappear, be destroyed as it were. But they will live in the causes as fine forms. Out of these fine forms they will emerge again as new earths, suns, moons, and stars.

There is one fact more to learn about this rising and falling. The seed comes out of the tree; it does not immediately become a tree, but has a period of inactivity, or rather, a period of very fine unmanifested action. The seed has to work for some time beneath the soil. It breaks into pieces, degenerates as it were, and regeneration comes out of that degeneration. In the beginning, the whole of this universe has to work likewise for a period in that minute form, unseen and unmanifested, which is called chaos, and out of that comes a new projection. The whole period of one manifestation of this universe − its going down into the finer form, remaining there for some time, and coming out again − is, in Sanskrit, called a Kalpa or a Cycle. . . . Evolution does not come out of zero; then, where does it come from? From previous involution. The child is the man involved, and the man is the child evolved. The seed is the tree involved, and the tree is the seed evolved. All the possibilities of life are in the germ. The problem becomes a little clearer. Add to it the first idea of continuation of life. From the lowest protoplasm to the most perfect human being there is really but one life. Just as in one life we have so many various phases of expression, the protoplasm developing into the baby, the child, the young man, the old man, so, from that protoplasm up to the most perfect man we get one continuous life, one chain. This is evolution, but we have seen that each evolution presupposes an involution. The whole of this life which slowly manifests itself evolves itself from the protoplasm to the perfected human being, the Incarnation of God on earth − the whole of this series is but one life, and the whole of this manifestation must have been involved in that very protoplasm. This whole life, this very God on earth, was involved in it and slowly came out, manifesting itself slowly, slowly, slowly. The highest expression must have been there in the germ state in minute form; therefore this one force, this whole chain, is the involution of that cosmic life which is everywhere. It is this one mass of intelligence which, from the protoplasm up to the most perfected man, is slowly and slowly uncoiling itself. Not that it grows. Take off all ideas of growth from your mind. With the idea of growth is associated something coming from outside, something extraneous, which would give the lie to the truth that the Infinite which lies latent in every life is independent of all external conditions. It can never grow; It was always there, and only manifests Itself.

The effect is the cause manifested. There is no essential difference between the effect and the cause.

Vivekananda, S. (1961) *Jnana-Yoga*, Calcutta: Advaita Ashrama, pp. 238–41, 276–7

See also GOD, KNOWLEDGE, *SAMSARA*

5 Shankara regards the effect as evidence of what exists potentially in the material cause:

Another point which must be grasped to understand Sankara's opposition to Sankhya is that both his and their theories share even more in common than the analogies. In essence, Sankara thinks that the rival theory makes a first good move, but does not go far enough. The first move is (i) to see that the effect already *preexists* in some way in the material cause, before it becomes manifest through the intervention of some efficient cause, the second move is (ii) to see that the effect is in fact *identical* with its material cause. The argument for Sankara's conclusion comes under BSB II.ii.18.

Sankara establishes (i) by a consideration familiar in Sankhya texts. Why, he asks, is it possible to produce a given effect from only a particular material cause? Why are curds produced only from milk, or a pot from clay?

If everything is be equally non-existent everywhere before creation, why should curds be produced from milk alone and not from clay; and why should a pot come out of clay and not out of milk? (BSB p. 339)

We need to say that milk has a special *potency* for curd, or equivalently that the curds are *latent* in milk. Curds therefore preexist in a latent form is that which is peculiarly suited to be their material cause. Moreover, we cannot say that the *potency* is a separate existence from either the milk or the curds: if milk exists independently of the potency, or the potency exists independently of the curds, why should the milk have a special tendency to give rise to that potency and no other, or the potency a special tendency to give rise to the curds and not something else? The existence of the milk, the potency and the curds must be an intimate one: 'the potency must be the very essence of the cause, and the effect must be involved in the very core of the potency'. (BSB p. 340) At least in this sense, therefore, the conclusion follows that the effect must preexist in the material cause, and become manifest through the activity of an efficient cause or agent.

Carr, B. (1997) "Sankaracarya" *Companion Encyclopedia of Asian Philosophy*, ed. I. Mahalingam and B. Carr, London: Routledge, 189–210, pp. 198–9

(BSB see Shankara in References)

Nagarjuna criticizes the whole idea of the necessity of causation as implying the solidity of things and their relations. The attempt to discover the 'essence' of cause and effect is to dignify a series of experiences with inappropriate terminology.   6

7. There is fruit (*phala*) when a process, a sprout, etc., starts from a seed;
   But without a seed that [process] does not proceed.
8. Inasmuch as the process is dependent on a seed and the fruit is produced from the process,
   The fruit, presupposing the seed, neither comes to an end nor is eternal.
9. There is a product (*phala*) when a mental process starts from a thought;
   But without a thought that [process] does not proceed.
10. Inasmuch as the process is dependent on a thought and the product (*phala*) is produced from the process,
    The product, presupposing the thought, neither comes to an end nor is eternal.
11. The ten pure "paths of action" are means for realizing the *dharma*.
    And the five qualities of desired objects [i.e., desire to know the form, sound, odor, taste, and touch of existence] are fruits (*phala*) of the *dharma* both now and after death.
[A third opponent argues for an imperishable element:]
12. There would be many great mistakes if that explanation [were accepted].
    Therefore, that explanation is not possible.
13. In rebuttal I will explain the interpretation which can be made to fit [the facts],
    That which is followed by the Buddha, the self-sufficient enlightened ones (*pratyekabuddha*) and the disciples [of Buddha].

14. As "that which is imperishable" is like a credit [on an account statement], so an action (*karma*) is like a debt.
    [The imperishable is] of four kinds in its elements (*dhatu*) [i.e., desire, form, non-form, and pure]; in its essential nature it cannot be analyzed.

15. [An imperishable force] is not destroyed *qua* destruction; rather it is destroyed according to spiritual discipline.
    Therefore, the fruit of actions originates by the imperishable force.

16. If [the imperishable force] were that which is destroyed by [usual] destruction or by transference of action,
    Fallacies [like] the destruction of action would logically result.

17. At the moment of transition that [imperishable force]
    Of all identical and different actions belonging to the same element (*dhatu*) originates.

18. That [imperishable force] is the *dharma*, having arisen by one action after another in visible existence;
    And it remains [constant] even in the development of all bifurcating action.

19. That [imperishable force] is destroyed by death and by avoiding the product (*phala*).
    There the difference is characterized as impure and pure.

20. "Emptiness," "no annihilation," existence-in-flux, "non-eternity,"
    And the imperishable reality of action: such was the teaching taught by the Buddha.

[Nāgārjuna refutes the above arguments:]

21. Why does the action not originate? Because it is without self-existence.
    Since it does not originate, it does not perish.

22. If an action did exist as a self-existent thing, without a doubt, it would be eternal.
    An action would be an unproduced thing; certainly, there is no eternal thing which is produced.

23. If the action were not produced, then there could be the fear of attaining something from "something not produced";
    Then the opposite to a saintly discipline would follow as a fallacy.

24. Then, undoubtedly, all daily affairs would be precluded.
    And even the distinction between saints and sinners is not possible.

25. Then an act whose development had taken place would develop again,

If an act, because it persists, exists through its own nature.

26. An action is that whose "self" (*ātma*) is desire, and the desires do not really exist.

If these desires do not really exist, how would the action really exist?

27. Action and desire are declared to be the conditioning cause of the body.

If action and desire are empty, what need one say about "body"?

[An opponent tries to establish an identifiable entity by saying:]

28. The man shrouded in ignorance, and chained by craving (*tṛṣṇa*)

Is one who seeks enjoyment. He is not different from the one who acts, nor identical to it.

[Nāgārjuna answers:]

29. Since action is not "originated presupposing the conditions" nor fails to arise from presupposing the conditions,

There is no one acting.

30. If there is no action, how could there be one who acts and the product of action?

And if there is no product, how can there be an enjoyer of the product?

31. Just as a teacher, by his magical power, formed a magical form,

And this magical form formed again another magical form –

32. Just so the "one who forms" is himself being formed magically; and the act performed by him

Is like a magical form being magically formed by another magical form.

33. Desires, actions, bodies, producers, and products

Are like a fairy castle, resembling a mirage, a dream.

Streng, F. (1967) *Emptiness: A Study in Religious Meaning*, Nashville: Abingdon Press, pp. 202–3

See also ACTION, DEPENDENT ORIGINATION, EMPTINESS, *KARMA*, MADHYAMAKA

7 Here Nagarjuna is poking fun at the idea of causation and at the conceptual claims which many philosophers make about how causation takes place. He is trying to draw the conclusion that any assertion about what causation precisely is would be a mistake since it offends the principle of emptiness:

5. If a cause, having given the cause for a product, is stopped,
   Then that which is "given" and that which is stopped would be two identities of the cause.

6. If a cause without having given the cause for a product is stopped
   Then, the cause being stopped, the product would be produced as something derived from a non-cause (*āhetuka*).

7. If the product would become visible concomitantly with the aggregate [of causes and conditions],
   Then it would logically follow that the producer and that which is produced [exist] in the same moment.

8. If the product would become visible before the aggregate,
   Then the product, without being related to causes and conditions, would be something derived from a non-cause.

9. If, when the cause of the product is stopped, there would be a continuation of the cause,
   It would logically follow that there would be another production of the previous producing cause.

10. How can that which is stopped, i.e., something which has disappeared, produce the arising of a product?
    How could a cause which is enclosed by its product, even though it persists, originate [that product]?

11. Or if that [cause] were not enclosed by the product, which product would it produce?
    For the cause does not produce the product, having seen or not having seen [the product].

12. There is no concomitance of a past product with a past cause, a future [cause] or present [cause].

13. Certainly there is no concomitance of the present product with future cause, past [cause] or present [cause].

14. Certainly there is no concomitance of a future product with a present cause, future [cause] or past [cause].

15. If there is no concomitance whatever, how would the cause produce the product?
    Or if a concomitance exists, how would the cause produce the product?

16. If the cause is empty of a product, how would it produce the product?

    If the cause is *not* empty of a product, how would it produce the product?

17. A non-empty product would not be originated, [and] a non-empty [product] would not be destroyed.

    Then that is non-empty which will not originate or not disappear.

18. How would that be produced which is empty? How would that be destroyed which is empty?

    It logically follows, then, that which is empty is not originated and not destroyed.

19. Certainly a oneness of cause and product is not possible at all.

    Nor is a difference of cause and product possible at all.

20. If there were a oneness of the cause and product, then there would be an identity of the originator and what is originated.

    If there were a difference of product and cause, then a cause would be the same as that which is not a cause.

21. Can a cause produce a product which is essentially existing in itself (*svabhāva*)?

    Can a cause produce a product which is not essentially existing in itself (*svabhāva*)?

22. It is not possible to have "what is by its nature a cause" (*hetutva*) of "that which is not producing."

    If "what is by its nature a cause" is not possible, whose product will exist?

23. How will that [aggregate of causes and conditions] produce a product when

    That which is the aggregate of causes and conditions does not produce itself by itself?

24. The product is not produced by the aggregate; nor is the product *not* produced by the aggregate.

    Without the product, how is there an aggregate of conditions?

Ibid., pp. 206–7

See also EMPTINESS, MADHYAMAKA

---

8   By contrast with the above views, some early Buddhist views were very respectful of causation and saw it as a vital part of the description of experience:

> The universal applicability of the causal law is recognized in early Buddhism when it uses this causal principle to explain every phenomenon. We come across many instances in which the causal principle is applied to explain the functioning of physical, both organic and inorganic, phenomena. Among events that receive causal explanations are the evolution and dissolution of the world-process, natural occurrences like drought and earthquakes, and also plant life. A special application of the causal principle is made with reference to the human personality, a problem of prime importance to the Buddha as well as to the pre-Buddhist thinkers. This twelvefold formula of causation became very popular in the early Buddhist texts. Psychological processes are also explained in terms of the causal principle. Furthermore, moral and social, as well as spiritual, behavior find causal explanations. As later scholiasts grouped them, there are five main spheres or realms in which causality predominates: (1) physical (inorganic) order (*utu-niyāma*), (2) physical (organic) order (*bīja-niyāma*), (3) psychological order (*citta-niyāma*), (4) moral order (*kamma-niyāma*), and (5) ideal spiritual order (*dhamma-niyāma*).
>
> These five groups appear to be so all-inclusive that nothing in experience is excluded. In short, everything in this universe comes within the framework of causality. Hence, to know causation is to know the truth. This explains the Buddha's statement, "He who perceives causation (*paṭiccasamuppāda*) perceives the *dhamma*."

Kalupahana, D. (1996) *Buddhist Philosophy: A Historical Analysis*, Honolulu: University of Hawaii Press, p. 30

See also DEPENDENT CO-ORIGINATION, *DHARMA*

COMPASSION

1   Compassion is linked with emptiness because it should be based on acting in the appropriate way, i.e. on the basis that the dualism between subject and object is empty:

We act on the basis of our understanding, our awareness, and if this is not open and alive, then our actions are necessarily clumsy and inappropriate.

This leads us to the subject of *karuna*. It seems that awareness is not just there for the fun of the thing, but it implies action. Action carried out in the light of the awareness of shunyata, that is, the action of prajna, is karuna. Karuna is usually translated as "compassion" and in many cases that may be correct. But the word itself derives from the Sanskrit root *kr*, which denotes action. Just as with prajna, we can speak of karuna on many levels. On the highest level, on the level of the Buddha, we speak of *mahakaruna*, "the greatest karuna." Buddha's awareness was that of the awakened state of mind. He could not act otherwise than in the light of that complete awareness. This complete awareness is the fundamental example of the indivisibility of shunyata and karuna.

Guenther, H. and Trungpa, C. (1975) *The Dawn of Tantra*, Berkeley: Shambhala, p. 31

See also EMPTINESS

These series of meditations direct the compassion of the individual to others in a selfless way, and also increase his spiritual awareness by making him mindful of the different ways in which we may go awry:

> O compassion on these suffering conscious beings
> Who wander in the life cycle, darkened with delusions,
> Not knowing their own minds as the infinite Truth Body –
> May all of them attain the Body of Truth!

> O compassion on these conscious beings, misguided in desires,
> Who wander in the life cycle, identifying with lust and
>   clinging,
> Not knowing their self-awareness as great bliss Beatific Body –
> May all of them attain the Body of Beatitude!

> O compassion on these misconceiving beings
> Who wander in the life cycle, with the dualistic mind of hate,

Not knowing their own minds as the born-free Emanation
　Body –
May they all attain the Body of Emanation!

O compassion on all beings who are not yet Buddhas,
Trapped by the presence-habit of addictive and objective veils,
Not knowing their own minds as the indivisible Three
　Bodies –
May they all attain the Three Bodies of Buddhahood!

Sambhava, P. (1994) *The Tibetan Book of the Dead*, trans. R. Thurman, London: Aquarian/Thorsons, pp. 102–3

See also SAMSARA

CONFUCIANISM

1　One of the key points of Confucianism is that there is no essential disparity between the 'self-cultivation' of the individual and the interests of the community. On the contrary, these should be part of one harmonious whole:

> The logic of taking the cultivation of the self and the regulation of the family as "roots" and the ordering of the community, the governance of the state, and universal peace as "branches," may give the impression that complex political processes are reduced to simple relationships explainable in personal familial terms. Yet the dichotomy of root and branch conveys the sense of a dynamic transformation from self to family, to community, to state, and to the world as a whole. Self-cultivation is the root, and harmony attained in the family is a natural outgrowth, like the branch, of our cultivated selves. Family is the root, and harmony attained in the community, the state, and the world is a natural outgrowth of the well-regulated families. In this sense what we do in the privacy of our own homes profoundly shapes the quality of life in the state as a whole.
>
> Nevertheless, it is important to note that the Confucians do not, by stressing the centrality of self-cultivation, undermine the corporate effort that is required for the family, the community, the state, and the world to become humane or fully human.

Just as the self must overcome egoism to become authentically human, the family must overcome nepotism to become authentically human. By analogy, the community must overcome parochialism, the state must overcome ethnocentrism, and the world must overcome anthropocentrism to become authentically human. In light of Confucian inclusive humanism, the transformed self individually and corporately transcends egoism, nepotism, parochialism, ethnocentrism, and anthropocentrism to "form one body with Heaven, Earth, and the myriad things."

Tu Wei-Ming *Centrality and Commonality: An Essay on Confucian Religiousness*, Albany: SUNY, 1988, pp. 115–16

See also HARMONY, HEAVEN

Good faith – *xin* (c) or *hsin* (WG) – typifies the behaviour of the gentleman, and is particularly appropriate for relationships between friends: 2

Confucius never gave up on the idea of virtue or nobility. He had opened up the education of nobles to everyone irrespective of class (*Analects* 15:38). In so doing, he changed *hsin* into a virtue among friends. *Hsin* is now a self-imposed virtue since the Confucian gentleman always aspires high (14:24) and demands more of himself (15:20). The inferior person aspires low and always blames others for his own failings. But *hsin* remains at the same time an other-directed virtue, so that instead of saying as Polonius did to his son Horatio in *Hamlet* – 'And above all, to thyself be true' – a Chinese father would say, 'Better it is to fail yourself than to fail others.' The Chinese father is being prudent, because 'it is better to sin against a gentleman (because he can be forgiving) than to ever offend a petty soul (who would exact his pound of revenge).' But more is involved here. The Chinese word for 'to fail' also means 'to bear, to carry, to shoulder' such that the expression *tzu-fu pi-fan* does not mean 'defeating oneself . . . ' but 'holding oneself up high above the crowd.' In that sense, it is always easier to 'fail oneself' than to 'fail others.'

The Confucian gentleman is self-demanding but also other-deferring. He is humble before his own ego ideal but steadfast and proud in his moral standing. This is what Confucius taught: a nobility not of birth but of character. In the process, loyalty and trust were redefined. Loyalty eventually became a devotion to all tasks as trustworthiness became a mark of personal integrity. Meanwhile as the scholar gave up the sword for the brush, he also gave up certain heroic (i.e. military) virtues that civic Greeks never totally did. Gone from China but not from Greece were the physical closeness of comrades in arms; the exhilaration of combat; the desire to die in glory and young; as well as the riotous eating and drinking following any hard-won battle. In their place, a new set of virtues modelled after the Master himself arose: a disregard for wealth and comfort, an acceptance of anonymity and poverty (4:2, 5; 8:13; 6:9; 11:18), and a general aloofness from intrigues and strife (15:21).

Whalen Lai (1996) "Friendship in Confucian China" in *Friendship East and West: Philosophical Perspectives*, ed. O. Leaman, Richmond: Curzon, p. 225

3   Differences emerge between the Confucian and the Daoist over the nature of self-development. For the former constant effort is required to bring it about, for the latter the best way to proceed might be through not making any efforts at all:

> For the Confucian, the religious problem is not so much to realign the layers of one's being as it is to cleanse oneself from the selfishness that blocks the right operation of one's responsiveness to the harmonies of Heaven and Earth. Like the Puritans, the Confucians see the religious problem to be a positive evil in individuals (the Confucians disagree among themselves about the origin of selfishness, and about whether an unselfish person would do right naturally or would need education). I believe the Confucian soteriological path has three roughly distinguishable elements. The first is that individuals are defined by their relations to other things, principally to other people, and that these relations are given social structure. The first element of the cause of mixture then is a proper harmony of the individual with the cosmos, especially with its social components. The second element comes from the ancient recognition that true social harmony is different from faked codified harmony that in reality can involve oppression and hide selfishness. The emphasis on humanity, *ren*, from Kongzi through Neo-Confucianism, is aimed to give authenticity, life, and spontaneity to the pursuit of social harmony. The rules of propriety are not the norms for social behavior; the norm rather is the authentic human spirit that inhabits them. It was for this reason that Kongzi was willing to wear the economical silk cap

rather than the ostentatious linen one, but was not willing to short cut respect for ancestors by eliminating the bow outside the temple (*Analects* 9:3). The third element is that the way to achieve harmony with the cosmos is through personal cultivation. Whereas the philosophical Daoist would be wary of making a project out of self-development, the Confucian believes that constant effort is required to identify and eliminate the pockets of selfishness blocking the way to harmony.

Neville, Robert 'The Chinese Case in a Philosophy of World Religions' 48–74, in Allinson, R. (ed.) (1989) *Understanding the Chinese Mind*, Hong Kong: Oxford University Press, p. 71

See also ACTION, DAOISM, HEAVEN, HUMANITY

CONSCIOUSNESS

See also SELF

Buddhists tend to criticize the notion of consciousness if this is taken to 1 imply the existence of a persisting self-consciousness. Their opponents like Shankara point out that we assume that our consciousness continues despite the changing nature of experience, since after all that changing experience is experience of a continuing subject:

One difficulty of this theory, as should be immediately obvious and as was pointed out by most anti–Buddhist philosophers, is that it fails to account for the unity of self-consciousness and for experiences such as memory and recognition. If every perception, every state of consciousness, is its own subject – which is what the theory amounts to, since on this theory every state of consciousness is also self-intimating – then it follows that two or more different states cannot be ascribed, except erroneously, to the same subject. There being no identical subject of experiences, one necessary condition of the possibility for memory and recognition would remain unsatisfied: this condition being that the present recollection and the past experience to which it relates should 'belong' to the same subject. I cannot recollect your experiences. I cannot recognize a person whom you have seen, not I. This sort of transcendental argument, it may be replied, assumes that memory and recognition are, at least in some cases, veridical and the Buddhist may very well question this assumption itself, thereby wanting to render the transcendental argument ineffective *ab initio*. The Buddhist may then contend that although ordinary experience is based on the claim of memory to be valid, in reality, from the metaphysical point of view, it is based on ignorance; so also is recognition. In both cases we are mistaking similarity and membership of a series as identity. Both fail to take note of discontinuity and surreptitiously substitute for it continuity. In the face of such a challenge, the Hindu philosophers argue that the radicality of this thesis (which holds not merely that memory and recognition are sometimes deceptive, but that they are, as a matter of principle, always deceptive) would vitiate all ordinary experience including perception, for perception, as a matter of essential necessity, is a possible basis for memory and recognition. In other words what is now perceived may be recollected and recognized as the same. Such a scepticism, instead of answering the question we set out to answer, would destroy the foundations on which that question was based. Furthermore, recognition of an external object may err; similarly may in fact be mistaken for sameness. But how can similarity be mistaken for sameness, if there is no non-illusory application for the concept of sameness? How can the judgement 'This is the same as that' be mistaken, if sometimes a judgement of that form is not true? Coming back now to the sense of 'I' how could my sense of self-identity be mistaken when even the possibility for its correct application is ruled out? As Śaṃkara argued, no one ever raises the doubt 'Do I exist?' No one is bothered by the doubt 'Am I the same person or not?'. One may concede that one's personality, character, self-image may radically change over time, but even in such cases an external observer would want to say, if he followed the route taken by that change, that they are but succeeding states of one and the same self, and, in principle, it is possible for the person himself to say 'I have changed a great deal', which implies that he is still the same I.

For the Hindu thinkers, the identity of the I is a condition of the possibility of knowledge, of social life and moral relationships, of suffering and enjoyment, of spiritual bondage and release from that bondage, or ignorance and illumination.

Mohanty, J. (1992) *Reason and Tradition in Indian Thought: An Essay on the Nature of Indian Philosophical Thinking*, Oxford: Clarendon Press, pp. 30–1

See also ADVAITA, *ANATMAN, ATMAN*

There is a whole continuum of views on the nature of consciousness, 2
ranging from the Charvakas who claim that the subject is really only the
body, to the Buddhists who argue that there is no subject at all:

> In the broad spectrum of views arising out of Indian speculations
> on this problem, the Cārvāka view that the 'I' in all these
> instances stands for one sort of thing, namely the body, stands at
> one end, while at the other end there is what may be called the
> Buddhist no-entity theory according to which the 'I' does not
> stand for any entity at all. In between these two extremes, there
> are, broadly speaking, two significant varieties of dualism: one of
> these holds the near-Cartesian view that physical properties
> are ascribed to the body and states of consciousness to the self
> (*ātmā*), which is a substance distinct from the body and its sense-
> organs as also from what may be roughly called the mind. For
> the other, the 'I' is not ambiguous as it is for the first view, but
> rather stands for a complex formed out of two heterogenous
> things: consciousness on the one hand and mind on the other.
> While this complex is the thing of which conscious states are
> directly predicated, physical states are only indirectly predicated
> of it – they are directly predicated of the body. The former view
> is defended, in spite of the other differences between them, by
> philosophers of both the Nyāya-Vaiśeṣika and Mīmāmsā schools;
> the latter by the Vedānta of Śaṃkara.

Ibid., p. 27

See also ADVAITA, *ANATMAN, ATMAN,* MATERIALISM,
MIMAMSA, NYAYA-VAISHESHIKA

The controversy over whether consciousness is formed or not is an 3
important part of the analysis of what it is:

> Let me begin with the first of the above questions: does
> consciousness have a form of its own, or is it formless? *ākāra* –
> which is translated here as 'form' but could also be rendered as
> 'shape' – is a function of the structural arrangement of the parts
> of a thing. Material things which are made up of parts are, in this
> sense, formed or *sākāra*. It is in this sense that the Nyāya and the

Mīmāmsā realists deny any form to consciousness. Since, in their view, consciousness is not a substance (*dravya*) but rather a quality (*guṇa*) or an action (*karma*) . . . it must be without parts. In the Nyāya ontology, only a substance can be made up of parts, a quality and an action cannot. The Buddhists who oppose this view and hold that consciousness is always formed (*sākāra*) have in their minds, curiously enough, the instantaneous events of consciousing, which, for them, is no less partless; it is the absolutely simple instantaneous consciousings, of which our conscious lives are in the long run constituted. It would seem, then, that while the realists reject the possibility of consciousness's having a form of its own on the ground of its not being a composite entity, the Buddhists do not consider this as counting against their thesis that consciousness, the simple event of consciousing, has a form of its own. Obviously they must be using the world *ākāra* in a sense different from the realist's. What then do the Buddhists mean by saying that consciousness is *sākāra*?

In relation to perceptual consciousness, the Buddhists hold that, for example, the cognition 'This is blue' has the form 'blue'. Now of course an event of consciousing, as the Buddhists construe it, cannot itself be blue, but is a consciousing–of–blue. In other words, being–of–blue is constitutive of it. In order to appreciate the precise nature of the Buddhist position, contrast it with a view pertinently expressed by G. E. Moore. Moore held that consciousness of blue and consciousness of yellow agree, i.e. are the same inasmuch as they are consciousnesses; they differ only with respect to their objects, i.e. blue and yellow. Since the objects fall outside consciousness, the two states of consciousness, *qua* consciousness, are the same. (They may, to be sure, differ in many other respects, such as their temporal location, owner-ship, etc.) This the Buddhists would regard as an intellectual abstraction. Being nominalists of a sort, they are unwilling to hypostatize 'consciousness as such'. Every event of consciousing is different from every other. Being idealists of a sort – and we are talking of the Yogācāras at present – they do not accept the independent existence of an external object, so a consciousing's being of blue is really, phenomenologically that is to say, being-of-blue. This being-of-blue as a constitutive feature of that event is its *ākāra* or form. It is a distinct concrete event with its inner distinctive feature that is not borrowed from an alleged external object, namely, the patch of blue over there I think I see.

Ibid., pp. 34–5

See also GUNAS, KARMA, YOGACHARA

Shankara presents an account of consciousness which differentiates it   4
sharply from its contents. While the latter may be changing and temporary,
the former is immutable and permanent:

> The Vedānta holds that the fact of consciousness is entirely
> different from everything else. So long as the assemblage of the
> physical or physiological conditions antecedent to the rise of any
> cognition, as for instance, the presence of illumination, sense-
> object contact, etc., is being prepared, there is no knowledge,
> and it is only at a particular moment that the cognition of an
> object arises. This cognition is in its nature so much different
> from each and all the elements constituting the so-called assem-
> blage of conditions, that it cannot in any sense be regarded as the
> product of any collocation of conditions. Consciousness thus,
> not being a product of anything and not being further analysable
> into any constituents, cannot also be regarded as a momentary
> flashing. Uncaused and unproduced, it is eternal, infinite and
> unlimited. The main point in which consciousness differs from
> everything else is the fact of its self-revelation. There is no
> complexity in consciousness. It is extremely simple, and its only
> essence or characteristic is pure self-revelation. The so-called
> momentary flashing of consciousness is not due to the fact that
> it is momentary, that it rises into being and is then destroyed
> the next moment, but to the fact that the objects that are
> revealed by it are reflected through it from time to time. But the
> consciousness is always steady and unchangeable in itself.

Dasgupta, S. (1932) *History of Indian Philosophy*, II, Cambridge: Cambridge
University Press, pp. 62–3

See also ADVAITA, *ATMAN*

Advaita Vedanta sought to defeat a variety of contrary views in Indian   5
philosophy on the nature of consciousness:

> The Vedānta had to refute three opponents in establishing its
> doctrine that the self is of the nature of pure consciousness and that

it is permanent and not momentary. The first opponent was the Buddhist, who believed neither in the existence of the self nor in the nature of any pure permanent consciousness. The Buddhist objection that there was no permanent self could be well warded off by the Vedānta by appealing to the verdict of our notion of self-identity – which could not be explained on the Buddhist method by the supposition of two separate notions of a past "that self" and the present "I am." Nor can consciousness be regarded as being nothing more than a series of passing ideas or particular awarenesses; for on such a theory it would be impossible to explain how we can react upon our mental states and note their differences. Consciousness has thus to be admitted as permanent. Against the second opponent, the Naiyāyika, the Vedānta urges that the self is not the inferred object to which awarenesses, volitions or feelings belong, but is directly and immediately intuited. For, had it not been so, how could one distinguish his own experiences as his own and as different from those of others? The internalness of my own experiences shows that they are directly intuited as my own, and not merely supposed as belonging to some self who was the possessor of his experiences. For inference cannot reveal the internalness of any cognition or feeling. Against the third opponent, the Mīmāṃsaka, the Vedānta urges that the self-revealing character belongs to the self which is identical with thought – as against the Mīmāṃsā view, that thought as a self-revealing entity revealed the self and the objects as different from it. The identity of the self and thought and the self-revealing character of it are also urged; and it is shown by a variety of dialectical reasoning that such a supposition is the only reasonable alternative that is left to us.

Ibid., pp. 71–2

See also ADVAITA, *ANATMAN, ATMAN,* MIMAMSA, NYAYA-VAISHESHIKA

---

6   Although the *Upanishads* talks about the self and consciousness, its precise nature still has to be determined, and the link it has with experience can be described in a variety of ways:

The nature of the self, as we have described it, is also attested by the verdict of the *Upaniṣads*. This self is directly revealed in its

94

own notion as "I," and pleasure, pain, attachment, antipathy are but its states, which are also revealed along with the revelation of its own self as the "I." This self is not, however, perceived by any of the senses or even by the organ *manas*, as Kumārila supposed. For the question arises as to when, if the self is believed to be perceived by the *manas*, that takes place? It cannot take place precisely at the moment when the knowledge of an object arises; for then the notions of the self and the objects, as they occur at the same moment, could not so appear that one (the self) was the cognizer or determiner, and the others (the objects) were the cognized or the determined. If the knowledge of the objects and the self arose at two different moments as separate acts, it would be difficult to conceive how they could be related as cognizer and cognized. So it cannot be held that the self, though it always manifests itself to us in self-consciousness, could yet be perceived by any of the senses or the *manas*. . . .

Some hold that the self is known from the objective consciousness and not directly by itself. It is easy to see that this can hardly be accepted as true; for how can objective consciousness, which refers to the objects, in any way produce the consciousness of the self? According to this view it is difficult to prove even the existence of knowledge; for this, since it is not self-manifested, requires something else to manifest it; if it is thought that it is self-manifesting, then we should expect it to be manifested to all persons and at all times. It may be said that, though knowledge is self-manifesting, yet it can be manifested only in connection with the person in whom it inheres, and not in connection with all persons. If that be so, it really comes to this, that knowledge can become manifested only through its connection with a someone who knows. If, in answer to this, it is said that knowledge does not require its connection with a person for its own existence, but only for its specific illumination as occurring with reference to a certain subject and object, then that cannot be proved. We could have accepted it if we had known any case in which pure consciousness or knowledge had been found apart from its specific references of subject and object. If it is still asserted that consciousness cannot be separated from its self-manifesting capacities, then it may also be pointed out that consciousness is never found separated from the person, the subject, or the knower who possesses it. Instead of conceding the self-manifesting power to the infinite number of states of consciousness, is it not better to say that the self-manifestation of consciousness proceeds from the self-conscious agent, the subject and determiner of all conscious experiences? Even if the states of consciousness had been admitted as self-manifesting, that would not explain how the self could be self-manifesting on the account.

Ibid., vol. III pp. 148–9

See also ANATMAN, ATMAN, MANAS, UPANISHADS

7 Shankara had to respond to the critique of the Lokayatika materialist doctrines which argued that there is no soul, only body:

Śankara, in interpreting the *Brahma-sūtra*, III, 3. 53, 54, tries to refute the *lokayatika* doctrine of soullessness. The main points in the *lokayatika* argument here described are that since consciousness exists only when there is a body, and does not exist when there is no body, this consciousness must be a product of the body. Life-movements, consciousness, memory and other intellectual functions also belong to the body, since they are experienced only in the body and not outside of it. To this Śankara's reply is that life-movements, memory, etc., do not sometimes exist even when the body exists (at death), therefore they cannot be the products of the body. The qualities of the body, such as colour, form, etc., can be perceived by everyone, but there are some who cannot perceive consciousness, memory, etc. Again, though these are perceived so long as the living body exists, yet there is no proof that it does not exist when this body is destroyed. Further, if consciousness is a product of the body, it could not grasp the body; no fire can burn itself and no dancer can mount his own shoulders. Consciousness is always one and unchangeable and is therefore to be regarded as the immortal self. Though ordinarily the self is found to manifest itself in association with a body, that only shows that the body is its instrument, but it does not prove that the self is the product of the body, as is contended by the Cārvākas.

Ibid., vol. III pp. 548–9

See also ADVAITA, MATERIALISM

CREATION

Although Shankara is happy to acknowledge God as the creator of the   1
world, the precise nature of that creation is problematic. If he created the
world for a purpose, then that would diminish him as an agent, since he
would have to follow some aim and act in accordance with it. On the other
hand, if he creates merely haphazardly the process looks rather ridiculous:

> When speaking of God, Śaṅkara sometimes refers to him as
> *saguṇa* Brahman (qualified Brahman), and sometimes as Īśvara
> (Lord). God is thus contrasted with *nirguṇa* Brahman, who has
> no properties whatsoever and cannot therefore be adequately
> described in language. The *saguṇa* Brahman or Īśvara serves a
> similar function to that of the demiurge in neo-Platonism. In
> this respect the Śaṅkaran God is viewed as directly related to the
> world, in other words, as *māyā*, and is therefore open to human
> understanding, both as the first cause of the world and as object
> of devotion. The Śaṅkaran God is, as Deutsch puts it, "that
> about which something can be said."[1]

Śaṅkara not only holds that God is the creator of the world,
but speaks of the specific way in which God carried out the act
of creation. Śaṅkara gives two examples in order to clarify the
nature of the process of creation:

> We see in everyday life that certain doings of princes
> or other men of high position who have no unfulfilled
> desires left have no reference to any extraneous purpose,
> but proceed from mere sportfulness as, for instance, their
> recreations in places of amusements. We further see that
> the process of inhalation and exhalation is going on with-
> out reference to any extraneous purpose, merely following
> the law of its own nature.

Śaṅkara then draws an analogy between these examples and
God's creation of the world:

> Analogously, the activity of the Lord also may be supposed
> to be mere sport (*līlā*), proceeding from its own nature,
> without reference to any purpose. For on the ground
> neither of reason nor of Scripture can we construe
> any other purpose of the Lord. Nor can his nature be
> questioned. Although the creation of this world appears to
> us a weighty and difficult undertaking, it is mere play
> to the lord, whose power is unlimited.[2]

97

Deutsch summarizes Śaṅkara's position with great clarity:

> The concept of *līlā*, of play or sport, seeks to convey that
> Īśvara creates (sustains and destroys) worlds out of sheer
> joy of doing so. Answering to no compelling necessity, his
> creative act is simply a release of energy for its own sake.
> Creation is not informed by any selfish motive. It is spon-
> taneous, without any purpose.[3]

At first glance the notion that the creation of the world took place
without any purpose seems implausible, if not absurd. It would
seem that there is no essential difference between the claim
that the world was created in play or sport and the claim that the
world exists out of sheer chance. Moreover, it would seem
that describing God as creating the world in play or sport makes
God a ridiculous figure and makes the very concept of God
meaningless. In fact, the *līlā* theory of creation was criticized along
these lines. For example, the Jainist school maintained that,

> If you say that he created to no purpose, because it was his
> nature to do so, then God is pointless.
> If he created in some kind of sport, it was the sport of a
> foolish child, leading to trouble.[4]

1 Deutsch, E. (1969) *Advaita Vedanta: A Philosophical Reconstruction*,
   Honolulu: East-West Center Press, p. 12
2 Thibaut, G. (tr) (1890) *The Vedanta Sutras of Badarayana, with the
   Commentary by Sankara*, Oxford: Clarendon Press, I, pp. 356–7
3 Deutsch, pp. 38–9
4 Mahapurana, in (1958) *Sources of Indian Tradition* ed. W. de Bary, New
   York: Columbia University Press, I, p. 77

Biderman, S. (1982) 'A "constitutive" God – an Indian solution', *Philosophy
East and West*, 32, 425–37, copyright University of Hawai'i Press, pp. 426–7

See also BRAHMAN, CAUSATION, GOD, *LILA*

---

2   The material requires shaping before it can take on a different form. It is
    appropriate to reason from the visible to the hidden:

> For neither earth etc. nor chariot etc. which are themselves
> insentient, are seen to have any tendency to behave in a particular
> way unless they are under the guidance of potters and others or
> horses and the like. The unseen has to be inferred from the seen.
> (BSB p. 371)

Shankara (1972) *Brahmasutrabhasya*, (BSB) trans. S. Gamhirananda, Calcutta: Advaita Ashrama, p. 371

See also CAUSATION

Al-Farabi argues that there could not have been a time when God existed and **3** the world did not exist. If God waited before creating the world then there must have been something standing in his way, which is impossible. If the world is worth creating, and God could create it at any time, then there could not have been a time at which he would not create it:

> What delays his making it is the obstacle to his making it, and the non-success which he thinks and knows will occur, if he makes the thing at that time is the obstacle which prevents his making it . . . If there is no cause of non-success, its non-existence is not preferable to its existence, and why did it not happen? . . . if he were personally the sole cause of the success, the success of the action should not be retarded in time, but both should happen together, and therefore when the agent is sufficient in himself alone for something to come into existence from him, it follows that the existence of the thing is not later than the existence of the agent.

Farabi (1961) *The fusul al-madani of al-Farabi* ('Aphorisms of the statesman') ed. and trans. D. Dunlop, Cambridge: Cambridge University Press, p. 66

See also CAUSATION, TIME

DAOISM

Our civilized lives takes us away from acting naturally in line with the **1** *dao*, the simple way in which things actually persist. Once we let go of the conceptual complication of what we regard as the world and acknowledge the emptiness of everything we can align ourselves harmoniously with what is around us:

> For the Daoist tradition, the religious (or cultural) problem is that our civilized life becomes detached from and out of harmony with the *dao*. In terms of our analysis this means that civilized life does not adequately acknowledge and express its roots in the relation between the eternal and named *dao*, in the originating impulse of

incipient non-being. The Daoist path thus is a celebration of emptiness, of nothingness, of relaxation into a womb-like unactive readiness. This rarely if ever has meant a pursuit of mystical fusion and bliss, of *samadhi*. Rather, the emptiness is to be recognized in the fullness of practical life, in the space between the spokes, in the hollow of the bowl. The esoteric Daoist cultivation of immortality in the form of the primeval infant is not a search for a transcendent, non-temporal blissful union with the *dao*, but a continuation of individual life reinforced and reorganized by the originating incipiency of infancy. In the practical life of philosophical Daoism, the search for the simple is not a yearning for ancient times, but an attitude shift about present life, a letting go of striving, a welcoming of the spontaneous impulses grounded ontologically in the eternal *dao*. The cause of mixture is conceived in Daoism as a vertical harmony among the various horizontal levels of reality, a harmony such that the more specific levels are given their truest operation by letting them express the creativity of the lower levels. The Daoist butcher did not gain expertise by ever more advanced courses in bovine anatomy. Rather, he learned to let the placing of the blade and the shove of his shoulder be in tune with the nothingness, the hollows and spaces, that pervade the ox as much as himself.

Neville, Robert 'The Chinese case in a philosophy of world religions' 48–74, in Allinson, R. (ed.) (1989) *Understanding the Chinese Mind*, Hong Kong: Oxford University Press, pp. 70–1

See also BUSHIDO, EMPTINESS

2   Daoists try to define the *dao* or the way, and emphasize that the main aim is to point out its paradoxical status. It is impossible to define it using language, yet being silent about it will not define it either:

"The Way cannot be thought of as being, nor can it be thought of as nonbeing. In calling it the Way we are only adopting a temporary expedient. 'Nothing does it,' 'something makes it like this' – these occupy a mere corner of the realm of things. What connection could they have with the Great Method? If you talk in a worthy manner, you can talk all day long and all of it will pertain to the Way. But if you talk in an unworthy manner, you can talk all day long and all of it will pertain to mere things. The perfection of the Way and things – neither words nor silence are worthy of expressing it. Not to talk, not to be silent – this is the highest form of debate."

Chuang Tzu (1968) *The Complete Works of Chuang Tzu*, trans. B. Watson, New York: Columbia University Press, p. 293

It is a central Daoist principle that it is dangerous to be useful. The best way 3 of living is to appear to be useless, and then everyone else leaves one alone. This is more than an interesting political point, though, and is based on the idea that what appears to be weak may well be strong, and vice versa:

Tzu-ch'i of Nan-po was wandering around the Hill of Shang when he saw a huge tree there, different from all the rest. A thousand teams of horses could have taken shelter under it and its shade would have covered them all. Tzu-ch'i said, "What tree is this? It must certainly have some extraordinary usefulness!" But, looking up, he saw that the smaller limbs were gnarled and twisted, unfit for beams or rafters, and looking down, he saw that the trunk was pitted and rotten and could not be used for coffins. He licked one of the leaves and it blistered his mouth and made it sore. He sniffed the odor and it was enough to make a man drunk for three days. "It turns out to be a completely unusable tree," said Tzu-ch'i, "and so it has been able to grow this big. Aha! – it is this unusableness that the Holy Man makes use of!"

The region of Ching-shih in Sung is fine for growing catalpas, cypresses, and mulberries. But those that are more than one or two arm-lengths around are cut down for people who want monkey perches; those that are three or four spans around are cut down for the ridgepoles of tall roofs; and those that are seven or eight spans are cut down for the families of nobles or rich merchants who want side boards for coffins. So they never get to live out the years Heaven gave them, but are cut down in mid-journey by axes. This is the danger of being usable.

Ibid., p. 65

The difficulties of naming the *dao* is explored. Since it is entirely beyond 4 language, language cannot successfully encapsulate it, and yet we have to use language to try to get close to it:

In the first chapter of the *Lao-tzu* we find the statement: "The *Tao* that can be comprised in words is not the eternal *Tao*; the name that can be named is not the abiding name. The Unnamable is the beginning of Heaven and Earth; the namable is the mother of all things." And in chapter thirty-two: "The *Tao* is eternal, nameless, the Uncarved Block. . . . Once the block is carved, there are names." Or in chapter forty-one: "The *Tao*, lying hid, is nameless." In the Taoist system, there is a distinction between *yu* (being) and *wu* (non-being), and between *yu-ming* (having-name, namable) and *wu-ming* (having-no-name, unnamable). These two distinctions are in reality only one, for *yu* and *wu* are actually simply abbreviated terms for *yu-ming* and *wu-ming*. Heaven and Earth and all things are namables. Thus Heaven has the name of Heaven, Earth the name Earth, and each kind of thing has the name of that kind. There being Heaven, Earth and all things, it follows that there are the names of Heaven, Earth, and all things. Or as Lao Tzu says: "Once the Block is carved, there are names." The *Tao*, however, is unnamable; at the same time it is that by which all namables come to be. This is why Lao Tzu says: "The Unnamable is the beginning of Heaven and Earth; the namable is the mother of all things."

Since the *Tao* is unnamable, it therefore cannot be comprised in words. But since we wish to speak about it, we are forced to give it some kind of designation. We therefore call it *Tao*, which is really not a name at all. That is to say, to call the *Tao* *Tao*, is not the same as to call a table table. When we call a table, we mean that it has some attributes by which it can be named. But when we call the *Tao* *Tao*, we do not mean that it has any such namable attributes. It is simply a designation, or to use an expression common in Chinese philosophy, *Tao* is a name which is not a name. In Chapter twenty-one of the *Lao-tzu* it is said: "From the past to the present, its [*Tao*'s] name has not ceased to be, and has seen the beginning [of all things]." The *Tao* is that by which anything and everything comes to be. Since there are always things, *Tao* never ceases to be and the name of *Tao* also never ceases to be. It is the beginning of all beginnings, and therefore it has seen the beginning of all things. A name that never ceases to be is an abiding name, and such a name is in reality not a name at all. Therefore it is said: "The name that can be named is not the abiding name."

Fung Yu-Lan (1948) *A Short History of Chinese Philosophy*, New York: Free Press, pp. 94–5

See also LANGUAGE

Another listing of apparent paradoxes which suggests that the best way to   5
attain an end is often not to try to attain it:

Lao Tzu warns us: "Not to know the invariable and to act blindly is to go to disaster." One should know the laws of nature and conduct one's activities in accordance with them. This, by Lao Tzu, is called "practicing enlightenment." The general rule for the man "practicing enlightenment" is that if he wants to achieve anything, he starts with its opposite, and if he wants to retain anything, he admits in it something of its opposite. If one wants to be strong, one must start with a feeling that one is weak, and if one wants to preserve capitalism, one must admit in it some elements of socialism.

Therefore Lao Tzu tells us: "The sage, putting himself in the background, is always to the fore. Remaining outside, he is always there. Is it not just because he does not strive for any personal end, that all his personal ends are fulfilled?" (*Lao-tzu* Ch. 7.) Again: "He does not show himself; therefore he is seen everywhere. He does not define himself; therefore he is distinct. He does not assert himself; therefore he succeeds. He does not boast of his work; therefore he endures. He does not contend, and for that very reason no one in the world can contend with him." (Ch. 22.) These sayings illustrate the first point of the general rule.

In the *Lao-tzu* we also find: "What is most perfect seems to have something missing, yet its use is unimpaired. What is most full seems empty, yet its use is exhaustible. What is most straight seems like crookedness. The greatest skill seems like clumsiness. The greatest eloquence seems like stuttering." (Ch. 45.) Again: "Be twisted and one shall be whole. Be crooked and one shall be straight. Be hollow and one shall be filled. Be tattered and one shall be renewed. Have little and one shall obtain. But have much and one shall be perplexed." (Ch. 22.) This illustrates the second point of the general rule.

Such is the way in which a prudent man can live safely in the world and achieve his aims. This is Lao Tzu's answer and solution to the original problem of the Taoists, which was, how to preserve life and avoid harm and danger in the human world. The man who lives prudently must be meek, humble, and easily content. To be meek is the way to preserve your strength and so be strong.

Ibid., p. 99

See also ACTION

6   A defence of the significance of being flexible:

> When people are born, they're supple and soft;
> When they die, they end up stretched out firm and rigid;
> When the ten thousand things and grasses and trees are alive,
>   they're supple and pliant;
> When they're dead, they're withered and dried out.
> Therefore we say that the firm and rigid are companions of
>   death,
> While the supple, the soft, the weak, and the delicate are
>   companions of life.
> If a soldier is rigid, he won't win;
> If a tree is rigid, it will come to its end.
> Rigidity and power occupy the inferior position;
> Suppleness, softness, weakness, and delicateness occupy the
>   superior position.

Laozi, trans. R. Henricks (1989) *Lao-Tzu: Te Tao Ching*, New York, Ballantine, Ch. 76 p. 47

7   Daoism is not to be identified with renouncing the world, but really with practical action:

> The Taoist philosophy is perhaps best summed up in the *Chuang Tzu*, which says, "To regard the fundamental as the essence, to regard things as coarse, to regard accumulation as deficiency, and to dwell quietly alone with the spiritual and the intelligent – herein lie the techniques of Tao of the ancients. Kuan Yin and Lao Tan (Lao Tzu) heard of them and were delighted. They built their doctrines on the principle of eternal non-being and held the idea of the Great One as fundamental. To them weakness and humility were the expression, and openness and emptiness that did not destroy anything were the reality."
>
> One should not be misled by its ideals of weakness and emptiness into thinking that Taoism is a philosophy of negativism or one of absolute quietism. The book advocates not only non-action, but also practical tactics for action. It teaches submission, but strongly opposes oppressive government. The philosophy of the *Lao Tzu* is not for the hermit, but for the sage–ruler, who does not desert the world but rules it with non-interference.

Taoism is therefore not a philosophy of withdrawal. Man is to follow Nature but in doing so he is not eliminated; instead, his nature is fulfilled. Any comparison of Taoism with Logos or Brahman must take these facts into account.

Chan, Wing-tsit (1963) *A Source Book in Chinese Philosophy*, Princeton, Princeton University Press, pp. 136–7

See also BRAHMAN

A central identification of *dao* with emptiness is explored: **8**

Tao is empty (like a bowl),
It may be used but its capacity is never exhausted.
It is bottomless, perhaps the ancestor of all things.
It blunts its sharpness,
It unties its tangles.
It softens its light.
It becomes one with the dusty world.
Deep and still, it appears to exist forever.
I do not know whose son it is.
It seems to have existed before the Lord.

Ibid., p. 141

See also EMPTINESS

DEATH

A fourteenth century Japanese thinker points out that while we are familiar **1** with the fact of death, its arrival is often regarded with surprise:

The four seasons, after all, have an appointed order. The hour of death waits not its turn. Death does not necessarily come from the front; it may be stealthily planning an attack from behind. Everyone knows of death, but it comes unexpectedly, when people feel they still have time, that death is not imminent. It is like the dry flats that stretch far out into the sea, only for the tide suddenly to flood over them onto the shore.

Kenko Yoshida, *Tsurezure-gusa, Essays in Idleness*, trans. D. Keene, New York: Columbia University Press 1967, p. 138

2 According to the *Dao dejing*, losing the fear of death is to become very strong, and yet at the same time to fall into danger:

> When normal decent people don't fear death,
> how can you use death to frighten them?
> Even when they have a normal fear of death,
> who of us dare take and kill the one who doesn't?
> When people are normal and decent and death-fearing,
> there's always an executioner.
> To take the place of that executioner,
> is to take place of the great carpenter.
> People who cut the great carpenter's wood
> seldom get off with their hands unhurt.

From the *Dao dejing*: Ch. 74, p. 47, *Parabola* Summer 1997 trans. U. Le Guin

---

See also ASCETICISM, FATALISM

---

3 An argument by Zhuangzi that we should not be upset when a loved one dies. Understanding the nature of death leads to awareness of its role in the world, and so alleviates our suffering:

> The mental torture inflicted upon man by his emotions is some-times just as severe as any physical punishment. But by the use of understanding, man can reduce his emotions. For example, a man of understanding will not be angry when rain prevents him from going out, but a child often will. The reason is that the man possesses greater understanding, with the result that he suffers less disappointment or exasperation than the child who does get angry. As Spinoza has said: "In so far as the mind understands all things are necessary, so far has it greater power over the effects, or suffers less from them." (*Ethics*, Pt. 5, Prop. VI.) Such, in the words of the Taoists, is "to disperse emotion with reason."
> A story about Chuang Tzu himself well illustrates this point. It is said that when Chuang Tzu's wife died, his friend Hui Shih went to condole. To his amazement he found Chuang Tzu sitting on the ground, singing, and on asking him how he could be so unkind to his wife, was told by Chuang Tzu: "When she had just died, I could not help being affected. Soon, however, I examined the matter from the very beginning. At the very beginning, she was not living, having no form, nor even substance. But somehow or other there was then her substance,

then her form, and then her life. Now by a further change, she has died. The whole process is like the sequence of the four seasons, spring, summer, autumn, and winter. While she is thus lying in the great mansion of the universe, for me to go about weeping and wailing would be to proclaim myself ignorant of the natural laws. Therefore I stop." (*Chuang-tzu*, ch. 18.) On this passage the great commentator Kuo Hsiang comments: "When ignorant, he felt sorry. When he understood, he was no longer affected. This teaches man to disperse emotion with reason." Emotion can be counteracted with reason and understanding. Such was the view of Spinoza and also of the Taoists.

Fung, Yu-Lan (1948) *A Short History of Chinese Philosophy*, New York: Free Press, pp. 108–9

Another approach to the topic by Zhuangzi which emphasizes the role of   4
death in the pattern of nature:

When Lao Tan died, Ch'in Shih went to mourn for him; but after giving three cries, he left the room.

"Weren't you a friend of the Master?" asked Lao Tzu's disciples.

"Yes."

"And you think it's all right to mourn him this way?"

"Yes," said Ch'in Shih. "At first I took him for a real man, but now I know he wasn't. A little while ago, when I went in to mourn, I found old men weeping for him as though they were weeping for a son, and young men weeping for him as though they were weeping for a mother. To have gathered a group like *that*, he must have done something to make them talk about him, though he didn't ask them to talk, or make them weep for him, though he didn't ask them to weep. This is to hide from Heaven, turn your back on the true state of affairs, and forget what you were born with. In the old days, this was called the crime of hiding from Heaven. Your master happened to come because it was his time, and he happened to leave because things follow along. If you are content with the time and willing to follow along, then grief and joy have no way to enter in. In the old days, this was called being freed from the bonds of God.

Chuang Tzu (1968) *The Complete Works of Chuang Tzu*, trans. B. Watson, New York: Columbia University Press, pp. 52–3

See also FATALISM

5   The Japanese thinker Motoori presents here a view of death which is distinct from that of Zhuang zi, whom he nevertheless generally admired. He argues that it is appropriate to be upset about death:

> Upon his death man must leave everything behind – his wife and children, relatives and friends, house and property – and depart forever from the world he has known. He must of necessity go to that foul land of death, a fact which makes death the most sorrowful of all events. Some foreign doctrines, however, teach that death should not be regarded as profoundly sorrowful, while others assert that one's actions and attitude of mind in this life can modify the situation after death. So comprehensive and detailed are these explanations that people have been deluded into thinking they are true. Once faith is established in these beliefs, grief over death is regarded as a superstition. Those who hold them profess to be ashamed of being concerned about death, and they try not to be superstitious or emotional about it. Some write deathbed poems to express their sense of supreme enlightenment. These are all gross deceptions contrary to human sentiment and fundamental truths. Not to be happy over happy events, not to be saddened by sorrowful events, not to show surprise at astonishing events – in a word, to consider it proper not to be moved by whatever happens – are all foreign types of deception and falsehood. They are contrary to human nature and extremely repugnant to me. Death in particular is and should be a sorrowful event. Even the deity Izanagi who had created the land and all things thereon, and who had first shown the way of life in this world, wept sorrowfully like a little child when death overtook his wife and, longing for her, followed her even to the land of death. That is an expression of true human nature and sentiment. The truth requires that man too must act likewise.
>
> In antiquity, before the confusion caused by the introduction of alien doctrines, man was honest. He did not indulge in the sophistication of inventing various and pointless theories about where he would go after death. He simply believed in the truth that at death he would go to the land of death, and death was cause for him to weep in sorrow. Now this may have no bearing on government, but it helps in understanding the relative truth of our Imperial Way and that of foreign lands.

Motoori, in de Bary, W. T. (c) (1958) in *Sources of Japanese Tradition*, II, Columbia University Press, pp. 26–7. Reprinted with permission of the publisher

See also DAOISM

DEPENDENT CO-ORIGINATION

The theory of dependent co-origination is based on the idea that all our **1** experience is dependent on something outside us, and so is lacking in reliability and solidity. Buddhism used this idea to dismantle the trust we have in our basic ideas and experiences:

> The theory of dependent origination, *pratitya-samutpāda*, which the Buddha expounded, advocated that anything experienced by us arises through dependence on something else. It involved a denial of the concept of substantiality, i.e., the concept that anything has a true substantial nature through which it can exist independently. The statement that phenomenal beings have no true selfhood (that there is nothing which has a permanent, true nature), a statement which is considered to be one of the basic teachings of Buddhism, well expresses this philosophy. Herein we can see a clear bud of the philosophy of 'Emptiness'. In early Buddhism, however, the theory of dependent origination and the philosophy of emptiness were still naively undifferentiated. It was Abhidharma Buddhism which awakened to a kind of philosophy of emptiness and set it up in the heart of Buddhism. But the method of its process of realization was to get rid of concepts of substantiality by analysing phenomenal things into diverse elements and thus advocating that everything is empty. Accordingly, Abhidharma Buddhism's philosophy of emptiness was based solely on *analytic* observation – hence it was later called the 'analytic view of emptiness'. It did not have a total realization of emptiness of the phenomenal things. Thus the overcoming of the concept of substantial nature or 'being' was still not thoroughly carried through. Abhidharma fails to overcome the substantiality of the analysed elements.

Abe, M. (1985) *Zen and Western Thought*, Basingstoke: Macmillan, pp. 92–3

See also ABHIDHARMA, CAUSATION, EMPTINESS

2   Nagarjuna suggests that the Buddhist concept of dependent co-origination is designed to replace the Upanishadic idea of *brahman*, the basic underlying reality. If everything is changing and dependent on something else then there is nothing solid in which to trust:

> A person might ask, however: Is there not a causal principle which is absolute and indeed is the ground for the forms that make up the phenomenal world? No, the denial of independent entities in the phenomenal world did not lead Nāgārjuna to accept a principle of causal relations as "the real" behind ephemeral phenomena. Rather, the denial of cause, as an ultimate self-existent reality, was inherently involved in denying the self-existence of the *dharmas*. In this chapter we want to show, first, Nāgārjuna's denial of the efficacy of any causal relations which assumed a self-existent reality (*svabhāva*); secondly, Nāgārjuna's interpretation of the notion "dependent co-origination" (*pratītyasamutpāda*), which had served for centuries to express the Buddhist understanding of the production of existence; and thirdly, the significance of this reinterpretation for the notion of *karma* (the causal force for, and the result of, action).
>
> The *Madhyamakakārikās* begins in the first chapter with an analysis of causal relations. "Causal relations" had been an important concern of the early Buddhists; and this concern took concrete form in the elaboration of *abhidharma* thought, which examined the elements and conditions from which the phenomenal world was constructed. The focus on causal relations is not surprising, for this notion took the place of a substantive substratum (*brahman*) underlying changing, phenomenal reality in Upanishadic thought, and accounted for the origination and cessation of phenomena. The Buddhist teachings of impermanance of every thing (*anitya*) and the absence of any "self" (*anātman*) required that another notion bear the explanation of "cause." In place of a causal notion based on an absolute "final cause" was the notion of "dependent co-origination," with its emphasis on the interdependency of different factors (*dharmas*) which combined to form existence as we experience it. From a subjective orientation, the construction of the phenomenal world was seen to depend on craving (*tṛṣṇa*) for illusory "things"; this construction, however, resulted in binding the energies of life, and this bondage is experienced as sorrow (*duḥkha*). As a means of correlating the human phenomenon of sorrow with the limiting power of producing forms in our experienced world,

"causal relations" had taken on a dual significance as representing (1) the states in the "phenomenal becoming" of every person, and (2) the course of the cosmos pulsating in and out of existence.

Denial of Any Self-substantiated Reality for Explaining Cause

Nāgārjuna regarded the causal relation, as conceived in early Buddhism, to be true only from the practical, conventional point of view. It accounted for phenomenal "becoming" and at least served to turn a person's attention away from positing independent reality within visible forms. However, it was far from perceiving the nature of phenomenal-becoming as empty, that is, empty of *any* self-existent conditions or relations. Nāgārjuna maintained that both practical truth and the highest truth affirm that all phenomena produced by causes are empty by inherent nature. From the latter point of view there is no cause or conditioning process at all; from the viewpoint of practical truth, production does not result in a self-substantiated entity because every production is conditioned. Nāgārjuna's denial of any self-sufficient entity does not entail an affirmation that dependency is itself an ultimate principle. From the standpoint of highest truth, the "causal process" is a mentally fabricated illusion.

Streng, F. (1967) *Emptiness: A Study in Religious Meaning*, Nashville: Abingdon Press, pp. 58–9

See also ABHIDHARMA, *ANATMAN, BRAHMAN,* CAUSATION, *DHARMA, DUHKHA*

DHARMA

The term *dharma* is probably the most ubiquitous in Buddhism, and underpins the identity between the practical and the theoretical aspects of the system: 1

The Buddha used the Sanskrit word "Dharma" to designate his Truth or Teaching. In the process he added a new dimension of meaning to the word. "Dharma" was derived from the verb / *dhr*, "to hold," and had a range of important meanings associated with holding. It could mean a distinct phenomenon, one that held a particular character, or also the particular character itself. It could mean a custom, duty, or law that held human behavior in a particular pattern. It could also mean religion, in the sense of a held pattern of belief and ritual. But the core of the Buddha's discovery was the essential reality of freedom – that underlying the lived reality of existence is the immediacy of total freedom, especially freedom from suffering, from bondage, from ignorance. This essential freedom can be realized by the human mind as its own deepest and most true condition. This realization makes it possible for freedom to prevail over the habitual suffering of personal experience. So the realized individual is thenceforth *held apart* from suffering; not *held in* anything, but *held out* of binding patterns. Thus the new range of meanings of "Dharma" concerned being *held away from* suffering. Dharma came to mean the Teaching, the path of practice of the Teaching, the virtue of that practice, the reality or Truth taught in that Teaching, and the freedom of that reality or Truth, nirvana itself. This Dharma as "Teaching" is divided into two branches: the Textual Dharma and the Experiential Dharma (the Teaching and its practice). Each of those is in turn divided into three: the Textual into three types of verbal teachings, the Discipline, Discourse, and Clear Science collections, and the Experiential into three types of higher learning, the Ethical, Meditational, and Wisdom higher educations. See figure 1.

The Buddha taught the Dharma far and wide throughout India for over forty-five years. Numerous people found his teachings beneficial, and they began to form a new community within the old society. This new community was called the "Sangha" – simply "the Community" – and it formed around a new institution at its core, a monastic order of monks and nuns. Before Buddha, there had been wandering ascetics and hermits in India, but he was the first to organize suburban communities of settled

Figure 1. Structure of the Buddha Dharma

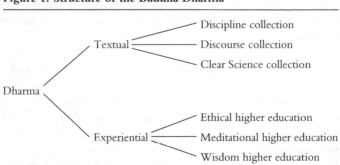

112

monastics. The community became very important in the history
of Buddhism, as it was the protective structure around the
individual who followed the Buddha's example and educated him-
or herself in the teachings. These three main aspects of Buddhism,
the Buddha, the Dharma, and the Sangha – Teacher, Teaching,
and Community – came to be known as the Three Jewels (Skt.
triratna) of Buddhism, that is, the three most precious things for
the individual seeking liberation from ignorance and suffering.

'Introduction' R. Thurman, in Sambhava, P. (1994) *The Tibetan Book of the
Dead*, tr. R. Thurman, London: Aquarian/Thorsons, pp. 14–15

See also DUHKHA, ENLIGHTENMENT, MOKSHA, NIRVANA

This is from the introduction to Kukai's 'Secret Key to the Heart Sutra', the **2**
Heart Sutra being the shortest of the Prajnaparamita Sutras. It deals with
the nature of transcendental knowledge, and argues that it is not hidden
from us, but is always available if we look for it properly:

The Buddha Dharma is nowhere remote. It is in our mind; it is
close to us. Suchness is nowhere eternal. If not within our body,
where can it be found? Since out of our own choice we either
remain deluded or attain enlightenment, once we set our mind
on enlightenment we will attain it. Since it is not by another's
will that we see light or sink into darkness, if we establish our
faith and devote ourselves to religious practice, we will at once
realize enlightenment.

trans. Hakeda, Y., (1972) *Kukai: Major Works*, New York, Columbia
University Press, p. 263. Reprinted with permission of the publisher.

See also ENLIGHTENMENT, TATHAGATA

Buddhists were often challenged with the question of whether they had **3**
ever seen the Buddha, and the appropriate reply from the monk Nagasena
to King Milinda is that he is known by his teaching, his *dhamma*, the Pali
term for *dharma*:

Milinda pressed the matter further when he asked, 'Have you
seen the Buddha?' And when Nāgasena admitted that neither
he nor his teachers had seen the Buddha, the king retorted

that there was no Buddha. This was the kind of elementary argument used earlier to refute those who had not seen Brahmā, and Nāgasena showed the absurdity of replying that since the king had not seen a famous river in the Himalayas there was no such river. But is the Buddha pre-eminent, since you have never seen him? Yes, just as a river plunges into the sea, so from those who have attained final Nirvāna we know that the Lord is pre-eminent. The Lord is known by his Dhamma, as past teachers are known from the writing they left.

Parrinder, G. (1997) *Avatar and Incarnation*, Oxford: Oneworld, p. 146

See also KNOWLEDGE

DHYANA

See also MEDITATION

1   Meditation came to have different meanings in India and China:

Literally, the name of the school should be Meditation, for the Sanskrit *dhyāna*, pronounced in Chinese "ch'an" and in Japanese "zen," means that. But meditation changed its character in China almost from the very inception of Buddhism, although the typically Indian form of sitting in meditation and concentrating one's mind to the point of ignoring the external world has continued in Chinese Buddhist schools. When Buddhism first came to China, it was mixed up with the Yellow Emperor-Lao Tzu cult. As a result, meditation was not understood in the Indian sense of concentration but in the Taoist sense of conserving vital energy, breathing, reducing desire, preserving nature, and so forth. . . . In the end, meditation meant neither sitting in meditation nor mental concentration, but simply the direct enlightenment of the mind.

Chan, Wing-tsit (1972) *A Source Book in Chinese Philosophy*, Princeton, Princeton University Press, p. 425

See also DAOISM, ZEN

2   Meditation is far from a simple process, and the different aspects of it require analysis:

dhāraṇā is essentially a *technique* which can be said to have as its characteristic feature the one-pointedness of the mind. . . . '[*Dhyāna*] is a deepened and creative *dhāraṇā*, in which the inner object is illumined mentally. The strict concentration on one object of consciousness is now supplemented with a searching-pensive contemplation of its actual nature. The object is, so to speak, placed before the contemplative consciousness in all its aspects and is apperceived as a whole. Its various characteristics are examined till its very essence is understood and becomes transparent [. . .] This is accompanied by a certain emotive disposition. Although the reasoning faculty functions acutely and clearly, it would be wrong to understand *dhyāna* merely as a logical-rational process: The contemplator must penetrate his object with all his heart, since he is after all primarily interested in a spiritual experience which is to lead him to ontic participation and the emancipation from all constricting and binding hindrances.'

Feuerstein, G. (1980) *The Philosophy of Classical Yoga*, Manchester: Manchester University Press, pp. 84–5

Meditation is difficult and it is easy to lose concentration: 3

Valid cognition (*pramāṇa*) and faulty cognition (*viparyaya*), both of which are dependent on an objective substratum, are the first to be eliminated in the internalisation procedure. There is no more contact with the external environment once meditative absorption (*dhyāna*) is established. *Vikalpa* or 'predicate-relation', is also soon restricted. Far more difficult is the elimination of sleep (*nidrā*). It is a common experience that during the first attempts at meditative absorption, the mind instead of reaching the restricted (*niruddha*) state often lapses into sleep. The untrained mind is unable to sustain the intense concentration required for more than brief spells only and quickly succumbs to exhaustion.

However, the greatest hindrance of all is the powerful human memory which constantly populates the consciousness space with thoughts, images and moods. Its complete control can only be achieved after extensive practice of *dhyāna*

Ibid., p. 73

See also IMAGINATION

DUHKHA/DUKKHA

1   Suffering according to Buddhism emerges from the variability of the world:

From the fact of the impermanence of the world, it follows that all things are unsatisfactory (*dukkha*). The word *dukkha* is rendered variously as 'ill', 'suffering', 'pain', and so on, which may be correct in certain contexts. But in other contexts, for example, where it is said that the five aggregates of grasping (*pañc' upādānakkhandha*) are *dukkha*, the term is used in the wider sense of 'unsatisfactory'. That this fact has been overlooked seems to be one of the main reasons why some Western interpreters considered Buddhism to be pessimistic. Early Buddhism never denied the satisfaction (*assāda*, Sk. *āsvāda*, from *ā* + √ *svad* 'to taste') that man can derive from worldly things. While not denying satisfaction, it emphasized the fact that this satisfaction is generally followed by evil or harmful consequences (*ādīnava*). This is true for several reasons. The nature of man is such that he craves for eternal or permanent happiness. But the things from which he hopes to derive such happiness are themselves impermanent. Happiness or satisfaction derived from impermanent or ephemeral things would surely be temporary and therefore fall short of his expectation, that is, permanent happiness. Hence his *suffering*.

Kalupahana, D. (1996) *Buddhist Philosophy: A Historical Analysis*, Honolulu: University Press of Hawaii, p. 37

See also ATMAN

2   Appropriate analysis of the nature of suffering can lead us to rise above it through meditation. But it is part and parcel of what we regard as ordinary experience:

For Patañjali this puzzle is no puzzle at all, but an eminently practical issue. As long as the 'correlation' (*saṃyoga*) between Self and world obtains, there is also suffering (*duḥkha*). Since the root of this correlation, or rather phantom correlation, between Self and non-self is nescience (*avidyā*), it is this which must be terminated. The prescribed expedient for the removal of the correlation condition is *viveka-khyāti*, the 'vision of discernment', a high-level enstasy which eliminates all one's false identities not by way of mere intellectual acrobatics but in a process of clarification and purification of consciousness. First the mind is withdrawn from the external stimuli, then all presented-ideas are obliterated and ultimately the subliminal traces (*vāsanā*) themselves are rooted out, which amounts to the total dispersion of the consciousness-of (*citta*).

Ordinary experience is possible only on account of the massive identity confusion arising from the overpowering influence of the subliminal traces which habitually throw the consciousness outside itself, thus forcing it to gather in continually new impressions, thereby replenishing the stock of subliminal traces (*vāsanā*) in the depths of the mind. In other words, the fundamental confusion about man's true identity is built into the psychomental organism whose growth and decay the individualised consciousness is witnessing. In fact, without this cognitive mix-up no experience would be possible.

Feuerstein, G. (1980) *The Philosophy of Classical Yoga*, Manchester: Manchester University Press, pp. 20–1

See also CONSCIOUSNESS, *DHYANA*

EDUCATION

The Mohists argue that the Daoists contradict themselves when they claim **1**
that learning is a waste of time. If learning is a waste of time, then it is also a waste of time to teach anyone anything, yet the Daoists have done precisely this in arguing that learning is a waste of time:

> The later Mohists also criticized the Taoists. In the second "Canon" we read: "Learning is useful. The reason is given by those who oppose it." (*Lao-tzu* Ch. 41.) The second "Exposition" comments on this: "Learning: By maintaining that people do not know that learning is useless, one is thereby informing them of this fact. This informing that learning is useless, is itself a teaching. Thus by holding that learning is useless, one teaches. This is perverse." (Ch. 43.)
>
> This is a criticism of a statement in the *Lao-tzu*: "Banish learning and there will be no grieving." (Ch. 20.) According to the later Mohists, learning and teaching are related terms. If learning is to be banished, so is teaching. For once there is teaching, there is also learning, and if teaching is useful, learning cannot be useless. The very teaching that learning is useless proves in itself that it is useful.

[References to the Canon are to the Mohist main work, the *Mojing*]

Fung Yu-Lan (1948) *A Short History of Chinese Philosophy*, New York: Free Press, p. 126

See also DAOISM, KNOWLEDGE

2   The point of education in Confucianism is to learn to be human. In fact, there is no essential disparity between Confucian and Daoist views, since both stress the importance of restraining our fascination with the self and urge the acquisition of a sense of public duty:

> In classical Confucian thought, the primary purpose of learning is for the sake of the self as a center of relationships. However, it is misleading to interpret the Confucian way of learning to be human as a form of social ethics, for the purpose of education in the Confucian tradition is self-cultivation. Social harmony and humane rulership are natural consequences of self-cultivation. Priorities are clearly established: only by strengthening the root (self-cultivation) will the branches (regulation of the family and governance of the state) flourish. If we reverse the order by first imposing peace upon society with the anticipation that people will learn to live harmoniously among themselves, we not only violate the natural process of moral education but rely on an external political ideology rather than the trust of a fiduciary community. This is ineffective, for social harmony can only be attained through personal self-cultivation.
>
> The common belief that Confucian self-cultivation is elitist in the sense that only the privileged few have access to the symbolic resources of the society – such as literary training – is also misleading. The primary concern of Confucian education is learning to be human. Education is more broadly conceived than merely learning to read and write. People who have no opportunity to learn to read or write, as well as those who do, can and should pursue their education as human beings. *Hsüeh* (learning), in its etymological sense, is *chüeh* (enlightening). To learn is to be enlightened; to teach is to enlighten.
>
> This classical Confucian sense of learning as enlightenment is compatible with the Taoist idea that in the pursuit of Tao we must learn to lose ourselves. The aspects of the self that both Confucians and Taoists would like to see us lose include self-centeredness, selfishness, opinionatedness, stubbornless, obsessiveness, possessiveness, material desires and attachment to mental or physical objects. To lose these acquired dispositions

in ourselves is not to practice self-denial, as in the spiritual discipline of inner-worldly asceticism, but to open ourselves to the experience of a deeper and more expansive selfhood. The two senses of the self, one private and limited and the other public and open, are shared by Confucians and Taoists even though their approaches to learning are significantly different.

Tu-Wei Ming 'Afterword' in Gregory, P. (ed.) (1987) *Sudden and Gradual: Approaches to enlightenment in Chinese thought*, Honolulu: University of Hawaii Press, p. 449

See also CONFUCIANISM, DAOISM, HARMONY, KNOWLEDGE

EMPTINESS

The *Commentary on the Chuang-tzu* by Guo Xiang (Kuo Hsiang) presents 1 a Daoist argument that there is no essential basis to the nature of the world:

The Hsiang-Kuo interpretation made several most important revisions in the original Taoism of Lao Tzu and Chuang Tzu. The first is that the *Tao* is really *wu*, i.e., "nothing" or "nothingness." Lao Tzu and Chuang Tzu also had maintained that the *Tao* is *Wu*, but by *Wu* they meant having no name. That is, according to them, the *Tao* is not a thing; hence it is unnamable. But according to the Hsiang-Kuo interpretation, the *Tao* is really literally nothing. "The *Tao* is everywhere, but everywhere it is nothing." (*Commentary on the Chuang-tzu*, ch. 6.)

The same text says: "In existence, what is prior to things? We say that the *Yin* and *Yang* are prior to things. But the *Yin* and *Yang* are themselves things; what then, is prior to the *Yin* and *Yang*? We may say that *Tzu Jan* [nature or naturalness] is prior to things. But *Tzu Jan* is simply the naturalness of things. Or we may say that the *Tao* is prior to things. But the *Tao* is nothing. Since it is nothing, how can it be prior to things? We do not know what is prior to things, yet things are continuously produced. This shows that things are spontaneously what they are; there is no Creator of things." (Ch. 22.)

Fung Yu-Lan *A Short History of Chinese Philosophy*, New York: Free Press, pp. 220–1

See also DAOISM, EMPTINESS, YIN and YANG

2　Is Nagarjuna a nihilist? Since he argues that the basis of everything is emptiness, is the doctrine of emptiness itself empty? This question was often
asked of the Madhymaka thinkers:

> Is there a vulnerable point in the *Kārikās* which undercuts all its
> conclusions – or rather its one conclusion – that all is empty?
> The last verse of the *Kārikās*, which summarizes all that has gone
> before, brings into clear relief the basis of my thesis:
>
> > To him possessing compassion, who taught the real *dharma*
> > For the destruction of *all* views – to him, Gautama, I
> > humbly offer reverence (27.30).[1]
>
> More explicitly supporting my thesis are these words earlier:
>
> > Emptiness is proclaimed by the victorious one as the
> > refutation of *all* viewpoints;
> > But those who hold "emptiness" as a viewpoint – [the true
> > perceivers] have called these "incurable" (*asādhya*) (13.8).[2]
>
> In both passages Nāgārjuna is declaring the emptiness – which
> is to say the non-substantiality, the ultimate meaninglessness – of
> all views (*dṛṣṭi*). In the second passage he lets us see how deter-
> minedly he is standing behind his thesis that all is empty: The
> thesis that all is empty is itself empty. This admission might at first
> strike us as nothing more than, let us say, thoroughly and
> "unselfishly" consistent. We would be right in thinking so, but,
> unfortunately, that is not all there is to the matter. There is a weak-
> ness – a weakness which, once it is pointed out, is all too obvious.
> If all is empty, then on what grounds can one meaningfully teach
> the emptiness of all views? On what grounds can he teach
> anything at all? Though "all too obvious," however, the difficulty
> is apparently not at all easy, as we shall learn, to *accept*.
>   Nāgārjuna himself saw the problem so clearly that he devoted
> the major part of his second most renowned short work, the
> *Vigrahavyāvartanī*, to it. He opens this treatise by placing the
> problem squarely before us. He has an opponent say,
>
> > If self-existence (*svabhāva*) does not exist anywhere in any
> > existing thing,
> > Your statement, [itself] being without self-existence, is not
> > able to discard self-existence.

But if that statement has [its own] self-existence, then your
  initial proposition is refuted;
There is a [logical] inconsistency in this, and you ought to
  explain the grounds of the difference [between the
  principle of validity in your statement and others]
  (vv. 1–2).[3]

Nāgārjuna's reply is that the very fact of the lack of self-existence
(*svabhāva*) in his thesis is *proof* of his thesis that all is empty: it just
goes to show, he would hold, that his thesis is no exception to
the universal law of emptiness: he says,

Just as a magically formed phantom could deny a phantom
  created by its own magic,
Just so would be that negation.

Here Nāgārjuna is being consistent (in a way) in maintaining that
all, even his thesis of emptiness, is empty, but he is not coming
to grips with the overruling, potentially lethal objection which
the objector has put forth. He has not addressed himself to the
challenge, "Your statement, [itself] being without self-existence,
is not able to discard self-existence." It is as if the objector had
said to Nāgārjuna, "You're wrong," and Nāgārjuna had answered,
"Of course I'm wrong; that's precisely what makes me right." As
alluring, as stunning, as Taoistically fascinating as such an answer
is, it is not really an answer; *it is not cogent in an argument where the
rules of logic apply*, as they do here. Nāgārjuna has evaded the issue;
he has *seen* the problem, but he has not treated it seriously: he has
not "accepted" it.

1 Translation of the *Karikas* from Streng *Emptiness*. Second italic author's
2 First italic author's
3 Translation from Streng *Emptiness* p. 222

Betty Stafford, L. (1983) "Nagarjuna's masterpiece – logical, mystical, both,
or neither?' *Philosophy East and West*, 33, 123–38, copyright University of
Hawaii Press, pp. 127–8

See also MADHYAMAKA

Emptiness is used in Daoism to represent being at peace with oneself: 3

Take emptiness to the limit;
Maintain tranquility in the center.

The ten thousand things – side-by-side they arise;
And by this I see their return.
Things come forth in great numbers;
Each one returns to its root.
This is called tranquility.
"Tranquility" – This means to return to your fate.
To return to your fate is to be constant;
To know the constant is to be wise.
Not to know the constant is to be reckless and wild;
If you're reckless and wild, your actions will lead to misfortune.

To know the constant is to be all-embracing;
To be all-embracing is to be impartial;
To be impartial is to be kingly;
To be kingly is to be like Heaven;
To be like Heaven is to be one with the Tao;
If you're one with the Tao, to the end of your days you'll suffer
   no harm.

Laozi, trans. R. Henricks (1989) *Lao-Tzu: Te Tao Ching*, New York,
Ballantine, Ch. 16 p. 68

See also DAOISM, FATALISM

---

4   The *dao* is empty and yet immensely powerful, as in the general Daoist
     thesis that what appears to be weakest is in fact strongest, so that what
     appears to be completely empty is really entirely full:

The Way is empty;
Yet when you use it, you never need fill it again.
Like an abyss! It seems to be the ancestor of the ten thousand
   things.

It files down sharp edges;
Unties the tangles;
Softens the glare;
And settles the dust.

Submerged! It seems perhaps to exist.
We don't know whose child it is;
It seems to have even preceded the Lord.

Ibid., Ch. 4 p. 56

ENLIGHTENMENT

See also MOKSHA, NIRVANA

Buddhist philosophy is naturally concerned with the nature of enlighten- **1**
ment and discusses the precise route to it, and the difficulties on the way:

"The Buddha said: 'It is one's mind which seeks after enlightenment and all-inclusive wisdom. Why? The original nature of
mind is pure and clean: it is neither within nor without; nor is it
obtainable between them. O Lord of Mysteries, the perfect
enlightenment of the Tathagata is neither blue, yellow, red, white,
pink, purple, nor of crystal color; neither is it long, short, round,
square, bright, dark; nor is it male, female, or androgynous.
O Lord of Mysteries, the mind is identical neither with the nature
of the world of desire, nor with that of the world of forms,
nor with that of the world of formlessness. . . . It does not rest
upon the world of perceptions of the ear, of the tongue, or of the
mind. There is in it neither seeing nor seen. Why? The mind,
whose characteristic is like that of empty space, transcends both
individuation and nonindividuation. The reason is that since the
nature [of the mind] is identical with that of empty space,
the nature is identical with the Mind; since the nature is identical
with the Mind, it is identical with enlightenment. Thus, O Lord
of Mysteries, these three – the mind, the characteristic of empty
space, and enlightenment – are identical. They [the mind and
enlightenment] are rooted in the spirit of compassion and are
fully endowed with the wisdom of means. O Lord of Mysteries,
I preach the doctrines in this way in order to make all bodhisattvas
whose *bodhicitta* (enlightened mind) is pure and clean realize their
mind. O Lord of Mysteries, if any man or woman wishes to
realize it, he should realize his own mind in this way. O Lord of
Mysteries, to realize one's own mind is to understand that the
mind is unidentifiable in all causally conditioned phenomena,
whether it is in colors, forms, objects, things, perceptions,
conceptions, predispositions, mind, I, mine, subjects of clinging,
objects of clinging, pure state, sense organs, sense data, etc. O Lord
of Mysteries, this teaching of the pure *bodhicitta* of the bodhisattvas
is called the preliminary way of clarifying the Dharma.'"

Kukai (1972) *Kukai: Major Works*, trans. Y. Hakeda, New York: Columbia
University Press, pp. 208–9

See also BODHICHITTA, BODHISATTVA, COMPASSION, DHARMA, TATHAGATA

2 Buddhism, Confucianism and Daoism all claim that we can become enlightened. This is linked to a central Chinese idea that human beings can perfect themselves:

> The Mencian line of Confucian teaching, the Taoist thought of Chuang Tzu, and the Ch'an of the subitist school all share one basic conviction: the spiritual resources at our disposal are necessary and sufficient for us to become enlightened. The ultimate ground of our self-realization and the actual process by which we become fully realized are inseparable. Our nature, an anthropocosmic reality, is not only our ground of being but also the creative and transformative activity that makes us dynamic, living, and growing persons. Despite our existential alienation from our true nature, we have never totally departed from it and should dedicate ourselves to fully return to it. We do not become what we are incrementally; we become, therefore we are. In the becoming process, suddenly and simultaneously, we see our true nature face to face.
>
> This is what Mencius recommended as the authentic way of learning to be human. We first establish that which is great in our nature. We do not depart from where we are here and now in order to appropriate what we do not have. Rather, the way is near at hand and inseparable from the ordinary experiences of our daily lives. Paradoxically, we must make the existential decision to find our way; otherwise, we will lose it to the extent that we become unaware that it is originally ours. Nevertheless, because it is originally ours, we can get it by simply exercising our will to do so. Willing is the necessary and sufficient condition for us to get it. The way is ours, suddenly and simultaneously, when we will that this be done.
>
> However, although the Confucians assume that ontologically the way is within us, they never underestimate the intellectual and spiritual discipline required for regaining the "lost heart." Chuang Tzu's "fasting of the heart," in this Confucian perspective, makes a great deal of sense. Its single-minded attention to "nourishing the heart," despite the vicissitude of emotions and discriminating consciousness, is in accord with the Mencian teaching of making our desires few. To get that which is

originally ours by simply willing is, in a common Ch'an expression, "the Great Matter." Existentially nothing is more urgent, difficult, and tormenting than this Great Matter. The strength of the subitists lies in their ontological insight into the original nature (the thusness) of this Great Matter and their existential awareness that, without commitment of body and soul, an external procedure, no matter how ingeniously designed, will not work.

The deep-rooted sinitic faith in the perfectibility of human nature through self-effort underlies the teachings of Mencian Confucianism, Chuang Tzu's Taoism, and the subitist Ch'an. This faith, informed by the ontological insight that human nature is not only a ground of being but also a transformative and creative activity, enables the Confucians to perceive human beings as earthbound yet striving to transcend themselves to join with heaven, the Taoists to perceive human beings as embodiments of the Tao taking part in the cosmic transformation as connoisseurs of undifferentiated wholeness, and the Ch'an Buddhists to perceive human beings as capable of true enlightenment in a living encounter with ordinary daily existence.

Tu Wei-Ming 'Afterword' in Gregory, P. (ed.) (1987) *Sudden and Gradual: Approaches to enlightenment in Chinese thought*, Honolulu: University of Hawaii Press, pp. 454–5

See also CONFUCIANISM, DAOISM, HUMANITY, ZEN

Enlightenment occupies the central point of teaching in all schools of Buddhism, Hīnayāna and Mahāyāna, "self-power" and "other-power," the Holy Path and the Pure Land, because the Buddha's teachings all start from his enlightenment experience, about 2,500 years ago in the northern part of India. Every Buddhist is, therefore, expected to receive enlightenment either in this world or in one of his future lives. Without enlightenment either already realized or to be realized somehow and sometime and somewhere, there will be no Buddhism. Zen is no exception. In fact, it is Zen that makes most of enlightenment, or *satori* (*wu* in Chinese).

Abe, M. (1985) *Zen and Western Thought*, Basingstoke: Macmillan, p. 6

See also MAHAYANA, ZEN

4 The subitist or sudden approach to enlightenment often employs shock tactics to achieve its end:

> When the student has reached the verge of Sudden Enlightenment, that is the time when the Master can help him the most. When one is about to make the leap, a certain assistance, no matter how small, is a great help. The Ch'an Masters at this stage used to practice what they called the method of "stick or yell" to help the leap to Enlightenment. Ch'an literature reports many incidents in which a Master, having asked his student to consider some problem, suddenly gave him several blows with a stick or yelled at him. If these acts were done at the right moment, the result would be a Sudden Enlightenment for the student. The explanation would seem to be that the physical act, thus performed, shocks the student into that psychological awareness of enlightenment for which he has long been preparing.
>
> To describe Sudden Enlightenment, the Ch'an Masters use the metaphor of "the bottom of a tub falling out." When this happens, all its contents are suddenly gone. In the same way, when one is suddenly enlightened, he finds all his problems suddenly solved. They are solved not in the sense that he gains some positive solution for them, but in the sense that all the problems have ceased any longer to be problems. That is why the *Tao* is called "the indubitable *Tao*."

Fung Yu-Lan (1948) *A Short History of Chinese Philosophy*, New York: Free Press, p. 262

See also ZEN

5 The *chan* view of cultivation through non-cultivation appears paradoxical, but it is based on the idea that achieving enlightenment is natural, and an absence of effort may be more effective in reaching *nirvana* than trying very hard:

> Thus the way to practice spiritual cultivation is to have adequate confidence in one's self and discard everything else. All one should do is to pursue the ordinary tasks of one's everyday life,

and nothing more. This is what the Ch'an Masters call cultivation through non-cultivation.

Here a question arises: Granted that this be so, then what is the difference between the man who engages in cultivation of this kind and the man who engages in no cultivation at all? If the latter does precisely what the former does, he too should achieve *Nirvana*, and so there should come a time when there will be no Wheel of Birth and Death at all.

To this question it may be answered that although to wear clothes and eat meals are in themselves common and simple matters, it is still not easy to do them with a completely non-purposeful mind and thus without any attachment. A person likes fine clothes, for example, but dislikes bad ones, and he feels pleased when others admire his clothes. These are all the attachments that result from wearing clothes. What the Ch'an Masters emphasized is that spiritual cultivation does not require special acts, such as the ceremonies and prayers of institutionalized religion. One should simply try to be without a purposeful mind or any attachments in one's daily life; then cultivation results from the mere carrying on of the common and simple affairs of daily life. In the beginning one will need to exert effort in order to be without effort, and to exercise a purposeful mind in order not to have such a mind, just as, in order to forget, one at first needs to remember that one should forget. Later, however, the time comes when one must discard the effort to be without effort, and the mind that purposefully tries to have no purpose, just as one finally forgets to remember that one has to forget.

Thus cultivation through non-cultivation is itself a kind of cultivation, just as knowledge that is not knowledge is nevertheless still a form of knowledge. Such knowledge differs from original ignorance, and cultivation through non-cultivation likewise differs from original naturalness. For original ignorance and naturalness are gifts of nature, whereas knowledge that is not knowledge and cultivation through non-cultivation are both products of the spirit.

Ibid., pp. 260–1

See also ZEN

ETHICS

1 Confucius had no doubts over the significance of family loyalty above other considerations:

> 18. The Duke of She told Master Kong: 'In my locality there is a certain paragon, for when his father stole a sheep, he, the son, bore witness against him.' Master Kong said: 'In my locality those who are upright are different from this. Fathers cover up for their sons and sons cover up for their fathers. Uprightness is to be found in this.'

Confucius, trans. R. Dawson (1993) *The Analects*, Oxford, Oxford University Press, Bk. 13 p. 51

See also CONFUCIANISM

2 A development of the earlier point, arguing that ethical links within the family are the basis for wider morality:

> The family context of Confucian ethics also is evidenced in Confucius' encounter with a local governor who, boasting of the high level of public morality in his part of the country, cited the son who testified against his father caught stealing a sheep. Confucius countered by saying that in his part of the country the father would shield the son and the son his father *Analects* 13:18). Here the point lies not in any tangible quid pro quo but in the inviolability of the family intimacy. If the most basic human relations cannot be respected and protected within the family where all virtue is nourished, if family members cannot trust one another, the whole fiduciary basis of society stands in jeopardy.
>
> The virtue at issue in this case is forthrightness or straight-forwardness (*chih*). It is one of several virtues associated with the gentleman and the latter's living by rites: "Courtesy not in keeping with what is rite becomes timidity; courage becomes brashness; and forthrightness becomes rudeness" (8:2). Here some translators render *li* as "the rules of property" (Legge), or "the prescriptions of ritual" (Waley), while Lau, apparently to avoid overdetermination, translates it as "the spirit of ritual." As before, we have difficulty combining form and spirit in one expression. In the earlier case of mourning for one's parents,

Confucius referred to the three-year period as both natural (given the normal term of infancy) and as the generally accepted practice throughout the country. Either way there was something of an objective norm to refer to. In the passage just cited, however, norms become a problem. On the one hand Confucius shows a clear distrust of mere instinct or impulse; some recourse must be had to an external norm or measure. On the other hand it is altogether unlikely that there would be a definite "rule" or "prescription" governing each of the cases cited, and even less so given Confucius' distrust of detailed regulation and legislated controls.

See also CONFUCIANISM, LEGALISM

In Tantric Buddhism the main ethical issue is the motive behind the nature 3 of action. It is the way in which things are done, rather than what is done itself, which is significant:

The main argument, to start with, is that to pass any ethical judgment on the nature of an action, it should always be remembered that an action, of whatsoever nature may it be, is by itself neither moral nor immoral; in its non-relational absolute nature it is purely colourless, and hence in itself it has got no value, that being always relative. Thus the moral, immoral and non-moral nature of an action is to be determined by the effect it produces in relation to the general scheme of life. To be strictly ethical, it is not even the effect that determines the nature of an action, – it is rather the motive behind that speaks either for or against it. The main emphasis of the Tāntric Buddhists seem to be on this vital point of ethics. If it be the motive behind the action itself, that determines the nature of an action, any and every action in the form of some religious practice is to be justified, provided, the motive behind is nothing but the attainment of some religious fulfilment. . . .

In the *Citta-viśuddhi-prakaraṇa* of Āryadeva we find a short ethical discussion on the nature of sin. There it is said that the mind is the real agent of all actions – nay, it is the antecedent factor of the *dharmas*, it is the most important, it is the quickest;

it is through the pleasure and displeasure of the mind that our speech and actions follow. It is, therefore, that the *citta* is solely responsible for the ethical nature of an action.

Thus the intention behind an action gives an action a moral or immoral colouring, and as this principle has got its sanction in the Scriptures, no pious man can have any objection to it. Then the author goes on to say that the Yogin, who has made a 'god' of himself by the universalisation of the self, and all of whose activities are prompted by a spirit of benevolence towards the world, attains liberation by the enjoyment of objects, and never is he bound down by any such enjoyment. As a man versed in the science of poison knows poison as poison and then swallows some quantity of it and yet he never falls swooning thereby, on the other hand, becomes cured of diseases, so also is the case with an expert Yogin, who attains liberation through enjoyment. . . .

It is pointed out that contradictory statements and injunctions are to be met with in the Tāntric texts; some actions are described somewhere as virtuous and vicious in other places. How then to reconcile these contradictory statements? It has been replied that in reality there is nothing virtuous and nothing vicious. Virtue and vice depend on the condition of the *citta*. There are three elements (*dhātu*) which generally combine together for the performance of an action; these are body (*kāya*), speech (*vāk*) and mind (*manas*). Of the three, body has no power to do anything without mind; speech is also never possible without mind; so, it stands that it is the *citta* that is doing all good and bad through body and speech. How then to define virtue and vice? It is said, whatever is done with a view to doing good to the world is right or virtuous, and whatever is done with any other motive is a sin. All the right and wrong are created by the *citta* and it is through the *citta* again that they are all destroyed. Charity is one of the universally recognised moral virtues; but the mere action of giving produces no virtue unless it is done with a charitable mind; the virtue of the action of giving depends solely on the attitude of the man. It is finally decided here that there is no other criterion of virtue than the benevolent spirit; any action prompted by such a spirit is moral, and any action done with a malicious spirit is immoral.

Dasgupta, S.B. (1974) *An Introduction to Tantric Buddhism*, Shambhala: Berkeley, pp. 179–80, 180–1, 182–3

See also ACTION, *MANAS*, *TANTRA*

There has been a development in the Hindu account of ethics from an   4
emphasis on prayer and sacrifice to meditation and self-understanding:

In the Vedic religion performance of sacrifices was considered as the primary duty. Virtue and vice consisted in obedience or disobedience to Vedic injunctions. It has been pointed out that these injunctions implied a sort of categorical imperative and communicated a sense of *vidhi* as law, a command which must be obeyed. But this law was no inner law of the spirit within, but a mere external law, which ought not to be confused with morality in the modern sense of the term. Its sphere was almost wholly ritualistic, and, though it occasionally included such commands as "One should not injure anyone" (*mā hiṃsyāt*), yet in certain sacrifices which were aimed at injuring one's enemies operations which would lead to such results would have the imperative of a Vedic command, though the injury to human beings would be attended with its necessary punishment. Again, though in later Sāṃkhya commentaries and compendiums it is said that all kinds of injuries to living beings bring their punishment, yet it is doubtful if the Vedic injunction "Thou shouldst not injure" really applied to all living beings, as there would be but few sacrifices where animals were not killed. The Upaniṣads, however, start an absolutely new line by the substitution of meditations and self-knowledge for sacrificial actions. In the primary stage of Upaniṣadic thoughts a conviction was growing that instead of the sacrificial performances one could go through a set form of meditations, identifying in thought certain objects with certain other objects (e.g. the dawn as the horse of horse-sacrifice) or even with symbolic syllables, OM and the like. In the more developed stage of Upaniṣadic culture a new conviction arose in the search after the highest and the ultimate truth, and the knowledge of Brahman as the highest essence in man and nature is put forward as the greatest wisdom and the final realization of truth and reality, than which nothing higher could be conceived. There are but few moral precepts in the Upaniṣads, and the whole subject of moral conflict and moral efforts is almost silently dropped or passes unemphasized.

Dasgupta, S. (1932) *A History of Indian Philosophy*, II Cambridge: Cambridge University Press, pp. 493–4

See also AHIMSA, BRAHMAN, MEDITATION,
SANKHYA-YOGA, *UPANISHADS*

5   The *Gita* identifies moral duties with caste positions, since only in this way
can a harmonious ethical climate be established:

> The *Gītā* is neither a practical guide-book of moral efforts nor a
> philosophical treatise discussing the origin of immoral tendencies
> and tracing them to certain metaphysical principles as their
> sources; but, starting from the ordinary frailties of attachment and
> desires, it tries to show how one can lead a normal life of duties
> and responsibilities and yet be in peace and contentment in a
> state of equanimity and in communion with God. The *Gītā* has
> its setting in the great battle of the *Mahā-bhārata.* . . .
>
>   The fundamental idea of the *Gītā* is that a man should always
> follow his own caste-duties, which are his own proper duties, or
> *sva-dharma.* Even if his own proper duties are of an inferior type,
> it is much better for him to cleave to them than to turn to other
> people's duties which he could well perform. It is even better to
> die cleaving to one's caste-duties, than to turn to the duties fixed
> for other people, which only do him harm. The caste-duties of
> Brahmins, Kṣattriyas, Vaiśyas and Śūdras are fixed in accordance
> with their natural qualities. Thus sense-control, control over
> mind, power of endurance, purity, patience, sincerity, knowledge
> of worldly things and philosophic wisdom are the natural
> qualities of a Brahmin. Heroism, bravery, patience, skill, not to
> fly from battle, making of gifts and lordliness are the natural
> duties of a Kṣattriya. Agriculture, tending of cattle and trade are
> the natural duties of a Śūdra. A man can attain his highest only
> by performing the specific duties of his own caste. God pervades
> this world, and it is He who moves all beings to work. A man
> can best realize himself by adoring God and by the performance
> of his own specific caste-duties. No sin can come to a man who
> performs his own caste-duties. Even if one's caste-duties were
> sinful or wrong, it would not be wrong for a man to perform
> them; for, as there is smoke in every fire, so there is some wrong
> thing or other in all our actions. Arjuna is thus urged to follow
> his caste-duty as a Kṣattriya and to fight his enemies in the
> battle-field. If he killed his enemies, then he would be the
> master of the kingdom; if he himself was killed, then since he
> had performed the duties of a Kṣattriya, he would go to Heaven.

If he did not engage himself in that fight, which was his duty; he would not only lose his reputation, but would also transgress his own *dharma*.

Ibid., pp. 501–3

See also BHAGAVAD GITA, CASTE

The *Gītā* ideal of conduct differs from the sacrificial ideal of **6** conduct in this, that sacrifices are not to be performed for any ulterior end of heavenly bliss or any other mundane benefits, but merely from a sense of duty, because sacrifices are enjoined in the scriptures to be performed by Brahmins; and they must therefore be performed from a pure sense of duty. The *Gītā* ideal of ethics differs from that preached in the systems of philosophy like the Vedānta or the Yoga of Patañjali in this, that, while the aim of these systems was to transcend the sphere of actions and duties, to rise to a stage in which one could give up all one's activities, mental or physical, the ideal of the *Gītā* was decidedly an ideal of work. The *Gītā*, as has already been pointed out, does not advocate a course of extremism in anything. However elevated a man may be, he must perform his normal caste-duties and duties of customary morality. The *Gītā* is absolutely devoid of the note of pessimism which is associated with early Buddhism.

Ibid., pp. 503–4

See also BHAKTI, YOGA

What is the general standpoint of Hindu Ethics? The Hindu **7** social system is based on a system of fourfold division of castes. The *Gītā* says that God Himself created the fourfold division of castes into Brahmins, Kṣattriyas, Vaiśyas and Śūdras, a division based on characteristic qualities and specific duties.

Over and above this caste division and its corresponding privileges, duties and responsibilities, there is also a division of the stages of life into that of *Brahma-cārin* – student, *gṛa-stha* – householder, *vāna-prastha* – retired in a forest, and *bhikṣu* – mendicant, and each of these had its own prescribed duties. The duties of Hindu ethical life consisted primarily of the prescribed caste-duties and the specific duties of the different stages of life, and this is known as *varṇāśrama-dharma*. Over and above this there were also certain duties which were common to all, called the *sādhāraṇa-dharmas*. Thus Manu mentions steadiness (*dhairya*), forgiveness (*kṣamā*), self-control (*dama*), non-stealing (*cauryā-bhāva*), purity (*śauca*), sense-control (*indriya-nigraha*), wisdom (*dhī*), learning (*vidyā*), truthfulness (*satya*) and control of anger (*akrodha*) as examples of *sādhāraṇa-dharma*. Praśastapāda mentions faith in religious duties (*dharma-śraddhā*), non-injury (*ahiṃsā*), doing good to living beings (*bhūta-hitatva*), truthfulness (*satya-vacana*), non-stealing (*asteya*), sex-continence (*brahma-carya*), sincerity of mind (*anupadhā*), control of anger (*krodha-varjana*), cleanliness and ablutions (*abhiṣecana*), taking of pure food (*śuci-dravya-sevana*), devotion to Vedic gods (*viśiṣṭa-devatā-bhakti*), and watchfulness in avoiding transgressions (*apramāda*). The caste-duties must be distinguished from these common duties. Thus sacrifices, study and gifts are common to all the three higher castes, Brahmins, Kṣattriyas and Vaiśyas. The specific duties of a Brahmin are acceptance of gifts, teaching, sacrifices and so forth; the specific duties of a Kṣattriya are protection of the people, punishing the wicked, not to retreat from battles and other specific tasks; the duties of a Vaiśya are buying, selling, agriculture, breeding and rearing of cattle, and the specific duties of a Vaiśya. The duties of a Śūdra are to serve the three higher castes.

Ibid., pp. 504–5

See also CASTE

---

8   It is the motive behind the action which is significant in the *Gita*. That motive needs to be one of lack of attachment, i.e. lack of selfishness:

The theory of the *Gītā* that, if actions are performed with an unattached mind, then their defects cannot touch the performer, distinctly implies that the goodness or badness of an action does not depend upon the external effects of the action, but upon the inner motive of action. If there is no motive of pleasure or self-gain, then the action performed cannot bind the performer; for it is only the bond of desires and self-love that really makes an action one's own and makes one reap its good or bad fruits. Morality from this point of view becomes wholly subjective, and the special feature of the *Gītā* is that it tends to make all actions non-moral by cutting away the bonds that connect an action with its performer. In such circumstances the more logical course would be that of Śaṇkara, who would hold a man who is free from desires and attachment to be above morality, above duties and above responsibilities.

Ibid., p. 507

See also BHAGAVAD GITA

The context is significant in deciding how to act, according to the *Gita*, and   9
virtues should not be taken to extremes:

Regarding also the practice of the virtues of non-injury, etc., Arjuna maintains that it is wrong to carry these virtues to extremes. Howsoever a man may live, whether as an ascetic or as a forester, it is impossible for him to practise non-injury to all living beings in any extreme degree. Even in the water that one drinks and the fruits that one eats, even in breathing and winking many fine and invisible insects are killed. So the virtue of non-injury, or, for the matter of that, all kinds of virtue, can be practised only in moderation, and their injunctions always imply that they can be practised only within the bounds of a common-sense view of things. Non-injury may be good; but there are cases where non-injury would mean doing injury. If a tiger enters into a cattle-shed, not to kill the tiger would amount to killing the cows. So all religious injunctions are made from the point of view of a practical and well-ordered maintenance of society and must therefore be obeyed with an eye to the results that may follow in their practical application. Our principal object is to maintain properly the process of the social order and the well-being of the people. It seems clear, then, that, when the *Gītā* urges again and again that there is no meaning in giving up our normal duties, vocation and place in life and its responsi-bilities, and that what is expected of us is that we should make our minds unattached, it refers to the view which Yudhiṣṭhira expresses, that we must give up all our works. The *Gītā* therefore repeatedly urges that *tyāga* does not mean the giving up of all works, but the mental giving up of the fruits of all actions.

Ibid., pp. 508–9

See also AHIMSA

10 Sometimes called the Golden Rule, Confucius is taken to argue that the central principle of ethics is not to do what you would not want to have done to you:

> [It is recorded in the *Analects* that] Tzu-kung asked, "Is there one word which may serve as a rule of practice for all one's life?" The Master said, "Is not 'reciprocity' such a word? What you do not want done to yourself, do not do to others." And when speaking about how to govern the state and bring peace to the world, [the commentary to] the *Great Learning* says no more than this: "What a man dislikes in his superiors, let him not display in the treatment of his inferiors; what he dislikes in his inferiors, let him not display in the service of his superiors."

Tai Chen (1990) *Tai Chen on Mencius: Explorations in Words and Meaning*, trans. A-p. Chin and M. Freeman, New Haven: Yale University Press, p. 75

See also CONFUCIANISM, GOLDEN MEAN

11 This entry in the index shows the significance of ethics in Chinese philosophy:

> ethics, 1; so much of Chinese philosophy is ethical that a complete list of all the references to 'ethical' subjects mentioned in this volume would be almost impossible

Fung Yu-Lan (1983) *A History of Chinese Philosophy*, trans. D. Bodde, Princeton: Princeton University Press, Index p. 429

12 Chinese philosophy is based on the importance of the social, by contrast with Western thought:

> Theory of mind, in turn, anchors theory of human nature and inspires, therefore, ethics and political theory. Subjectivism in theory of language – the theory that language is tied to internal, private, conceptual, or mental states – yields subjectivism in theory of mind. If the mind works in robust aloofness from society, this fact affects ethical and political theory. Individualism, in its strictest versions, may be intelligible only if we reject the

classical Chinese theories. Awareness of the social nature of language and mind may undermine Western ethics.

Chinese theory of language and mind shows a realistic appreciation of the effect of society on the *xin*'s functioning. The social nature of language and the importance of language in the heart-mind may help explain the non-individualist formulation of ethical questions. Mozi, for example, does not ask how *I* should govern *my* action, but how *we* (society) should govern *ours*. His reflective doubt of convention thus differs from Socrates' scepticism.

Hansen, Chad 'Language in the Heart-mind' 75–124 in Allinson, R. (ed.) (1989) *Understanding the Chinese Mind*, Hong Kong: Oxford University Press, p. 119

See also CONFUCIANISM, DAOISM

The account of moral action in Mengzi is based on a particular capacity of   13
the human mind, a capacity which is universal:

> For (human) mouths, there is the common form of taste; for the ears, there is the common form of sound; for the eyes, there is the common form of colour. Is there nothing common to the mind? What is common to the mind is the *logos*, the right. The sage only achieves what is common to all of our minds. Therefore, the *logos* and the right satisfy the mind just as good food satisfies the mouth. (Mengzi)

This paragraph shows that the moral capacity or *xing* is universal to all members of the human race.

More important and well known is the paragraph about 'the four beginnings'. Mengzi said:

> Every human being has a sense of commiseration in his mind. . . . What I mean can be illustrated in this way: when a man suddenly sees a child about to fall into a well, he immediately feels alarmed and worried; this is not because he wants to make friends with the parents, nor because he wants to get a good reputation among his acquaintances, nor because he dislikes the crying. (This response to human suffering belongs to his *xing*.) Seeing it in this way,

a human being who has no sense of commiseration is not a human being at all. Similarly, a human being without the sense of shame and abhorrence (of evils), or without the sense of unacceptability (of improper things), or without the sense of right and wrong, ceases to be a human being. The sense of commiseration is the beginning of *ren*, the sense of shame and abhorrence is the beginning of *yi*, the sense of unacceptability is the beginning of *li*, and the sense of right and wrong is the beginning of wisdom. Every human being has the four beginnings in his mind, just as he has the four limbs in his body. One, possessing these four beginnings but saying that he cannot achieve these virtues, is self-destroying.

Here, Mengzi pointed out the four *a priori* modes of moral consciousness, or four concrete manifestations of the innate moral capacity.

Following this view, the incentive to achieving moral and cultural values, both for the person and human society, is simply natural. Evils arise only because human beings sometimes follow animal desires and fail to maintain their *xing*. To develop the innate capacity, we need education. But such details are not to be discussed here. Now we can move to Mengzi's political thought, to show his ideas of moral order for society.

Although Mengzi seemed to put little emphasis on the human body, this does not imply that he did not care for actual society. On the contrary, it is the primary goal of Confucian philosophy to create a cultural and moral order for the actual world. Unlike the Daoists who taught about 'not-doing', when they advocated their social and political philosophy, Kongzi and Mengzi placed all the emphasis upon the concept of duty, namely, the things we must try to do.

Lao Sze-Kwang 'On Understanding Chinese Philosophy: An Inquiry and a Proposal' in Allinson, R. (ed.) (1989) *Understanding the Chinese Mind*, Hong Kong: Oxford University Press; 265–93, pp. 286–7

See also CONFUCIANISM, DAOISM, HUMAN NATURE

14 These are precepts by Buddaghosa, a 5th century CE commentator in Pali within the Theravada tradition:

I. THE FIVE PRECEPTS

'I UNDERTAKE to observe the rule
to abstain from taking life;
to abstain from taking what is not given;
to abstain from sensuous misconduct;
to abstain from false speech;
to abstain from intoxicants as tending to cloud the mind.'

The first four precepts are explained by Buddhaghosa as follows:

(1) 'Taking life' means to murder anything that lives. It refers to the striking and killing of living beings. 'Anything that lives' – ordinary people speak here of a 'living being', but more philosophically we speak of 'anything that has the life-force'. 'Taking life' is then the will to kill anything that one perceives as having life, to act so as to terminate the life-force in it, in so far as the will finds expression in bodily action or in speech. With regard to animals it is worse to kill large ones than small. Because a more extensive effort is involved. Even where the effort is the same, the difference in substance must be considered. In the case of humans the killing is the more blameworthy the more virtuous they are. Apart from that, the extent of the offence is proportionate to the intensity of the wish to kill. Five factors are involved: a living being, the perception of a living being, a thought of murder, the action of carrying it out, and death as a result of it. And six are the ways in which the offence may be carried out: with one's own hand, by instigation, by missiles, by slow poisoning, by sorcery, by psychic power.

(2) 'To take what is not given' means the appropriation of what is not given. It refers to the removing of someone else's property, to the stealing of it, to theft. 'What is not given' means that which belongs to someone else. 'Taking what is not given' is then the will to steal anything that one perceives as belonging to someone else, and to act so as to appropriate it. Its blameworthiness depends partly on the value of the property stolen, partly on the worth of its owner. Five factors are involved: someone else's belongings, the awareness that they are someone else's, the thought of theft, the action of carrying it out, the taking away as a result of it. This sin, too, may be carried out in six ways. One may also distinguish unlawful acquisition by way of theft, robbery, underhand dealings, stratagems, and the casting of lots.

(3) 'Sensuous misconduct' – here 'sensuous' means 'sexual', and 'misconduct' is extremely blameworthy bad behaviour. 'Sensuous misconduct' is the will to transgress against those whom one should not go into, and the carrying out of this intention by unlawful physical action. By 'those one should not go into', first of all men are meant. And then also twenty kinds of women. Ten of them are under some form of protection, by their mother, father, parents, brother, sister, family, clan, co-religionists, by having been claimed from birth onwards, or by the king's law. The other ten kinds are: women bought with money, concubines for the fun of it, kept women, women bought by the gift of a garment, concubines who have been acquired by the ceremony which consists in dipping their hands into water, concubines who once carried burdens on their heads, slave girls who are also concubines, servants who are also concubines, girls captured in war, temporary wives. The offence is the more serious, the more moral and virtuous the person transgressed against. Four factors are involved: someone who should not be gone into, the thought of cohabiting with that one, the actions which lead to such cohabitation, and its actual performance. There is only one way of carrying it out: with one's own body.

(4) 'False' – this refers to actions of the voice, or actions of the body, which aim at deceiving others by obscuring the actual facts. 'False speech' is the will to deceive others by words or deeds. One can also explain: 'False' means something which is not real, not true. 'Speech' is the intimation that that is real or true. 'False speech' is then the volition which leads to the deliberate intimation to someone else that something is so when it is not so. The seriousness of the offence depends on the circumstances. If a householder, unwilling to give something, says that he has not got it, that is a small offence; but to represent something one has seen with one's own eyes as other than one has seen it, that is a serious offence. If a mendicant has on his rounds got very little oil or ghee, and if he then exclaims, 'What a magnificent river flows along here, my friends!', that is only a rather stale joke, and the offence is small; but to say that one has seen what one has not seen, that is a serious offence. Four factors are involved: something which is not so, the thought of deception, an effort to carry it out, the communication of the falsehood to someone else. There is only one way of doing it: with one's own body.

'To abstain from' – one crushes or forsakes sin. It means an abstention which is associated with wholesome thoughts. And it is threefold: (I) one feels obliged to abstain, (II) one formally undertakes to do so, (III) one has lost all temptation not to do so.

(I) Even those who have not formally undertaken to observe the precepts may have the conviction that it is not right to offend against them. So it was with Cakkana, a Ceylonese boy. His mother was ill, and the doctor prescribed fresh rabbit meat for her. His brother sent him into the field to catch a rabbit, and he went as he was bidden. Now a rabbit had run into a field to eat of the corn, but in its eagerness to get there had got entangled in a snare, and gave forth cries of distress. Cakkana followed the sound, and thought: 'This rabbit has got caught there, and it will make a fine medicine for my mother!' But then he thought again: 'It is not suitable for me that, in order to preserve my mother's life, I should deprive someone else of his life.' And so he released the rabbit, and said to it: 'Run off, play with the other rabbits in the wood, eat grass and drink water!' On his return he told the story to his brother, who scolded him. He then went to his mother, and said to her: 'Even without having been told, I know quite clearly that I should not deliberately deprive any living being of life.' He then fervently resolved that these truthful words of his might make his mother well again, and so it actually happened.

(II) The second kind of abstention refers to those who not only have formally undertaken not to offend against the precepts, but who in addition are willing to sacrifice their lives for that. This can be illustrated by a layman who lived near Uttaravarddhamana. He had received the precepts from Buddharakkhita, the Elder. He then went to plough his field, but found that his ox had got lost. In his search for the ox he climbed up the mountain, where a huge snake took hold of him. He thought of cutting off the snake's head with his sharp knife, but on further reflection he thought to himself: 'It is not suitable that I, who have received the Precepts from the venerable Guru, should break them again.' Three times he thought, 'My life I will give up, but not the precepts!' and then he threw his knife away. Thereafter the huge viper let him go, and went somewhere else.

(III) The last kind of abstention is associated with the holy Path. It does not even occur to the Holy Persons to kill any living being.

Conze, E. (ed.) (1976) *Buddhist Scriptures*, Harmondsworth, Penguin, 1959, pp. 70–3

See also *AHIMSA*, ASCETICISM

EVIL

See also ETHICS

1   What counts as evil varies according to context. We need to examine the context carefully before we can grasp precisely what is supposed to be evil or good:

> Good and evil are not constant – they change according to time and circumstance. For example, an arrow is good if it penetrates its object, while armor is good if it is impenetrable. In the heat of a summer day coolness is good, while in the cold of winter heat is good. For the man who treads the road at night darkness is bad, but for the one who seeks to conceal himself moonlight is bad. In such a way all things may be good or bad. Thus too the good and bad in man's mind and in his acts may not be as opposed to each other as they seem: they differ according to the doctrines one follows. What Confucianism deems good Buddhism may not; and what Buddhism considers good Confucianism might regard as evil. Likewise, references to good and evil in the *Tale* may not correspond to Confucian or Buddhist concepts of good and evil. Then what is good or evil in the realm of human psychology and ethics according to the *Tale of Genji?* Generally speaking, those who know the meaning of the sorrow of human existence, i.e., those who are in sympathy and in harmony with human sentiments, are regarded as good; and those who are not aware of the poignancy of human existence, i.e., those who are not in sympathy and not in harmony with human sentiments, are regarded as bad. Regarded in this light, good and evil in the *Tale* may not appear to be especially different from that in Confucianism or Buddhism. However, if examined closely it will be noted that there are many points of difference, as, for example, in the statement about being or not being in harmony with human sentiment. The *Tale* presents even good and evil in gentle and calm terms unlike the intense, compelling, dialectical manner of Confucian writings.

Motoori in de Bary, W.T. (c) in *Sources of Japanese Tradition*, II, 1958, Columbia University Press, pp. 28–9. Reprinted with permission of the publisher

---

See also CONFUCIANISM

Evil is not caused by God, according to Zoroastrianism, everything has free   **2** will and can act in evil ways:

> This does not, however, mean that God created evil, for Zoroastrianism is the religion of free will *par excellence*. The Evil Spirit *chooses* to do the worst things: his initial act of *will* is evil, not necessarily his nature. In Zoroastrianism no rational being, whether human or angelic, is created with an unfree will, and this must be true of the Evil Spirit too. He chooses evil of his own accord, and once he has chosen, his choice is irrevocable. He becomes the Destructive Spirit who brings death into the world. For the Zoroastrians as for the Jews man was created immortal in body and in soul. But physical death is not due to man's own sin as in the Jewish legend, but to the wickedness of a more than human power which seeks to blot out the 'existence of mortal man'. For the Zoroastrian salvation does not consist in extricating the soul from the body before death as it does for the Buddhist: it consists in reuniting soul and body after they have been separated. This is expressed by the words 'wholeness' (*haurvatāt* from the same root as *salva*-tion) and 'immortality'; and there can be no wholeness if one half of a man, even the less noble one, has perished for ever.

Zaehner, R. (1958) *At Sundry Times: An Essay in the Comparison of Religions*, London: Faber, pp. 142–3

See also AFTERLIFE, DEATH

The Zoroastrian view is that the world represents the site for a battle   **3** between good and evil:

> For medieval Zoroastrianism, too, the world has a purpose. It is a deadly serious battle between good and evil – a battle in which the scales are not quite equally balanced. The good has the advantage, not because it is more powerful, but because it is

orderly and wise. Evil on the other hand must ultimately be annihilated because it is a disorderly motion, brutish, foreseeing nothing, and therefore carrying the seeds of its own destruction within itself. Creation, otherwise so great a mystery, is not only no mystery to these rationalistic epigones of the Prophet; it is a sheer necessity imposed on God as a measure of self-defence against the diabolic attack which cannot fail to materialize since Ahriman, the Devil, is by nature an aggressor. The conflict, once joined, must finally be won by Ohrmazd since the anarchy inherent in the diabolic camp must finally destroy itself. After the inevitable defeat of the Devil the millennium will set in, in which heaven and earth are made anew and man enjoys eternal fellowship with God.

Ibid., p. 151

4   One of the problems with zen sayings is that they often appear to claim precisely the reverse of what they should mean. To say that what is evil includes the good is not to assert that there is no difference between evil and good, just that the traditional dualisms need to be replaced with an understanding of the unity of being:

> The monk further asked Tōsu: "Am I in the right when I understand the Buddha as asserting that all talk, however trivial or derogatory, belongs to ultimate truth?" The master said, "Yes, you are in the right." The monk went on, "May I then call you a donkey?" The master thereupon struck him. . . .
>
> Even when a great teacher is decried as reminding one of an ass, the defamation must be regarded as reflecting something of ultimate truth. All forms of evil must be said somehow to be embodying what is true and good and beautiful, and to a contribution to the perfection of Reality. To state it more concretely, bad is good, ugly is beautiful, false is true, imperfect is perfect, and also conversely. This is, indeed, the kind of reasoning in which those indulge who conceive the God-nature to be immanent in all things.

Suzuki, D. (1973) *Zen and Japanese Culture*, Princeton: Princeton University Press, p. 33

See also ZEN

For Mencius evil is a matter of forgetting that one is human: 5

> Man then, must act in accordance with reason and righteousness so that he may 'follow that part of himself which is great.' Thus will he preserve that which makes of him a man, and be in accordance with the essential definition of the word man. If not, he will lose that whereby he is human, and become one with the beasts. Mencius says:
> "And so of what properly belongs to man, shall it be said that his mind is lacking in human-heartedness and righteousness? The way in which a man loses his goodness of mind (*liang hsin*) is like the way in which trees are denuded by axes and bills. Hewn down day after day, can they retain their beauty? But there is a restoration of its (the mind's) life every night, and in the calm atmosphere of early morning it feels to a close degree those desires and aversions which are proper to humanity, but the feeling is not strong, and is fettered and destroyed by what takes place during the day. This fettering taking place again and again, the restorative influence of the night is not sufficient to preserve (the mind's natural goodness), and when this proves insufficient it becomes not much different from that of the irrational animals, and is then held never to have possessed those powers (which I assert). But is this the reality regarding humanity?" (VI*a*, 8).
> 'The restorative influence of the night' means mans 'heart of human-heartedness and righteousness' which has not yet been completely destroyed. And if man does not preserve this, he loses that whereby he is human, and so becomes no more than an animal. The reason why Mencius stressed the need for seeking for one's lost mind, and not losing one's fundamental mind is because these are necessary before one can really be a man.

> [Quotations from the *Mengzi*]

Fung Yu-Lan (1983) *A History of Chinese Philosophy*, trans. D. Bodde, Princeton: Princeton University Press, pp. 123–4

According to the Legalist thinker Han Fei it is the human capacity for 6
selfishness which is the basis of society:

> All men, Han Fei Tzŭ insists, act from motives of selfishness and self-profit, and so 'show calculating minds in their attitude'

toward one another. It is this fact that makes the system of rewards and punishments possible.

Ibid., p. 327

See also LEGALISM

7   The Legalist critique of other theories is based on their lack of realism:

Men of ancient times and of the present day differ in conduct because of their altered environments, and not because of difference in their natures. It is permissible to say that the customs of ancient people were gentle, but not to say that this means that their natures were better.

Human nature being like this, men must be led by governmental organization and kept in their place by punishments, if the world is to be properly ordered. But if, as Confucius and Mencius urged, people were to be led by virtue and kept in place by the traditional *li*, the government would be without authority and would reach nowhere.

Ibid., pp. 329–30

See also CONFUCIANISM, HUMANITY, LEGALISM, POLITICS AND POWER

8   The existence of good and evil is dependent on our links with *maya* or illusion, the ways in which we misrepresent what is real:

So long as the self is in association with the covering of *māyā* it experiences good and evil. The association of consciousness with matter is thus effected through the manifestation of a special energy of God by which the self is made to undergo the various experiences through its association with *māyā*. As soon as the bond is broken, the self as pure consciousness becomes one with Brahman.

Dasgupta, S. (1940) *A History of Indian Philosophy*, III, Cambridge: Cambridge University Press, p. 26

See also BRAHMAN, MAYA, SELF

Hsun-Tzu (Xunzi) was a Confucian, but with distinctive views on the nature 9
of humanity:

> The nature of man is evil; his goodness is the result of his activity.
> Now, man's inborn nature is to seek for gain. If this tendency is
> followed, strife and rapacity result and deference and compliance
> disappear. By inborn nature one is envious and hates others. If
> these tendencies are followed, injury and destruction result and
> loyalty and faithfulness disappear. By inborn nature one possesses
> the desires of ear and eye and likes sound and beauty. If these
> tendencies are followed, lewdness and licentiousness result, and
> the pattern and order of propriety and righteousness disappear.
> Therefore to follow man's nature and his feelings will inevitably
> result in strife and rapacity, combine with rebellion and disorder,
> and end in violence. Therefore there must be the civilizing
> influence of teachers and laws and the guidance of propriety and
> righteousness, and then it will result in deference and compli-
> ance, combine with pattern and order, and end in discipline.
> From this point of view, it is clear that the nature of man is evil
> and that his goodness is the result of activity. . . .
>   Mencius said, "Man learns because his nature is good." This
> is not true. He did not know the nature of man and did not
> understand the distinction between man's nature and his effort.
> Man's nature is the product of Nature; it cannot be learned and
> cannot be worked for. Propriety and righteousness are produced
> by the sage. They can be learned by men and can be accom-
> plished through work. What is in man but cannot be learned or
> worked for is his nature. What is in him and can be learned
> or accomplished through work is what can be achieved through
> activity. This is the difference between human nature and human
> activity. Now by nature man's eye can see and his ear can hear.
> But the clarity of vision is not outside his eye and the distinctness
> of hearing is not outside his ear. It is clear that clear vision and
> distinct hearing cannot be learned. Mencius said, "The nature
> of man is good; it [becomes evil] because man destroys his
> original nature." This is a mistake. By nature man departs from
> his primitive character and capacity as soon as he is born, and he
> is bound to destroy it. From this point of view, it is clear that
> man's nature is evil.

Chan, Wing-tsit (1972) *A Source Book in Chinese Philosophy*, Princeton, Princeton University Press, pp. 128, 129

See also HUMANITY

10 Mencius had a more optimistic view:

> Mencius said, "In good years most of the young people behave well. In bad years most of them abandon themselves to evil. This is not due to any difference in the natural capacity endowed by Heaven. The abandonment is due to the fact that the mind is allowed to fall into evil. Take for instance the growing of wheat. You sow the seeds and cover them with soil. The land is the same and the time of sowing is also the same. In time they all grow up luxuriantly. When the time of harvest comes, they are all ripe. Although there may be a difference between the different stalks of wheat, it is due to differences in the soil, as rich or poor, to the unequal nourishment obtained from the rain and the dew, and to differences in human effort. Therefore all things of the same kind are similar to one another. Why should there be any doubt about men? The sage and I are the same in kind. Therefore Lung Tzu said, 'If a man makes shoes without knowing the size of people's feet, I know that he will at least not make them to be like baskets.' Shoes are alike because people's feet are alike.

Ibid., p. 55

See also HUMANITY

11 In Zoroastrian thought, good and evil are essential metaphysical concepts which characterize reality:

> (49) 'More wonderful is this that we send our children to school and teach them good conduct and keep them far from evil. Yet when you consider, they still come to know evil before good. But good is good in the sight of God and before men; and evil is evil before the Creator and before men. And in man there is good and evil; and in the world there is good and evil; and in the firmament there is good and evil; and in the spiritual world there is heaven and hell. (50) We were created by the Creator, and to Him is our return. Had it not been necessary, the Creator would not have created us. And with regard to the fact that evil should never have been created and yet exists, a veil is drawn

over this, or else our intelligence cannot attain it. Yet since this is so, we must leave what is God's concern to God.'

Zaehner, (1955) *Zurvan: A Zoroastrian Dilemma* NY, Biblio & Tanven, pp. 415–16

EXISTENCE

Buddhists deny that there is anything essential about what we take to be   1
existence:

> For the Buddhist thesis that existence is not a real predicate, I will quote the following statement from Vasubandhu: "We say matter 'is produced', 'it exists', but there is no difference between existence and the element which exists." The point of the argument is thus developed by Vācaspati Miśra in *Nyāyavārttikatāt-paryatīkā*: consider the existential affirmative judgement 'The cow exists' and the existential negative judgement 'The cow does not exist'. In both cases, the predicate is 'existence'. But of what is 'existence' predicated? If the word 'cow' designated a real existent, then affirmation of existence would be tautologous (*punarukti*), and denial of existence self-contradictory (*virodha*) Therefore 'existence' is not a predicate of the real; it is affirmed or denied of a conceptual construction. Of what is real, 'existence' need not be affirmed and cannot be denied. In fact, the existent and its existence are one and inseparable. As Vasubandhu said, "there is no difference between existence and the element which exists".

Mohanty, J. (1992) *Reason and Tradition in Indian Thought: An Essay on the Nature of Indian Philosophical Thinking*, Oxford: Clarendon Press, p. 158

The Nyaya and Advaita both disagree with the Buddhists on the nature of   2
existence:

> If, for the Nyāya, *sattā* is the most general predicate, the extensionally widest real universal (*parājāti*), and if, according to the Buddhist, there is no existence as such but only the unique occurrence, the Advaita Vedānta, as contrasted with these schools, regards 'existence' as the ultimate subject of all predication, the enduring substratum of all qualification. The Advaita Vedānta agrees with the Nyāya that 'existence' is the highest

generality, but it differs in regarding it not as a universal but as a substance (*dravya*); it agrees with the Buddhist that it is not a predicate, but differs in regarding it not as an instantaneous occurrence but as a timeless, simple substance underlying all things and permitting them to borrow their existence–claims from their 'association' with it. Again, another of its affinities to the Buddhist thesis is apparent: just as, according to the Buddhist, any empirical judgement derives its validity from the uniquely existing occurrence that underlies and supports the mental constructions constituting the judgement, so also for Advaita Vedānta, any existential judgement, in fact any judgement, presupposes the self–manifesting being as the ground of its possibility. . . .

According to the Advaita thesis, whenever we assert of anything that it exists, its existence is of the nature of *brahman*, but only as limited by the content of 'it'. Likewise, whenever we say of anything that it appears, the bare element of manifestation as abstracted from the content that is manifested is the *brahman*. It is also the same in the case of value-judgements. This shows, according to Advaita Vedānta, that being is as much immanent as transcendent with regard to ordinary experience: it is immanent as the indwelling condition of its possibility; it is transcendent inasmuch as in its purity it is beyond the limitations of contents encountered in experience.

Ibid., p. 161

See also ADVAITA, *BRAHMAN*, NYAYA

FA

The Chinese term for law, a crucial term in the thought of Legalism and its leading thinker Han Fei. He is well-known for his book named after him, the *Han Fei Tzu* (WG) or *Han Feizi*.

See also LEGALISM

---

1   The ruler works according to law just as Heaven does:

Han Fei believed that neither power (*shih*), methods of government (*shu*), nor laws (*fa*), can be neglected, one for another. Therefore he says in the *Han-fei-tzŭ* (ch. 48):

"*Shih* is the means for gaining supremacy over the masses. . . . Therefore the intelligent ruler carries out his regulations as would Heaven, and employs men as if he were a spirit. Being like Heaven, he commits no wrong, and being like a spirit, he falls into no difficulties. His *shih* enforces his strict teachings, and nothing that he encounters resists him. . . . Only when this is so can his laws be carried out in concert" (*chüan* 18, p. 8).

By comparing the ruler with heaven, Han Fei Tzŭ means that he acts only according to the law, fairly and impartially. That 'he employs men as if he were a spirit' means that he makes use of them according to his 'methods' or *shu*, secretly and unfathomably; while with the awe which he inspires through the use of rewards and penalties, he 'carries out his laws in concert.' There is no state that cannot be governed when these three, authority, methods and laws, are practised together.

Fung Yu-Lan (1983) *A History of Chinese Philosophy*, trans. D. Bodde, Princeton: Princeton University Press, pp. 320–1

See also HEAVEN, POWER AND POLITICS

The law is the framework within which all appropriate action takes place: 2

The *Han-fei-tzŭ* (ch. 6) says:
"Therefore the intelligent ruler sees to it that his multitude of subjects do not allow their minds to wander beyond the scope of the law; do not perform acts of favoritism within the scope of the law; and make no act not in accord with the law" (*chüan* 2, p. 3). Again (ch. 37):
Although a ruler employs men, he must measure them according to standards, and watch them according to the function of their offices. Affairs in accord with the law he allows to proceed; those not in accord with the law, he puts a stop to" (*chüan* 15, p. 9).

Ibid., p. 322

See also POLITICS AND POWER

FATALISM

See also DEATH

1 The doctrine of *karma* is inconsistent with the idea of free will or personal responsibility, at least in this life:

> The theory of *karma* thus involves a belief in the mysterious existence and ripening of the sinful and virtuous elements of our actions, which alone in their course of maturity produce effects. If the theory that sins bring their punishment, and virtues produce their beneficial effects, of themselves, is accepted, its logical consequences would lead us to deny the possibility of mere physical actions modifying the fruition of these *karmas*. So the acceptance of the moral properties of actions leads to the denial of their direct physical consequences. If through my honest efforts I succeed in attaining a happy state, it is contended that my success is not due to my present efforts, but it was predestined, as a consequence of the good deeds of my previous birth, that I should be happy. For, if the fruition was due to my ordinary efforts, then the theory that all happy or unhappy experiences are due to the ripening of the *karmas* of the previous births falls to the ground. If, on the other hand, all success or failure is due to our proper or improper efforts, then the capacity of sins or virtues to produce misery or happiness may naturally be doubted, and the cases where even our best efforts are attended with failure are not explained. But, if our ordinary efforts cannot effect anything, and if the modes of our experiences, pleasures and sufferings, and the term of our life are already predestined, then none of our efforts are of any use in warding off the calamities of this life, and the purpose of the science of medicine is baffled.

Dasgupta, S. (1932) *A History of Indian Philosophy*, II, Cambridge: Cambridge University Press, p. 404

See also ETHICS, *KARMA*

2 Mozi argues that fatalism is a dangerous doctrine and results in inaction:

> Now, the fatalists say: "Whoever is rewarded by the superior is destined to be rewarded. It is not because of his virtue that he

is rewarded." Under these conditions the people would not be filial to their parents at home, and respectful to the elders in the village or the district. They would not observe propriety in conduct, moderation in going out and coming in, or decency between men and women. And, if they were made to look after the court they would steal, if they were made to defend a city they would raise an insurrection. If the lord met with death they would not commit suicide, and if the lord were banished they would not accompany him. This is what the superior will punish, and what the people will condemn. The fatalists say: "Whoever is punished by the superior is destined to be punished. It is not because of his vice that he is punished." Believing in this, the ruler would not be righteous, the minister would not be loyal, the father would not be affectionate, the son would not be filial, the elder brother would not be brotherly, and the younger brother would not be respectful. The unnatural adherence to this doctrine is responsible for pernicious ideas and is the way of the wicked. . . .

If the doctrine of the fatalist were put to practice, the superiors would not attend to government and the subordinates would not attend to work. If the superior does not attend to government, jurisdiction and administration will be in chaos. If the subordinates do not attend to work, wealth will not be sufficient.

Mozi (1974) *The Ethical and Political Works of Motse*, trans. Yi-Pao Mei, Taipai: Ch'eng Wen Publishing Company, pp. 186–7

A Zoroastrian text which emphasizes balance between trust in fate and   **3**
individual action:

Do the things that happen to man happen through fate or through action? Fate and action together are like body and breath-soul. For the body without the breath-soul is a useless carcase, and the breath-soul without the body an impalpable wind. But when they are fused together, they are powerful and exceedingly beneficial.

What is fate and what is action? Fate is the cause and action the occasion for the things that happen to man. . . .

Know for certain that whosoever neglects to make efforts and puts his trust in fate and destiny makes himself contemptible; and whosoever continually exerts himself and makes efforts and denies fate and destiny is a fool and puffed up with pride. The wise man must find the mean between effort and fate, and not be content with one of them. For fate and effort are like two bales of a traveller's baggage on the back of a mule. If one of them is heavier and the other lighter, the load falls to the ground, and the back of the mule is broken, and the traveller suffers embarrassment and does not reach his destination. But if both bales are equal, the traveller does not need to worry, the mule is comfortable, and both arrive at their destination.

'Epistle of Tansar'

Zaehner (1955) *Zurvan: A Zoroastrian Dilemma* NY, Biblio & Tanven, p. 405

GENDER

1   Nichiren derives what many Buddhists would regard as radical consequences from the *Lotus Sutra*. Becoming Buddha is not limited to men, and that possibility is open to all men and women:

[The second admonition concerns the fact that the Dragon King's daughter attained Buddhahood.] When she attained Buddhahood, this does not mean simply that one person did so. It reveals the fact that all women will attain Buddhahood. In the various Hinayana sutras that were preached before the Lotus Sutra, it is denied that women can ever attain Buddhahood. In the Mahayana sutras other than the Lotus Sutra, it would appear that women can attain Buddhahood or be reborn in the Pure Land. But they may do so only after they have changed into some other form. It is not the kind of immediate attainment of Buddhahood that is encompassed in the doctrine of *ichinen sanzen*. Thus it is an attainment of Buddhahood or rebirth in the Pure Land in name but not in reality. The Dragon King's daughter is, as the phrase has it, "one example that stands for all the rest." When the Dragon King's daughter attained Buddhahood, it opened up the possibility of attaining Buddhahood for all women of later ages.

Confucianism preaches filial piety and care for one's parents, but it is limited to this present life. It provides no way for one to assist one's parents in their future lives, and the Confucian sages and worthies are therefore sages and worthies in name only and not in reality. Brahmanism, though it recognizes the existence of past, present, and future lives, similarly offers no means to assist one's parents to a better life in the future. Buddhism alone can do so, and thus it is the true way of sages and worthies. But in the Hinayana and Mahayana sutras preached before the Lotus Sutra, and in the sects based on these sutras, to gain salvation even for oneself is impossible. One can hardly hope to do anything for one's parents either. Though the texts of these sutras may say [that they can bring about salvation], in reality that is not the case. Only with the preaching of the Lotus Sutra, in which the Dragon King's daughter attained Buddhahood, did it become evident that the attainment of Buddhahood was a possibility for all the mothers of the world. And when it was revealed that even an evil man such as Devadatta could attain Buddhahood, it became evident that Buddhood was a possibility for all the fathers of the world.

Nichiren (1990) *Selected writings of Nichiren*, ed. P. Yampolsky (c) Nichiren Shoshu International Center, trans. B. Watson et al, New York: Columbia University Press, pp. 121–2. Reprinted with permission of the publisher.

See also AMIDA, CONFUCIANISM, *LOTUS SUTRA*

GOD

For ibn Sina (Avicenna) God is the ultimate cause of everything, but he does 1 not have any power over whether things can exist or not:

> It is clear that for Avicenna a contingent thing can only exist if it is brought into existence by something else, and we would get an infinite regress of such causes were there not in existence a thing which is necessary in itself and which therefore does not require a causal push into existence. Now, many views of God and his creation would interpret this relation as one of God considering which of the possible states of affairs he could bring into existence if he is to fulfil his aims in constructing the world. God can select any possible state of affairs as desirable and then bring it into existence in the world. But this is not Avicenna's view at all. Contingent things are obliged to wait before they exist in a kind of metaphysical limbo which is entirely independent of God's will. All God can do is determine whether contingent things will exist or not; he cannot affect their

possibility. This has interesting consequences. Avicenna distinguishes between possible material and possible immaterial
substances. The former are essentially as they are before God's
causal powers get to work on them; were they to be otherwise,
on Avicenna's familiar argument, they would not be possible
because 'whatever comes to exist, before it came to exist was
either possible as an existent or impossible. Now, whatever is
opposed to existence will never exist, and what is possible as
an existent, surely its possibility as an existent preceded it . . .
There has therefore already preceded everything which begins
to be matter.' God's control over even existence is severely
circumscribed with regard to the possible immaterial substances
which are dependent upon him for their existence and not
necessary in themselves, but for whom there was not time when
they were not in existence. They are necessary but only necessary
through another thing, God, and they exist in tandem with him.
In so far as the contents of the material world go, though, God
is confined to willing the possible to exist. He cannot will the
possible to be existent *and* possible. He is rather in the position of
the customer in a restaurant who has no choice as to what he can
order. He can and indeed must order the fixed menu, and he has
no control over the selection which is set before him.

Leaman, O. (1985) *An Introduction to Medieval Islamic Philosophy*, Cambridge:
Cambridge University Press, pp. 30–1

See also CREATION, EXISTENCE

---

2   The Mimamsa argue against the existence of God, while Shankara suggests
    that the references to *brahman* in the Upanishads are about an ultimate
    cause:

The Mīmāṃsists do not admit the existence of Īśvara. Their
antitheistic arguments, which we have not considered, can be
dealt with here in contrast to Yāmuna's doctrine of Īśvara. They
say that an omniscient Īśvara cannot be admitted, since such an
assumption cannot be proved, and there are, indeed, many
objections to the hypothesis. For how can such a perception of
omniscience be acquired? Surely it cannot be acquired by the
ordinary means of perception; for ordinary perception cannot
give one the knowledge of all things present and past, before and

far beyond the limits of one's senses. Also the perception of
Īśvara generally ascribed to the Yogins cannot be admitted; for
it is impossible that the Yogin should perceive past things and
things beyond the limits of his senses, by means of his sense-
organs. If mind (*antaḥkaraṇa*) be such that it can perceive all
sense-objects without the aid of the senses, then what is the use
at all of the senses? Of course it is true that by great concentration
one can perceive things more clearly and distinctly; but no
amount of concentration or any other process can enable a
man to hear by the eye or to perceive things without the help of
the senses. Omniscience is therefore not possible, and we have
not by our senses seen any such omniscient person as Īśvara. His
existence cannot be proved by inference; for, since He is beyond
all perceptible things, there cannot be any reason (*hetu*) which
we could perceive as being associated with Him and by reason
of which we could make Him the subject of inference. It is urged
by the Naiyāyikas that this world, formed by collocation of parts,
must be an effect in itself, and it is argued that, like all other
effects, this also must have taken place under the superintendence
of an intelligent person who had a direct experience of world
materials. But this is not necessary; for it may very well be
conceived that the atoms, etc., have all been collocated in their
present form by the destinies of men (*adṛṣṭa*) – according to the
karma, of all the men in the world. The *karmas* of merit and
demerit exist in us all, and they are moulding the world-process,
though these cannot be perceived by us. The world may thus
be regarded as a product of the *karmas* of men and not of *Īśvara*,
whom no one has ever perceived. Moreover, why should *Īśvara*,
who has no desire to satisfy, create this world? This world, with
all the mountains, rivers and oceans, etc., cannot be regarded as
an effect produced by any one. . . .

The Śaṅkarites had held that, when the Upaniṣads say that
nothing exists but one Brahman, it means that Brahman alone
exists and the world is false; but that is not the sense. It means
simply that there is no other Īśvara but Īśvara, and that there is
none else like Him. When the Upaniṣads declare that Brahman
is all that we see and that He is the sole material of the world, it
does not mean that everything else does not exist and that the
qualityless Brahman is the only reality. If I say there is one sun, it
does not mean that He has no rays; if I say there are the seven
oceans, it does not mean that the oceans have no ripples, etc.
The only meaning that such passages can have is that the world

has come out of Him, like sparks from fire, and that in Him the world finds its ultimate rest and support; from Him all things of the world – the fire, the wind, the earth – have drawn their powers and capacities, and without His power they would have been impotent to do anything. If, on the contrary, it is held that the whole world is false, then the whole experience has to be sacrificed, and, as the knowledge of Brahman also forms a part of this experience that also has to be sacrificed as false.

Dasgupta, S. (1940) *A History of Indian Philosophy*, III, Cambridge: Cambridge University Press, pp. 152–3

See also ADVAITA, *BRAHMAN*, *KARMA*, MIMAMSA, NYAYA-VAISHESHIKA, *UPANISHADS*

3   The Nyaya argue for the existence of God because of the way in which the world is designed. By contrast, Buddhists generally argue against eternal and unchanging entities, and so could not accept the existence of God:

One of the chief arguments of the Naiyāyika theists in favour of the existence of God is based on the fact that the specific forms and shapes of the different objects in the world cannot be explained except on the supposition of an intelligent organizer or shaper. . . .

The general Buddhist arguments against the existence of any eternal entity will also apply against the existence of any eternal God. The argument that, since a state of arrest breaks up into a state of motion or production in all natural phenomena, there must be an intelligent creator, is wrong; for there is no state of arrest in nature; all things in the world are momentary. Again, if things are happening in succession, at intervals, through the operation of a causal agent, then God also must be operating at intervals and, by the arguments of the opponents themselves, He must have another being to guide His operations, and that another, and that another, and there would thus be a vicious infinite. If God had been the creator, then everything would have sprung into being all at once. He ought not to depend on accessory assistance; for, He being the creator of all such accessory circumstances, they could not render Him any assistance in His creation. Again, if it is urged that the above argument does not hold, because God only creates when He wishes, then it may be replied that, since God's will is regarded as eternal and one, the old objection of simultaneous production holds good. Moreover, since God is eternal and since His will depends only on Him and Him alone, His will cannot be transitory. Now, if He and His will be always present, and yet at the moment of the production of any particular phenomenon all other phenomena are not produced, then those phenomena cannot be regarded as being caused by God or by His will. Again, even if for argument's sake it may be granted that all natural objects, such as trees, hills, etc., presuppose intelligent creators, there is no argument for supposing that one intelligent creator is the cause of all diverse natural objects and phenomena. Therefore there is no argument in favour of the existence of one omniscient creator.

Dasgupta, S. (1932) *A History of Indian Philosophy*, II, Cambridge: Cambridge University Press, pp. 176–7

See also CREATION, NYAYA

The Sankhya do not find a role for God in their thought, in the sense of a   4
creator of the universe:

As classically formulated, however, Yoga appears as the technique used for realizing the truth of the so-called Sāṁkhya philosophy: it is the technique whereby it is possible to separate the eternal soul from all its mortal trappings. It is not concerned with God, for there is no God in the Sāṁkhya system. It is true that in Patañjali's *Yoga-Sūtras*, a being called 'the Lord' is introduced; but this 'Lord', *īśvara*, is not at all what we would call God. Like all other souls he is eternal, but he is not the creator and sustainer of the universe, nor anything like it. He is simply the only soul that never comes into contact with matter and who is thereby able to help other souls out of their bondage to the body. Yet though the *īśvara* of Patañjali is certainly not God, he does prefigure, however dimly, the fully developed divine figure of the Bhagavad-Gītā.

Zaehner, R. (1958) *At Sundry Times: An Essay in the Comparison of Religions*, London: Faber, p. 41

See also BHAGAVAD GITA, CREATION, SANKHYA-YOGA

GOLDEN MEAN

1   This comment on *Analects* 4:15 represents an argument by Confucius on the importance of balance and reciprocity:

> *Comment.* It is often said that Confucianism teaches only the "negative golden rule," not to do to others what one does not want them to do to him. However, the golden rule is here positively stated, that is, to do to others what one expects others to do to him. There is no question about the positive character of the Confucian doctrine which is clearly stated in terms of conscientiousness and altruism.
>
> 14. The superior man does what is proper to his position and does not want to go beyond this. If he is in a noble station, he does what is proper to a position of wealth and honorable station. If he is in a humble station, he does what is proper to a position of poverty and humble station. If he is in the midst of barbarian tribes, he does what is proper in the midst of barbarian tribes. In a position of difficulty and danger, he does what is proper to a position of difficulty and danger. He can find himself in no situation in which he is not at ease with himself. In a high position he does not treat his inferiors with contempt. In a low position he does not court the favor of his superiors. He rectifies himself and seeks nothing from others, hence he has no complaint to make. He does not complain against Heaven above or blame men below. Thus it is that the superior man lives peacefully and at ease and waits for his destiny.

Chan, Wing-tsit (1972) *A Source Book in Chinese Philosophy*, Princeton, Princeton University Press, p. 101

See also CONFUCIANISM, ETHICS, HEAVEN

2   This explication of the Confucian rule discusses the sort of person who would develop out of a rigorous adherence to another formulation of the Golden Mean:

> *Question*: The *Doctrine of the Mean* says, "the superior man is cautious over what he does not see and apprehensive over what he does not hear." It also says, "The superior man is watchful over himself when he is alone." Based on these statements, later Confucianists have developed the theory that principle should

be preserved and that desires should be curbed or suppressed. Now you say that desires may be compared to the flow of water, which certainly cannot be dammed; if water is truly allowed to flow in its channel, then no matter where it goes, it will be in accordance with its natural principle. If we have this in mind when we try to prevent our desires from overflowing, then it is quite reasonable. Thus the above statements from the *Doctrine of the Mean* are not merely saying that we should control our desires so that they do not overflow. Is it possible for you to elucidate the meaning of these statements?

Answer: In speaking of "being cautious" and "being apprehensive," the *Doctrine of the Mean* had reference to the difference between being serious and being heedless. Most people are cautious in their manners and behavior when they are on public view. They are careful not to say something wrong when others are listening. The superior man maintains this attitude even when not in the presence of others; he is serious and dares not be the least heedless. This is what is meant by the statement in the final chapter of the *Doctrine of the Mean*, "The superior man, even when he is not moving, is serious, and while he speaks not, he has the feeling of truthfulness."

"Being cautious when alone" is in reference to what is wrong and what is right. The beginning of any action commences with a will or an intent, just as the beginning of what is visible commences with what is hidden, and the beginning of what is manifest commences with what is subtle. A person's will or intent may be activated, but others do not see it. This is the meaning of the statement in the final chapter of the *Doctrine of the Mean*, "The superior man examines his heart, that there be nothing wrong there, and that he has bad intentions. It is in what he does that the superior man cannot be equaled – what he does others cannot see."

The fact is that before one responds to an event, there is a difference whether in his attitude he is serious or heedless. When something arises and he responds to it, there is a difference as to whether [his actions] are wrong or right. One who is serious is always self-disciplined, whereas one who is heedless is just the opposite. Right actions are those in which selfish motives are not involved, whereas wrong actions are just the opposite. It is necessary that one be serious in intent and correct in action, but should one be partial in his opinions, he cannot be said to have grasped principle. Although his intelligence may suffice him to understand principle, unless he is serious, he will make many mistakes, and unless he is correct, he will be a complete hypocrite. There are three cautions one must observe, each of which has its special point: first, one must avoid making mistakes, second, one must strictly refrain from hypocrisy, and third, one must turn away from becoming partial.

Tai Chen (1990) *Tai Chen on Mencius: Explorations in Words and Meaning*, trans. Ann-ping Chin and M. Freeman, New Haven: Yale University Press, pp. 86–7

See also ACTION, CONFUCIANISM, ETHICS

GUNA/GUNAS

1   According to the ancient view, the dynamics of *prakṛti* are governed by the interactions of the three *guṇas*, which are the three basic types of constituent of physical substance. The three *guṇas* are *sattva*, *rajas* and *tamas*, which correspond roughly with 'transparency and buoyancy,' 'energy and activity,' and 'inertia and obstruction.' All physical phenomena are believed to consist of unstable mixtures of these three types of constituent, and the instability of these mixtures is responsible for the evolution and transformations of the material world. Thus the conceptual processes sustained by the mind are governed by the mechanical and unconscious interplay of the *guṇas*, and to this extent, mental phenomena are viewed in purely 'physicalistic' or mechanical terms. The unfolding of thought-forms is an integral part of the evolution of *prakṛti*, and mental processes are simply the result of appropriate transformations of unconscious material substance. It is worth noting at this point that the Sāṅkhya-Yoga view thereby avoids one of the most serious pitfalls of Cartesian dualism, since on the Indian account, mental causation does not violate physical conservation laws. By including the mind in the realm of matter, mental events are granted causal efficacy, and are therefore able to directly initiate bodily motions.

Schweitzer. P. (1993) 'Mind/Consciousness Dualism in Sankhya-Yoga Philosophy', *Philosophy and Phenomenological Research*, LIII, 4, 845–59, p. 849

See also PRAKRITI, SANKHYA-YOGA

Prakriti, which is the interplay of three fundamental modes of   2
its working, three qualities, Gunas. And what is the medium? It
is the complex system of existence created by a graded evolution
of the instruments of Prakriti, which, as they are reflected here
in the soul's experience of her workings, we may call successively
the reason and the ego, the mind, the senses and the elements of
material energy which are the basis of its forms. These are all
mechanical, a complex engine of Nature, *yantra*; and from our
modern point of view we may say that they are all involved
in material energy and manifest themselves in it as the soul
in Nature becomes aware of itself by an upward evolution of
each instrument, but in the inverse order to that which we
have stated, matter first, then sensation, then mind, next reason,
last spiritual consciousness. Reason, which is at first only pre-
occupied with the workings of Nature, may then detect their
ultimate character, may see them only as play of the three Gunas
in which the soul is entangled, may distinguish between the soul
and these workings; then the soul gets a chance of disentangling
itself and of going back to its original freedom and immutable
existence. In Vedantic language, it sees the spirit, the being;
it ceases to identify itself with the instruments and workings of
Nature, with its becoming; it identifies itself with its true Self and
being and recovers its immutable spiritual self-existence. It is
then from this spiritual self-existence, according to the Gita, that
it can freely and as the master of its being, the Ishwara, support
the action of its becoming.

Aurobindo (1987) *The Essential Aurobindo*, ed. R. McDermott, Great
Barrington, MA: Lindisfarne Press, p. 125

See also BHAGAVAD GITA, PRAKRITI

GURU

The teacher has to impart not just knowledge but also must possess the   1
skill to transmit knowledge. This is not just an intellectual skill, but has to be
spiritual also:

Every soul is destined to be perfect, and every being, in the end, will attain the state of perfection. Whatever we are now is the result of our acts and thoughts in the past; and whatever we shall be in the future will be the result of what we think and do now. But this, the shaping of our own destinies, does not preclude our receiving help from outside; nay, in the vast majority of cases such help is absolutely necessary. When it comes, the higher powers and possibilities of the soul are quickened, spiritual life is awakened, growth is animated, and man becomes holy and perfect in the end.

This quickening impulse cannot be derived from books. The soul can only receive impulses from another soul, and from nothing else. We may study books all our lives, we may become very intellectual, but in the end we find that we have not developed at all spiritually. It is not true that a high order of intellectual development always goes hand in hand with a proportionate development of the spiritual side in man. In studying books we are sometimes deluded into thinking that thereby we are being spiritually helped; but if we analyse the effect of the study of books on ourselves, we shall find that, at the utmost, it is only our intellect that derives profit from such studies, and not our inner spirit. This inadequacy of books to quicken spiritual growth is the reason why, although almost every one of us can *speak* most wonderfully on spiritual matters, when it comes to action and the living of a truly spiritual life, we find ourselves so awfully deficient. To quicken the spirit, the impulse *must* come from another soul.

The person from whose soul such impulse comes is called the Guru – the teacher; and the person to whose soul the impulse is conveyed is called the Shishya – the student. To convey such an impulse to any soul, in the first place, the soul from which it proceeds must possess the power of transmitting it, as it were, to another; and in the second place, the soul to which it is transmitted must be fit to receive it. The seed must be a living seed, and the field must be ready ploughed; and when both these conditions are fulfilled, a wonderful growth of genuine religion takes place.

Vivekananda. S. (1959) *Bhakti-Yoga*, Calcutta: Advaita Ashrama, pp. 24–5

See also EDUCATION

HAPPINESS

Although Buddhism sees happiness as the basis of action, it is not selfish [1]
happiness achieved through expanding personal pleasures but rather
through escaping suffering by thinking and living in the appropriate ways:

Now it will be possible to examine the basis of ethical judgment
according to Buddhism. One way of deciding whether an action
is right or wrong, good or bad is by finding out whether it
leads to detachment (*virāga*) or attachment (*rāga*). Very often the
Buddha remarked that such and such an action ought not to have
been done (*akaraṇīyaṃ*), the *reason* being that that action does not
lead to detachment (*virāga*) and pacification (*vūpasama*) of desires.
Yet this is not the final criterion of good and bad.

Why are those things or actions that lead to nonattachment
(*virāga*) considered good and those that lead to attachment (*rāga*)
considered bad? The reason is that the former lead to happiness
(*sukhudrayaṃ, sukhavipākaṃ*) and freedom, while the latter are
conducive to suffering (*dukkhudrayaṃ, dukkhavipākaṃ*) and
bondage. The emphasis on happiness as the goal of ethical
conduct seems to give the Buddhist theory a utilitarian character. But a major difference between the early Buddhist and the
utilitarian analyses of happiness is that according to the latter,
happiness includes pleasures derived from the senses, while
according to the Buddhists, sense pleasures lead finally to suffering rather than to happiness. Of course the Utilitarians, though
they included pleasures under happiness, still distinguished
between animal pleasures and the more exalted forms of human
pleasure.

The noblest happiness, according to early Buddhism, is to be
achieved through the control of all hankering for the world (of
sense pleasures), all coveting of its false values, together with the
dejection to which their impermanence and lack of enduring
satisfaction give rise. This is achieved through right, complete,
or perfect mindfulness.

Kalupahana, D. (1996) *Buddhist Philosophy: A Historical Analysis*, Honolulu:
University Press of Hawaii, pp. 60–1

See also DUHKHA, ETHICS

2   We tend to think that happiness is a matter of doing a lot and getting many things, but according to Zhuangzi it is rather achieved by doing as little as possible:

> Is there such a thing as perfect happiness in the world or isn't there? Is there some way to keep yourself alive or isn't there? What to do, what to rely on, what to avoid, what to stick by, what to follow, what to leave alone, what to find happiness in, what to hate?
>
> This is what the world honors: wealth, eminence, long life, a good name. This is what the world finds happiness in: a life of ease, rich food, fine clothes, beautiful sights, sweet sounds. This is what it looks down on: poverty, meanness, early death, a bad name. This is what it finds bitter: a life that knows no rest, a mouth that gets no rich food, no fine clothes for the body, no beautiful sights for the eye, no sweet sounds for the ear.
>
> People who can't get these things fret a great deal and are afraid – this is a stupid way to treat the body. People who are rich wear themselves out rushing around on business, piling up more wealth than they could ever use – this is a superficial way to treat the body. People who are eminent spend night and day scheming and wondering if they are doing right – this is a shoddy way to treat the body. Man lives his life in company with worry, and if he lives a long while, till he's dull and doddering, then he has spent that much time worrying instead of dying, a bitter lot indeed! This is a callous way to treat the body. . . .
>
> What ordinary people do and what they find happiness in – I don't know whether such happiness is in the end really happiness or not. I look at what ordinary people find happiness in, what they all make a mad dash for, racing around as though they couldn't stop – they all say they're happy with it. I'm not happy with it and I'm not unhappy with it. In the end is there really happiness or isn't there?
>
> I take inaction to be true happiness, but ordinary people think it is a bitter thing. I say: perfect happiness knows no happiness, perfect praise knows no praise. The world can't decide what is right and what is wrong. And yet inaction can decide this. Perfect happiness, keeping alive – only inaction gets you close to this!
>
> Let me try putting it this way. The inaction of Heaven is its purity, the inaction of earth is its peace. So the two inactions combine and all things are transformed and brought to birth.

Wonderfully, mysteriously, there is no place they come out of. Mysteriously, wonderfully, they have no sign. Each thing minds its business and all grow up out of inaction. So I say, Heaven and earth do nothing and there is nothing that is not done. Among men, who can get hold of this inaction?

Chuang Tzu (1968) *The Complete Works of Chuang Tzu*, trans. B. Watson, New York: Columbia University Press, pp. 190, 191

See also ACTION, DAOISM

Happiness according to Confucius is a matter of living simply: 3

Neo-Confucianism attempted to find happiness in *ming-chiao* (morals, institutions). The search for happiness, indeed, is one of the professed aims of the Neo-Confucianists. Ch'eng Hao says, for example: "When we studied under Chou [Tun-yi], he always asked us to find out wherein lay the happiness of K'ung [Confucius] and Yen [Hui], and what they found enjoyable." (*Literary Remains of the Two Ch'engs, chüan* 2a.) There are, in fact, many passages in the *Analects* recording the happiness of Confucius and his disciple. Those commonly quoted by the Neo-Confucianists include the following:

"Confucius said: 'With coarse rice to eat, with only water to drink, and my bended arm for a pillow, I am happy in the midst of these things. Riches and honor acquired by means that I know to be wrong are to me as a floating cloud.'" (*Analects*, VII, 15.)

About Yen Hui, Confucius said: "Incomparable indeed was Hui. A handful of rice to eat, a gourdful of waters to drink, and living in a mean street: these, others would have found unbearably depressing, but for Hui's happiness they made no difference at all. Incomparable indeed was Hui." (*Ibid.*, VI, 9.)

Another passage says that once when Confucius was sitting with several of his disciples, he asked each of them to express his desires. One replied that he would like to be minister of war in a certain state, another to be minister of finance, and still another to be master of ceremonies. But the fourth, Tseng Tien, paid no attention to what others were saying, but continued to strum his lute. When the others had finished, Confucius asked him to speak. He replied: "[My desire would be], in the last month of spring, with the dress of the season all complete, along with five or six young men, and six or seven boys, to go to wash in the river Yi, enjoy the breezes among the rain altars, and return home singing." Whereupon Confucius said: "I am with Tien." (XI, 25.)

Fung Yu-Lan (1948) *A Short History of Chinese Philosophy*, New York: Free Press, pp. 289–90

See also CONFUCIANISM

HARMONY

1   Gu Mu, chairman of a conference of the Chinese Communist Party, presents this interesting argument that socialism, Confucianism and social harmony are part of the same political philosophy:

> The Chinese nation has had a long history and brilliant ancient culture. For a long period of time in human history, the Chinese culture, with the Confucian school of thought as the main stream, glittered with colorful splendor . . .
>
> Culture serves both as the emblem of the level of civilization of a nation or a country and the guidance for its political and economic life. To promote prosperity and peace of a nation and for mankind in general, it is necessary to develop a compatible culture. In this regard, a proper attitude toward the traditional national culture is very important. It is inadvisable either to be complacent about the past or to discard the past and the tradition. The correct attitude is to inherit the essence and discard the dross.
>
> The Chinese people are working hard to build socialist modernization and a prosperous and strong socialist country. In order to reach this goal, we must develop and improve our new culture, which, we believe, should be national, patriotic, scientific, and democratic. This calls for inheriting and reforming the traditional culture of our nation and parallel efforts to courageously and yet selectively assimilate the advanced cultures of the outside world, merging the two into an integral whole.
>
> As for the attitude toward the traditional culture and foreign cultures, there is no doubt that the traditional culture should be kept as the mainstay. . . .

As is known to all, the idea of harmony is an important component of the Chinese traditional culture. As early as in the last years of the West Zhou dynasty three thousand years ago, ancient scholars elucidated the brilliant idea of "harmony making prosperity." Later, Confucius and the Confucian school put forward the proposition of "harmony above all," and established theories on the coordination of interpersonal relations, the protection of the natural environment, and the maintenance of ecological balance. These thoughts not only made positive contributions to the prosperity of ancient Chinese society, but also have profound practical significance for the survival and development of mankind today.

de Bary, W.T. (1991) *The Trouble with Confucianism*, Cambridge, Mass.: Harvard University Press, pp. 107–8

See also CONFUCIANISM

HEAVEN

Right action according to Mozi is what leads the world to flourish, and so is   1
naturally favoured by Heaven:

Now, what does Heaven desire and what does it abominate? Heaven desires righteousness and abominates unrighteousness. Therefore, in leading the people in the world to engage in doing righteousness I should be doing what Heaven desires. When I do what Heaven desires, Heaven will also do what I desire. Now, what do I desire and what do I abominate? I desire blessings and emoluments, and abominate calamities and misfortunes. When I do not do what Heaven desires, neither will Heaven do what I desire. Then I should be leading the people into calamities and misfortunes. But how do we know Heaven desires righteousness and abominates unrighteousness? For, with righteousness the world lives and without it the world dies; with it the world becomes rich and without it the world becomes poor; with it the world becomes orderly and without it the world becomes chaotic. And Heaven likes to have the world live and dislikes to have it die, likes to have it rich and dislikes to have it poor, and likes to have it orderly and dislikes to have it disorderly. Therefore we know Heaven desires righteousness and abominates unrighteousness.

Mozi (1974) *The Ethical and Political Works of Motse*, trans. Yi-Pao Mei, Taipai: Ch'eng Wen Publishing Company, p. 136

See also ETHICS

2   Heaven has organized everything to accord with our needs, and does not even demand anything in return:

> Moreover I know Heaven loves men dearly not without reason. Heaven ordered the sun, the moon, and the stars to enlighten and guide them. Heaven ordained the four seasons, Spring, Autumn, Winter, and Summer, to regulate them. Heaven sent down snow, frost, rain, and dew to grow the five grains and flax and silk that so the people could use and enjoy them. Heaven established the hills and rivers, ravines and valleys, and arranged many things to minister to man's good or bring him evil. He appointed the dukes and lords to reward the virtuous and punish the wicked, and to gather metal and wood, birds and beasts, and to engage in cultivating the five grains and flax and silk to provide for the people's food and clothing. This has been taking place from antiquity to the present. Suppose there is a man who is deeply fond of his son and has used his energy to the limit to work for his benefit. But when the son grows up he returns no love to the father. The gentlemen of the world will all call him unmagnanimous and miserable. Now Heaven loves the whole world universally. Everything is prepared for the good of man. The work of Heaven extends to even the smallest things that are enjoyed by man. Such benefits may indeed be said to be substantial, yet there is no service in return. And they do not even know this to be unmagnanimous. This is why I say the gentlemen of the world understand only trifles but not things of importance.

Ibid., pp. 145–6

See also ETHICS, EVIL

3   It is important to stress that the role of Heaven in Chinese philosophy is very different from what in the Western tradition would be regarded as a specifically religious concept:

> Heaven (*tian*). Although there is much in the *Analects* about the

observance of ritual both in religious and secular contexts, the work does not include specifically religious teaching and Master Kong is depicted as displaying an agnostic attitude towards ghosts and spirits, although they are seen as part of the general experience of life. On the other hand he is very conscious of the role of Heaven who 'created the virtue' in him, and upon whom all riches and honours depend, while others are described in the *Analects* as believing that Heaven is using the Master and will grant that he becomes a sage. A more impersonal 'fate' or 'destiny' (*ming*), a word which is also used in its more literal sense of 'decree' or command', also occurs commonly. It reflects the feeling which must be common to all cultures that, despite all our efforts, what happens is really out of our hands (although commands and decrees can of course be disobeyed and one can, for example, lay down one's life and so not accept one's predestined span).

Confucius, trans. R. Dawson (1993) *The Analects*, Oxford: Oxford University Press, p. xxvi

See also FATALISM

For Zhuangzi heaven stands for what is natural, and human the reverse: 4

"Hence it is said: the Heavenly is on the inside, the human is on the outside. Virtue resides in the Heavenly. Understand the actions of Heaven and man, base yourself upon Heaven, take your stand in virtue, and then, although you hasten or hold back, bend or stretch, you may return to the essential and speak of the ultimate."

"What do you mean by the Heavenly and the human?"

Jo of the North Sea said, "Horses and oxen have four feet – this is what I mean by the Heavenly. Putting a halter on the horse's head, piercing the ox's nose – this is what I mean by the human. So I say: do not let what is human wipe out what is Heavenly; do not let what is purposeful wipe out what is fated; do not let [the desire for] gain lead you after fame. Be cautious, guard it, and do not lose it – this is what I mean by returning to the True."

Chuang Tzu (1968) *The Complete Works of Chuang Tzu*, trans. B. Watson, New York: Columbia University Press, pp. 182–3

See also DAOISM

HUA YAN/HUA YEN

Hua Yan (Hua Yen) or the Flower (Garland) School is a form of Buddhism which especially flourished in China:

1   The whole Hua-yen philosophy centers around its fundamental concept, the Universal Causation of the Realm of Dharmas (elements of existence). The Realm of Dharmas (*Dharmadhātu*) connotes the whole universe, which in the belief of the school, is fourfold. It involves the Realm of Facts, the Realm of Principle (*Li*), the Realm of Principle and Facts harmonized, and the Realm of All Facts interwoven and mutually identified. Principle is static, spaceless, formless, characterless, Emptiness, the noumenon; while facts are dynamic, have specific forms and specific characters, are in an unceasing process of transformation, and constitute the phenomenal world. They interact and interpenetrate and thus form a Perfect Harmony.

The basic principle underlying this perfect harmony is the simple idea of interpenetration and mutual identification. It is based on the theory of the Ten Mysterious Gates, according to which all things are coexistent, interwoven, interrelated, interpenetrating, mutually inclusive, reflecting one another, and so on. This doctrine in turn rests on the theory of the Six Characters to the effect that each dharma possesses the six characteristics of universality, specialty, similarity, difference, integration, and disintegration, so that each dharma is at once one and all and the world is in reality a Perfect Harmony. Consequently, when one dharma rises, all dharmas rise with it, and vice versa. In short, the entire universe rises at the same time. This is the meaning of the Universal Causation of the Realm of Dharmas.

Fung Yu-Lan (1948) *A Short History of Chinese Philosophy*, New York: Free Press, p. 407

See also CAUSATION, *DHARMA*, HARMONY, TIAN TAI

HUMAN NATURE/HUMANENESS/HUMANITY

1   An account of human nature as consisting of balance, a familiar Confucian idea:

Human nature may be compared to water, and the desires to the flow of the water. If one keeps his desires within bounds, he is acting in accordance with Heavenly principle. This is the way of mutual development and nourishment. It is analogous to water flowing in its own channel. When a man indulges his desires to the point where "his mind becomes perverted and deceitful, and he commits wicked acts and causes disturbances," his actions are analogous to a flood out of control inundating the Middle Kingdom. The sages taught us to examine ourselves and think how we would feel should others treat us in the same way we were treating them. This standard of restraint is analogous to the way in which Yü directed the rivers into their natural channels instead of damming them, for fear that they would overflow their banks. As for those who are clever in advancing the theory of damaging the rivers lest they should overflow, actually what they are doing is to cut off the source of the rivers. This is analogous to putting a stop to desires or to having no desires.

Tai Chen (1990) *Tai Chen on Mencius: Explorations in Words and Meaning*, trans. Ann-ping Chin and M. Freeman, New Haven: Yale University Press, pp. 85–6

See also GOLDEN MEAN

Mencius extended the Confucian principle that human beings should seek 2
to link themselves with each other by adding the idea that we are naturally
good, and so have an obvious motive to help others and be concerned
about their welfare:

Confucius spoke very much about *jen* (human heartedness), and made a sharp distinction between *yi* (righteousness) and *li* (profit). Every man should, without thought of personal advantage, unconditionally do what he ought to do, and be what he ought to be. In other words, he should "extend himself so as to include others," which, in essence, is the practice of *jen*. But though Confucius held these doctrines, he failed to explain *why* it is that a man should act in this way. Mencius, however, attempted to give an answer to this question, and in so doing developed the theory for which he is most famed: that of the original goodness of human nature.

Whether human nature is good or bad – that is, what, precisely, is the nature of human nature – has been one of the most controversial problems in Chinese philosophy. According to Mencius, there were, in his time, three other theories besides his own on this subject. The first was that human nature is neither good nor bad. The second was that human nature can be either good or bad (which seems to mean that in the nature of man there are both good and bad elements), and the third was that the nature of some men is good, and that of others is bad. (*Mencius*, VIa, 3–6).

Fung Yu-Lan (1948) *A Short History of Chinese Philosophy*, New York: Free Press, p. 69

See also CONFUCIANISM, ETHICS, EVIL

---

3 It is important, Mencius argues, for government to share the common human distaste for seeing the suffering of others:

Mencius said, "All men have the mind which cannot bear [to see the suffering of] others. The ancient kings had this mind and therefore they had a government that could not bear to see the suffering of the people. When a government that cannot bear to see the suffering of the people is conducted from a mind that cannot bear to see the suffering of others, the government of the empire will be as easy as making something go round in the palm."

Chan, Wing-tsit (1972) *A Source Book in Chinese Philosophy*, Princeton, Princeton University Press, p. 69

See also EVIL

---

4 An account of what is distinctive about Confucius' approach:

Confucius' contribution to the redefining of traditional virtue centered on the concept of humaneness (*jen*). He still talks about virtue as *te*, but humaneness as the perfection of virtue becomes the predominant theme of the *Analects*, in frequency-count outdoing all other concepts by a large margin. As a result, humaneness takes over as the operative personal virtue conjoined to rites and becomes the quality most definitive of Confucius' new understanding of the *chün-tzu* as noble man. One might plausibly interpret this change as taking place under the aegis of Heaven, the sacred canopy legitimating rational, moral rule on a more universal scale. But it also means, humanly speaking, that no government can succeed or be considered legitimate, if it does not rest on an adequate conception of what it means to be fully human; only such a regime can enlist voluntary cooperation and tap the energies of the people.

de Bary, W.T. (1991) *The Trouble with Confucianism*, Cambridge, Mass.: Harvard University Press, pp. 30–1

See also CONFUCIANISM, ETHICS

Although Confucius speaks a lot about pursuing humaneness, he does not 5 provide much detail about it. This is because he wants to remain open about what it means, and does not wish to restrict it in a parochial way:

The key to humaneness is, for Confucius, empathy or mutuality (*shu*). Though rarely mentioned in itself, Confucius speaks of it, along with "being true" (*chung*), as the "one thread that runs through" his teaching (*Analects* 4:15). This is because one comes to understand what it means to be truly human through a process of introspection and self-examination, along with observation and understanding of others. It calls for judging, not oneself as others might see us, but one's actions as others might be affected by them. "What you do not want done to you, do not do to others" (12:2, 15:24). The self-understanding at the heart of *jen*, which some have translated as "human-heartedness," also comes from observing others and learning from this what to emulate in them or avoid in oneself. "When walking in a party of three, I always have teachers. I can take the good qualities of one for imitation, and the bad qualities of the other for correction in myself" (7:21).

As the quintessence of virtue, humaneness is, strictly speaking, open-ended and indefinable; in the full magnitude of its empathetic feeling, *jen* reaches out to all men and even to Heaven itself. Hence Confucius is reluctant to pin it down, or to cite any paragon of such comprehensive virtue. Yet he knows exactly where the cultivation of humaneness begins, and from this standpoint there is nothing vague, elusive, or mysterious about it. It starts with the self in feeling contact with others, following a reliable method – likening oneself to others – that operates through all the virtues, inasmuch as these are bound up with human relations, and all such relations involve some element of reciprocal obligation. "The humane man, desiring to establish himself, seeks to establish others; desiring himself to succeed, he helps others to succeed. To judge others by what one knows of oneself is the method of achieving humanity" (6:28).

Ibid., pp. 32–3

See also CONFUCIANISM, HEAVEN

6   Humaneness (*ren*). This word is pronounced the same as and is closely related to *ren* meaning 'man'. It is the key virtue in the *Analects*. It has had a variety of translations, e.g. perfect virtue, kindness, goodness, human-heartedness, benevolence; but it seems to me to be necessary for the version used to render the connection with human beings. The graph consists of 'man' plus 'two' and the word summarizes how a human being should ideally behave towards other human beings, i.e. it embraces all the social virtues. Although it does refer to the individual's attainment of ideal human qualities, it is important not to think of it as merely indicating the psychology of the human being, such as a translation like 'magnanimity' or 'compassion' might suggest. It rather refers to the practical manifestations of being humane. Since it is a supreme and all-embracing virtue, it is not surprising that Master Kong is often depicted as reluctant either to define it or to agree that people have succeeded in achieving it. On the other hand, since the virtue does after all derive from a person's essential humanity, it is sometimes depicted as within easy reach if only one would make the effort to grasp it. Before Master Kong's time the word did not have ethical importance, and its centrality is one of the great innovations of the *Analects*.

Confucius, trans. R. Dawson (1993) *The Analects*, Oxford, Oxford University Press, p. xxi

See also CONFUCIANISM

The pursuit of humaneness is an essential task for human beings: 7

2. The Master said: 'It is impossible for those who are not humane to dwell for a long time in adversity, and it is also impossible for them to dwell for long in pleasurable circumstances. Those who are humane rest content with humaneness and those who are wise derive advantage from humaneness.'

3. The Master said: 'Only one who is humane is able to like other people and able to dislike other people.'

4. The Master said: 'If one sets one's heart on humaneness, one will be without evil.'

5. The Master said: 'Riches and honours, these are what men desire, but if this is not achieved in accordance with the appropriate principles, one does not cling to them. Poverty and obscurity – these are what men hate, but if this is not achieved in accordance with the appropriate principles, one does not avoid them. If a gentleman abandons humaneness, how does he make a reputation? The gentleman never shuns humaneness even for the time it takes to finish a meal. If his progress is hasty, it is bound to arise from this; and if his progress is unsteady, it is bound to arise from this.'

6. The Master said: 'I have never come across anyone who loved humaneness and hated inhumaneness. As far as anyone who loved humaneness is concerned, there would be no way of surpassing him. As far as anyone who hated inhumaneness is concerned, in his practice of humaneness he would not let the inhumane come near his person. Does there exist anyone who is capable of devoting his energies to humaneness for a single day? I have never come across anyone whose energies were inadequate. Surely such people exist, but I have never come across them.'

7. The Master said: 'People's mistakes all come in the same category in that, if one contemplates a mistake, then one gains an understanding of humaneness.'

Ibid., p. 13–14

See also CONFUCIANISM

Confucius links humaneness with ritual and modesty: 8

1. Yan Hui asked about humaneness. The Master said: 'To subdue oneself and return to ritual is to practise humaneness. If someone subdued himself and returned to ritual for a single day, then all under Heaven would ascribe humaneness to him. For the practice of humaneness does surely proceed from the man himself, or does it proceed from others?' Yan Hui said: 'I beg to ask for the details of this.' The Master said: 'Do not look at what is contrary to ritual, do not listen to what is contrary to ritual, do not speak what is contrary to ritual, and make no movement which is contrary to ritual.' Yan Hui said: 'Although I am not clever, I beg to put this advice into practice.'

2. Zhonggong asked about humaneness. The Master said: 'When you are away from home, behave as if receiving an important guest. Employ the people as if you were officiating at a great sacrifice. Do not impose on others what you would not like yourself. Then there will be no resentment against you, either in the state or in the family.' Zhonggong said: 'Although I am not clever, I beg to put this advice into practice.'

3. Sima Niu asked about humaneness. The Master said: 'The humane person is hesitant in his speech.' He said: 'Hesitant in his speech! Is that all that is meant by humaneness?' The Master said: 'To do it is difficult, so in speaking about it can one avoid being hesitant?'

Ibid., p. 44

See also CONFUCIANISM, GOLDEN MEAN

IMAGINATION

1 Buddhists criticize sense experience because of its strong links with imagination and the concepts this involves. If we import imaginative ideas into our
analysis of experience then we are acting inappropriately, and we end up
talking about all sorts of ideas and things for which we have no direct evidence:

There is a strong and widespread philosophic view (not often
stressed) that claims all seeing is seeing-as . . . The Buddhist in the
Dinnāga–Dharmakīrti school holds the counter-thesis: no seeing
is seeing-as . . . This implies that the cases of our seeing-as . . .
should not be properly called seeing, because what constitutes
seeing-truly should be free from conceptual or imaginative
construction (*kalpanā*), and our seeing-as . . . necessarily involves

the intervention of a construction. Dinnāga's definition of perception as what is free from construction may in this way be taken as almost a stipulative or prescriptive definition. The claim seems to be that the verbal report of proper perception would be strictly impossible. For in the verbal report of what we normally take to be perceptual experience we invariably construct or conceptualize, but such awareness is not, properly speaking, perceptual! . . .

First, if perception is a cognitive event arising from sense and object, then being a representation of that object, it is incapable of being joined with a verbal expression, or word. For notwithstanding what Bhartṛhari has said, what is seen does not carry a word or a name on its body as its label. Our sense faculty cannot grasp a concept, or a name, or a word. If I have never seen a camel, never heard about it, or seen its picture, then in my first encounter I do not certainly see IT *as a camel*, although I do see IT. For neither the concept camel nor the word 'camel' (and these are more or less two sides of the same coin, according to Bhartṛhari's notion of words and concepts) are attached to the animal I see. Since the word 'camel' and the corresponding concept are unattached to the object, neither can be part of the cognitive (perceptual) awareness – awareness that is derived from the object. In other words since awareness arises from the object, it will represent the object not the word/concept. If a sensory awareness arises from the colour (or the visual form), it will represent only that colour. It does not represent that colour accompanied by another object, say, a taste. When a particular blue is present in the visual field, I see blue, not blue plus bitter taste. Hence when I see the object *x*, I cannot say truly that I *see* a tomato without having recourse to *vikalpa* (concepts).

Matilal, B. (1986) *Perception: An Essay Classical Indian Theories of Knowledge*, Oxford: Clarendon Press, p. 316–17

See also INFERENCE, KNOWLEDGE

INFERENCE

Buddhist philosophy from India had a powerful impact on subsequent Tibetan philosophy, and in particular the problem of explaining how one can take sense experience as being evidence for the existence of something outside of that experience:

Dharmakīrti illustrates his point by a double example: the apprehension of the light of a lamp as being taken as a jewel and the apprehension of the light of a jewel as being taken as a jewel. The first example illustrates how a conception can be wrong: If we mistake the light of a lamp for an actual jewel, no useful result can be expected. Misled by a partial similarity, we project inappropriate concepts. Dharmakīrti says: "When [one sees] the glitter of a jewel, one rushes [impelled] by the belief that [this is] a jewel. Although both [cognitions] are equally wrong, there is a difference in [their ability] to perform a function." This unusual example has excited the imagination and exegetical skill of commentators. Let us examine Go-ram-ba's summary of the different positions in turn. He distinguishes three interpretations: one can take Dharmakīrti's example to be about (1) an inference, (2) a perception, or (3) a wrong cognition.

1. According to Go-ram-ba, Dharmakīrti's direct disciple Devendrabuddhi and his student Śākyabuddhi hold that Dharmakīrti's example as well as its meaning concerns the validity of inference. The example is an inference from effect to cause: We infer the presence of a jewel from the light of that jewel. The light is the evidence that indicates the presence of the cause, the jewel. This example illustrates, according to this interpretation, the more general point that inference is nondeceptive despite being mistaken (since it does not apprehend real individual objects but only unreal constructs).

2. According to Go-ram-ba, the later commentator Prajñākaragupta holds the example to be a perception of the light of a jewel as an actual jewel. The example illustrates the validity of inference by comparing inference to a perception that is partially mistaken, but practically nondeceptive. Kay-drup disagrees with this rendering of this second interpretation, for he thinks that it is unlikely that an accomplished thinker such as Prajñākaragupta would take as perception a mental episode apprehending a glitter as an actual jewel. According to Kay-drup, Prajñā-karagupta's position is that the example refers to the perception holding the glitter and inducing the inference of the presence of the jewel. Kay-drup holds that, in fact, Devendrabuddhi, Śākyabuddhi, and Prajñākaragupta explain Dharmakīrti's example in the same way.

3. According to Go-ram-ba, Dharmottara takes the example to involve a comparison between the pragmatic value of an erroneous cognition (*log shes*) and that of an inference. When we see the glowing light of a jewel, we think "this is a jewel." This is a mistake, however, for the light of a jewel is not a real jewel. Nevertheless, if we act on our mistake, we can obtain the real jewel. Similarly, inference is pragmatically valid. Although both inference and wrong conception are mistaken, since they apprehend constructed properties that are not part of the fabric of reality, they can be the support of successful practical actions.

Go-ram-ba criticizes (1) for not fitting the example closely enough. The inference of the light of a jewel does not match the example, which requires holding the glitter to be an actual jewel. An inference does not hold the glitter to be an actual jewel, for then it would be a false conception. Moreover, he says, the example of an inference does not answer the opponent's objections to which Dharmakīrti is responding in the text. The adversary is arguing that since all inferences are mistaken they cannot be valid. It would not be convincing to argue that inference in general is valid because some particular inferences are valid, for this is precisely what the adversary denies!

Against (2) Go-ram-ba argues that a perception also does not fit the example because a perception does not hold the glitter to be a jewel. The perception of a jewel's glitter is no more the perception of a jewel than the vision of a coiled rope is the perception of a snake. If the example is about the judgment induced by the perception, then it is not about a perception but about a wrong conception. This is indeed, according to Go-ram-ba, what the example is about.

Following Dharmottara, Go-ram-ba explains that if we were to see the glitter through the chink of a door, we might react in different ways. The careful person understands that this is not a real jewel but may indicate the presence of a jewel. Others might get excited and think that there really is a jewel. Such a conception can lead to successful action despite being erroneous. For Go-ram-ba, the apprehension of a jewel with respect to a jewel's glitter is no less erroneous than a similar apprehension with respect to a lamp's light. They are equally mistaken. They are also equally unable by themselves to cause us to obtain a real jewel. What then is the difference between valid and nonvalid conceptions? Go-ram-ba answers: "Although the inference realizing the impermanence of sound and the wrong apprehension of sound as permanent are equally mistaken, there is a difference in their being valid cognitions or not. For example, the mind that apprehends a jewel's glitter as a jewel and the mind that apprehends a lamp's light as a jewel are equally wrong cognitions. Nevertheless, there is a difference in their being [able] or not to support further valid cognitions [enabling one] to appropriate their objects of application. Such is the unequaled thought of [Dharmakīrti's] root text. Let the ones who rely on the meaning investigate." Despite the puzzling details of Dharmakīrti's example, the gist of his answer is clear: The only factor that differentiates the conceptions we hold to be factual from others is their practical success. This success consists of its capacity to bring forth a more valid mode of cognition; namely, perception. Valid conceptions, that is, inferences, allow us to gain experience of things as they are through perception.

We are now able to explain in relation to inference what Dharmakīrti means when he describes valid cognitions as being "nondeceptive with respect to the purpose [of the action] in the application [toward an object] after having determined it." Let us take the example of the inference of the presence fire from the presence of smoke. This determination is valid, not because it truly mirrors reality, but because it relates adequately to the perceptions of smoke and fire. It is caused by the perception of smoke and leads to the perception of fire. These relations to perception make the conceptual determination of an object adequate.

Dreyfus, G. (1997) *Recognizing Reality: Dharmakirti's Philosophy and its Tibetan Interpretations*, Albany: State University of New York Press, pp. 317–19

See also ANALYSIS, IMAGINATION, KNOWLEDGE

`IRFAN

1   In illuminationist (*ishraqi*) thought the notion of a direct access to the truth is crucial:

> . . . the experienced unitary consciousness of the mystic is creative enough to reconstruct, through illumination, all the beautiful

mystical stages that he has already witnessed in the vertical dimension of emanation during his self-realization. This reconstructive act of representation, which directly and introvertively overflows from the depth of the ineffable mystical knowledge by presence, is the introvertive knowledge by representation (knowledge by correspondence), referred to by the Sufi authorities as "`irfān`."

`Irfān` is thus a kind of knowledge by representation, illuminated and acquired from mystical knowledge by presence through the illuminative relationship. Since this introspective knowledge by representation (`irfān`) was set down for the first time in the history of the Sufi tradition by Muhyī al-Dīn ibn al-'Arabī (1164–1240) with such thoroughness and in such a systematic way, it quickly became popular and well known as the linguistic science of mysticism.

Obviously such a direct access to the truth of mysticism is not possible through a philosophical way of thinking concerned only with a logical, semantic, and epistemological justification of the truth and falsity of mystical statements and paradoxical assertions. All philosophy can do concerning mysticism is to take that language of the mystics – `irfān` – as the subject of its investigation.

Ha'iri Yazdi, M. (1992) *The Principles of Epistemology in Islamic Philosophy: Knowledge by presence*, Albany: State University of New York Press, pp. 162–3

See also KNOWLEDGE, SUFISM

JAINISM

Jain philosophy has a distinct approach to epistemology: 1

For the Jain, negation is an essential aspect of every real. Everything, on his view, is a unity in multiplicity; as a unity, it is different from everything else, while as a multiplicity, it resembles and is to that degree the same as everything else. Negation is merely the former aspect. It is not an independent entity as the Nyāya-Vaiśeṣika holds, nor is it an "unreal" mental construction as, for example, the Advaitin holds. It has as much reality as any aspect of things has. . . .

The topic of error was significant for Buddhists, Mīmāṃsakas, and Naiyāyikas because they all accepted the doctrine that ignorance is a necessary condition of bondage and its eradication the path to freedom. To show that ignorance is avoidable is, for them, to show that freedom is possible. But this criticism is not to the point, for the Jain accepts the same doctrine. He is not saying that knowledge is not relevant for the attainment of freedom – on the contrary, he thinks it essential. But he doesn't think that the kind of knowledge that is essential is the kind of knowledge that we seek in every-day situations. . . .

Jain philosophers tend to distinguish at least five "levels" of knowledge, of which only the first two are capable of literal linguistic expression in the form of judgments. Arranged in an ascending series, these five "levels" are (1) the level of sensory cognitions (*matijñāna*) ; (2) the level of revealed knowledge (*śrutajñāna*) ; (3) the level of knowledge of modes (*avadhijñāna*); (4) the level of knowledge of mental states (*manaḥparyāyajñāana*); and (5) omniscience (*kevalajñāna*). By (1), we are able to make judgments of sensory perception, more or less adequate as our sense-organs are more or less well-trained. By (2), we become able to make general judgments about the nature of the things known by (1), the difference being that (2) allows us to make universal judgments whereas (1) properly speaking is limited to specific reports of presented sensory contents. When we get to (3), however, there is no appropriate verbal means of expression. Through (3) we know the shapes of things not given to us through the senses. Through (4) we come to know the essential nature and interrelationships of such subtle items as minds, light, speech (conceived as neither auditory nor visual but as that which lies behind speech-sounds and written words), and *karma*, that subtle stuff of infinite variety which constitutes the material of bondage. Finally, in (5) we come to know the exhaustive interrelationships of all the contents entertained in the previous four levels. These five kinds of knowledge are not levels in the sense that one graduates from one to the next; each one is capable of greater or less adequacy in a given individual.

Besides these five varieties of knowledge (*jñāna*) there are several varieties of intuition (*darśana*). The difference between knowledge and intuition seems to be that knowledge is outer-directed while intuition is inner-directed. Most Jain writers seem to agree that in the fifth stage knowledge and intuition coincide, but that they are distinct outside of that stage. . . .

At any level of knowledge or intuition, the model is not that common "scientific" knowing. As far as we know the *verification* of a knowledge on the first level has nothing to do with its *adequacy* metaphysically, i.e., in terms of self-realization. We are reminded of Dharmakīrti's introduction of yogic perception and his consequent inability to provide a criterion for distinguishing valid yogic knowledge from invalid empirical knowledge. The path to a more adequate knowledge is for Jainism primarily *moral* and not intellectual at all. One prepares himself for freedom by practising such all-important virtues as *ahiṃsā* (non-violence), celibacy, and the like, but in Jainism there is no suggestion that one can see how well one is succeeding by testing his judgments by experimental means. For all we can see, a scientifically *false* theory may well be the theory the holding of which leads to metaphysical *truth*.

Potter, K. (1972) *Presuppositions of India's Philosophies*, Westport, Conn.: Greenwood Press, pp. 212–14

See also *AHIMSA*, KNOWLEDGE, MIMAMSA, NYAYA-VAISHESHIKA, *PRAJNA*

JIVA/JIVANMUKTA

Jiva is often referred to as the soul when it is still within the confines of samsara, the world of corruption and generation:

1

The Atman never comes nor goes, is never born nor dies. It is nature moving before the Atman, and the reflection of this motion is on the Atman; and the Atman ignorantly thinks it is moving, and not nature. When the Atman thinks that, it is in bondage; but when it comes to find it never moves, that it is omnipresent, then freedom comes. The Atman in bondage is called Jiva. Thus you see that when it is said that the Atman comes and goes, it is said only for facility of understanding, just as for convenience in studying astronomy you are asked to suppose that the sun moves round the earth, though such is not the case. So the Jiva, the soul, comes to higher or lower states. This is the well-known law of reincarnation; and this law binds all creation.

Vivekananda, S. (1961) *Jnana-Yoga*, Calcutta: Advaita Ashrama, p. 823

See also AFTERLIFE, *ATMAN*, *SAMSARA*

2   Can the individual, the *jiva*, reach the state of liberation while still alive, i.e. achieve the status of *jivanmukta*? Not according to the Nyaya, for whom the body must be entirely separated from the soul for liberation to be feasible:

> The different Indian systems are not all agreed regarding the possibility of the *jīvan-mukta* state. Thus, according to the Nyāya, *apavarga*, or emancipation, occurs only when the soul is absolutely dissociated from all the nine kinds of qualities (will, antipathy, pleasure, pain, knowledge, effort, virtue, vice and rooted instincts). Unless such a dissociation actually occurs, there cannot be emancipation; and it is easy to see that this cannot happen except after death, and so emancipation during the period while the body remains is not possible. The point is noticed by Vātsyāyana in a discussion on *Nyāya-sūtra*, IV. 2. 42–45, where he raises the question of the possibility of knowledge of external objects through the senses and denies it by declaring that in emancipation (*apavarga*) the soul is dissociated from the body and all the senses, and hence there is no possibility of knowledge; and that with the extinction of all knowledge there is also ultimate and absolute destruction of pain. The Vaiśeṣika holds the same view on the subject. Thus Śrīharṣa says that, when through right knowledge (*paramārtha-darśana*) all merit ceases, then the soul, being devoid of the seeds of merit and demerit, which produce the body and the senses, etc., and the present body having been destroyed by the exhaustive enjoyment of the fruits of merit and demerit, and there being no further production of any new body by reason of the destruction of all the seeds of *karma*, there is absolute cessation of the production of body, like the extinction of fire by the burning up of all the fuel; and such an eternal non-production of body is called *mokṣa* (emancipation).

Dasgupta, S. (1932) *A History of Indian Philosophy*, II, Cambridge: Cambridge University Press, pp. 248–9

See also AFTERLIFE, *KARMA*, *MOKSHA*, NYAYA, *SAMSARA*

KARMA

1   *Karma yoga* is the attempt to work and yet at the same time not work out of selfish motives which result in distancing ourselves from liberation. The

point is to seek to achieve a result out of impersonal intentions, and then the activity will be pure:

> To find the way out of the bondages of the world we have to go through it slowly and surely. There may be those exceptional persons about whom I just spoke, those who can stand aside and give up the world as a snake casts off its skin and stands aside and looks at it. There are no doubt these exceptional beings; but the rest of mankind have to go slowly through the world of work. Karma-Yoga shows the process, the secret, and the method of doing it to the best advantage.
>
> What does it say? "Work incessantly, but give up all attachment to work." Do not identify yourself with anything. Hold your mind free. All this that you see, the pains and the miseries, are but the necessary conditions of this world; poverty and wealth and happiness are but momentary; they do not belong to our real nature at all. Our nature is far beyond misery and happiness, beyond every object of the senses, beyond the imagination; and yet we must go on working all the time. "Misery comes through attachment, not through work." As soon as we identify ourselves with the work we do, we feel miserable; but if we do not identify ourselves with it, we do not feel that misery. If a beautiful picture belonging to another is burnt, a man does not generally become miserable; but when his own picture is burnt, how miserable he feels! Why? Both were beautiful pictures, perhaps copies of the same original; but in one case very much more misery is felt than in the other. It is because in one case he identifies himself with the picture, and not in the other. This "I and mine" causes the whole misery. With the sense of possession comes selfishness, and selfishness brings on misery. Every act of selfishness or thought of selfishness makes us attached to something, and immediately we are made slaves. Each wave in the Chitta that says "I and mine" immediately puts a chain round us and makes us slaves; and the more we say "I and mine", the more slavery grows, the more misery increases. Therefore Karma-Yoga tells us to enjoy the beauty of all the pictures in the world, but not to identify ourselves with any of them. Never say "mine". Whenever we say a thing is mine, misery will immediately come. Do not even say "my child" in your mind. Possess the child, but do not say "mine". If you do, then will come the misery.

Vivekananda, S. (1960) *Karma-Yoga*, Calcutta: Advaita Ashrama, pp. 114–15

See also ACTION, *BHAGAVAD GITA, MOKSHA*

2   This story represents one account of how Tibetan Buddhism saw scope for working within the framework of *karma* to overcome the forces of evil, Mara:

> When the young prince-turned-mendicant, Siddhartha, sat down on a seat of soft grass on the east side of a pipal tree, he vowed not to arise until he had attained full awakening. Because of his meditative experience, he knew what lay before him. He knew that in a certain way, awakening was direct and simple, a spontaneous experience of clarity and radiance, born of lifetimes of a settled discipline of mind. But he also knew that he must be strong and resolute for he would be attacked by Mara, the demon lord of death and destruction, and his awakening depended upon maintaining an open but unyielding attitude toward these attacks. Mara represented the unacknowledged or unfinished karmic tendencies, emotionality, and conceptuality inherent in Siddhartha himself and in all human experience. . . .
>
> Having proclaimed the fearlessness which he had discovered in his practice, Milarepa followed the training given him by his guru. He invited the demons to stay with him and to receive his hospitality. He also challenged them to a friendly contest of teachings.

> Ye ghosts and demons, enemies of the
> Dharma, I welcome you today!
> It is my pleasure to receive you!
> I pray you, stay; do not hasten to leave;
> We will discourse and play together.
> Although you would be gone, stay the night;
> We will pit the Black against the White
> Dharma,
> And see who plays the best.
> Before you came, you vowed to afflict me.
> Shame and disgrace would follow
> If you returned with this vow unfulfilled.

> We may notice that when Milarepa invited the demons, he displayed several moods successively. This can be understood in terms of the Tibetan tantric expression of four enlightened stages of skillful, appropriate action, called the four *karmas*. These

karmas are the strategies employed by the realized yogin when working with intractable situations, whether they be in practice or in daily life. These methods are based on "not accepting, not rejecting" in the sense that the most threatening situations are excellent opportunities for practice.

The first karma is "pacifying," in which one opens fully to negativity, with the line "I welcome you today!" When we open to the shadow in this way, we reverse the habitual tendency to ignore or hide it. Next, the yogin inspires the unacknowledged aspects with confidence by creating an atmosphere of celebration, free from aggression, in an action called "enriching" ("It is my pleasure to receive you!"). Taking the attitude of enriching, we affirm the power of the shadow rather than discounting it as we usually do. Then, with the third karma of "magnetizing," the yogin draws the negativity toward him or her with an actual invitation: "Do not hasten to leave; we will discourse and play together . . . stay the night." In this way, the shadow is charmed into relationship and its power is harnessed.

The last karma, "destroying," is the final resort for an accomplished yogin like Milarepa. Often the shadow material does not require this final step, for its ferocity has rested primarily on our denial of it, and the inviting nature of the first three karmas removes its threatening qualities. However, when negativities are entrenched in conceptual justifications and defenses, we must employ "destroying," in which we challenge and threaten the crystallized, residual negativity with extinction. Milarepa did this with the challenge, "we will pit the Black against the White Dharma, and see who plays the best." Here he was referring to the black magic and sorcery of his past training, his central shadow, directly confronted by the white magic of Buddhism, which can accommodate and purify the black. Having challenged the demons, Milarepa arose and rushed with great confidence directly at them. They shrank in terror, rolling their eyes and trembling violently, and then swirled together into a single vision and dissolved. With this, the destroying was completed, and Milarepa the black sorcerer was reclaimed by Milarepa the white sorcerer.

Simmer-Brown, J. (1997) "Inviting the Demon" *Parabola, The Magazine of Myth and Tradition*, XXII, No. 2 Summer, pp. 12, 16–17

See also DHARMA, GURU

3 Karma plays a central role in both Buddhism and philosophies linked to Hinduism:

> The recognition that "cause" is "empty" has implications for the doctrine of *karma*. The significance of *karma* as a soteriological term in Indian thought seems originally to have been related to the efficacy in magic, or to ritual origination of reality, and in purification through repetition of formulas. *Karma* (action) is the fabrication of reality which has the efficacy for both good and bad existence. In early Buddhism final release (*nirvāṇa*) was conceived as the exhaustion of *karma*, for the turmoil (*duḥkha*) of existence was the result of *karma*.
>
> In the centuries preceding Nāgārjuna, the term *karma* had been used to designate the potential for future existence as well as the result of past actions.

Streng, F. (1967) *Emptiness: A Study in Religious Meaning*, Nashville: Abingdon Press, p. 66

See also CAUSATION, *DUHKHA*, EMPTINESS, EXISTENCE, MADHYAMAKA

4 Karma can be seen as the source of evil, or just as an aspect of actions. According to the *Gita*, what is important is how we act within the context of karma, in the sense of the motives which move us, as compared with what karma actually results in happening:

> There are two contradictory views of *karma*: one view in which *karma* is regarded as the cause which brings about all inequalities in life, and another view which does not attribute any value to good or bad actions. The only way in which the two views can be reconciled in accordance with the spirit of the *Gītā* is by holding that the *Gītā* does not believe in the objective truth of virtue or vice (*puṇya* or *pāpa*). There is nothing good or bad in the actions themselves. It is only ignorance and foolishness that regards them as good or bad; it is only our desires and attachments which make the actions produce their bad effects with reference to us, and which render them sinful for us. Since the actions themselves are neither good nor bad, the performance of

even apparently sinful actions, such as the killing of one's kinsmen on the battle-field, cannot be regarded as sinful, if they are done from a sense of duty; but the same actions would be regarded as sinful, if they were performed through attachments or desires.

Dasgupta, S. (1932) *A History of Indian Philosophy*, II, Cambridge: Cambridge University Press, p. 522

See also BHAGAVAD GITA, ETHICS, EVIL

KNOWLEDGE

The Yogachara thinker emphasizes the significance of sense experience at the expense of where that experience may be held to originate. Thus Vasubandhu has difficulties in accounting for any real distinction between experiences of reality and experiences which are only imaginary:

> The subjective idealist has strong arguments on its side. His position is familiar to all who have survived a standard introduction to philosophy: there is no "external" reality which operates as a causal factor in determining our cognitions, even the purest ones; the causal factors of sensation as well as cognition are exhausted by items within the knower. Knowing is a relation between the knower and himself. If it be objected that knowledge is never known to know itself, since it is always knowledge *of* something, the idealist has the handy example of dreams in his favor. When we dream we apprehend contents whose cause is not elsewhere than in the mind of the knower himself. Does this then mean that there is no difference between imagined and "real" experiences? No, replies Vasubandhu; although all experiences are our creations, some of them are not *present* creations, but rather stem from past traces (*vāsanās*) stored up in the unconscious or subconscious (*ālayavijñāna*). As Dharmakīrti rightly holds, error in knowing consists in attributing externality to the causes of our consciousness; where Dharmakīrti makes his mistake is in supposing there are exceptions to this. In truth, *all* the causes of our consciousness are ours, and although not all of them are under our direct control, they are all indirectly under our control since all experiences are the result of previous *karma* which laid down the traces. Therefore we don't need

Dharmakīrti's yogic knowledge; to destroy ignorance one needs only realize the nonexternality of the causes of knowledge and he will consequently realize his own complete freedom. All *judgments* are indeed false, because a judgment is something which contains an element of prediction or implication concerning something assumed to be out of control in an "external" world.

Potter, K. (1972) *Presuppositions of India's Philosophies*, Westport, Conn., Greenwood Press, pp. 195–6

See also KARMA

---

2   Buddhist theorists of knowledge are frequently critical of the confusion between what we perceive and the constructions we make out of our ideas which we then assume to be real:

According to the Buddhist, the Nyāya claim that we grasp the same object through sight and touch is based upon a confusion. It confuses what is immediately perceived through the senses with what is indirectly, i.e. *mentally*, grasped (cf. *manobuddhih smṛtyupasthāpitatvāt*, Diṅnāga). For instance, as Diṅnāga has argued, the sense of sight grasps the colour white, not what is white. The adjectival use of 'white' (*śveta*) to designate the thing perceived is either a metaphorical extension or is due to a grammatical peculiarity, viz. elision of a possessive suffix (*matuv-lopa*, as permitted by Pāṇini). In other words, when I use 'white' to designate the thing-substance *constructed* in my perception, I use it either metaphorically to designate not the colour white directly, but the physical location where the colour white is supposedly present (the non-metaphorical meaning of 'white' being only the colour white; or this particular use of 'white' is in fact a contracted form from the expression 'white-possessing' (*śveta + matup*, followed by elision etc.). In this way, 'I see white' would unpack, according to Diṅnāga, as 'I see something possessing the colour white', and therefore *seeing* here is no longer a sensory awareness but a mental (constructive) awareness aided by memory (*manobuddhi* etc.). Otherwise, Diṅnāga argues, looking at a flower we may have an awareness of fragrance, seeing honey we may have an awareness of sweetness, but in neither case can we say that we *see* that it is fragrant or that it is sweet. Both cases are constructions of the form '*x* is fragrance-possessing' or '*x* is sweetness-possessing'. The qualifiers, fragrance and sweetness, are not percepts in the given case, they are only remembered properties. Therefore these are cases of mental awareness, mistakenly confused as sensory awareness. The case of *seeing* a white thing is similar.

Matilal, B. (1986) *Perception: An Essay on Classical Indian Theories of Knowledge*, Oxford: Clarendon Press, pp. 373–4

See also IMAGINATION, NYAYA

An expression of Daoist suspicion of the great status given to knowledge: **3**

No need to leave your door to know the whole world;
No need to peer through your windows to know the Way of
  Heaven.
The farther you go, the less you know.

Therefore the Sage knows without going,
Names without seeing,
And completes without doing a thing.

Laozi, trans. R. Henricks (1989) *Lao-Tzu: Te Tao Ching*, New York: Ballantine, ch. 47, p. 16

See also ACTION, DAOISM

Perfection is knowing that one is not perfect, according to Daoism. **4**
Similarly, knowing that one does not know is the finest kind of knowledge:

To know you don't know is best.
Not to know you don't know is a flaw.
Therefore, the Sage's not being flawed
Stems from his recognizing a flaw as a flaw.
Therefore, he is flawless.

Ibid., ch. 71, p. 42

See also DAOISM

5   Han Fei is presenting here the popular Chinese slogan that action is much harder than knowledge. It is one thing to formulate abstract ideas, and quite another to do anything useful with them:

> Once there was a rich man of Sung. When the dirt wall around his house collapsed in a heavy rain, his son said, "If you don't rebuild it, thieves will surely break in," and the old man who lived next door told him the same thing. When night fell, thieves actually broke in and made off with a large share of the rich man's wealth. The rich man's family praised the son for his wisdom, but eyed the old man next door with suspicion.
>
> Both these men – the high official Kuan Ch'i-ssu and the old man next door – spoke the truth, and yet one was actually executed for his words, while the other cast suspicion on himself. It is not difficult to know a thing; what is difficult is to know how to use what you know.

Han Fei Tzu (1964) *Han Fei Tzu: Basic Writings*, trans. B. Watson, New York: Columbia University Press, pp. 77–8

See also ACTION

---

6   Although knowledge is important and useful, it can also stand in the way of what we naturally can do. Daoism criticizes the ways in which we use knowledge to try to do things which are too complicated for our needs and actually get in the way of what we could do anyway:

> As long as men in high places covet knowledge and are without the Way, the world will be in great confusion. How do I know this is so? Knowledge enables men to fashion bows, crossbows, nets, stringed arrows, and like contraptions, but when this happens the birds flee in confusion to the sky. Knowledge enables men to fashion fishhooks, lures, seines, dragnets, trawls, and weirs, but when this happens the fish flee in confusion to the depths of the water. Knowledge enables men to fashion pitfalls, snares, cages, traps, and gins, but when this happens the beasts flee in confusion to the swamps. And the flood of rhetoric that enables men to invent wily schemes and poisonous slanders, the glib gabble of "hard" and "white," the foul fustian of "same" and "different" bewilder the understanding of common men. So the world is dulled and darkened by great confusion. The blame lies in this coveting of knowledge.

In the world everyone knows enough to pursue what he does not know, but no one knows enough to pursue what he already knows. Everyone knows enough to condemn what he takes to be no good, but no one knows enough to condemn what he has already taken to be good. This is how the great confusion comes about, blotting out the brightness of sun and moon above, searing the vigor of hills and streams below, overturning the round of the four seasons in between. There is no insect that creeps and crawls, no creature that flutters and flies that has not lost its inborn nature. So great is the confusion of the world that comes from coveting knowledge!

Zhuangzi (1968) *The Complete Works of Chuang Tzu*, trans. B. Watson, New York: Columbia University Press, pp. 112–13

See also DAOISM

Increasing knowledge leads to increasing dissatisfaction, according to Laozi.   7
Instead of helping us gain our ends, it increases our ambitions and comes to control us:

Likewise Lao Tzu emphasizes that people should have little knowledge. Knowledge is itself an object of desire. It also enables people to know more about the objects of desire and serves as a means to gain these objects. It is both the master and servant of desire. With increasing knowledge people are no longer in a position to know how to be content and where to stop. Therefore, it is said in the *Lao-Tzu*: "When knowledge and intelligence appeared, Gross Artifice began." (Ch. 18.)

Fung Yu-Lan (1948) *A Short History of Chinese Philosophy*, New York: Free Press, pp. 101–2

See also DAOISM

A modern account of the links between action and practice in Chinese   8
philosophy which follows closely the classical formulation of the issue:

Discover the truth through practice, and again through practice verify and develop the truth. Start from perceptual knowledge and actively develop it into rational knowledge; then start from rational knowledge and actively guide revolutionary practice to change both the subjective and the objective world. Practice, knowledge, again practice, and again knowledge. This form repeats itself in endless cycles, and with each cycle the content of practice and knowledge rises to a higher level. Such is the whole of the dialectical-materialist theory of knowledge.

Mao (1967) *Selected works of Mao Tse-Tung*, Beijing: Foreign Languages Press, I, 308

See also ACTION

9　Averroes (ibn Rushd) replies to the charge from Abu Hamid al-Ghazali that the philosophers believe that God cannot know anything about particular things. The reply takes the form of arguing that God can know particulars, but in a unique sort of way:

In addition to all this we hold that Abū Ḥāmid was mistaken about the Peripatetic philosophers, in ascribing to them the assertion that God, Holy and Exalted, does not know particulars at all. In reality they hold that God the Exalted knows them in a way which is not of the same kind as our way of knowing them. For our knowledge of them is an effect of the object known, originated when it comes into existence and changing when it changes; whereas Glorious God's Knowledge of existence is the opposite of this: it is the cause of the object known, which is existent being. Thus to suppose the two kinds of knowledge similar to each other is to identify the essences and properties of opposite things, and that is the extreme of ignorance. And if the name of 'knowledge' is predicated of both originated and eternal knowledge, it is predicated by sheer homonymy, as many names are predicated of opposite things: e.g. *jalal* of great and small, *ṣarīm* of light and darkness. Thus there exists no definition embracing both kinds of knowledge at once, as the theologians of our time imagine. We have devoted a separate essay to this question, impelled by one of our friends.

But how can anyone imagine that the Peripatetics say that God the Glorious does not know particulars with His eternal Knowledge, when they hold that true visions include premonitions of particular events due to occur in future time, and that this warning fore-knowledge comes to people in their sleep from the eternal Knowledge which orders and rules the universe? Moreover, it is not only particulars which they say God does not know in the manner in which we know them, but universals as well; for the universals known to us are also effects of the nature of existent being, while with His Knowledge the reverse is true. Thus the conclusion to which demonstration leads is that His Knowledge transcends qualification as 'universal' or 'particular'. Consequently there is no point in disputing about this question, i.e. whether to call them unbelievers or not.

Averroes (1976) *On the Harmony of Religion and Philosophy*, trans. G. Hourani, London: Luzac, pp. 54–5

See also GOD, LANGUAGE

KOAN

The paradox points in the direction of expressing the inexpressible, and **1** hence is often illogical or absurd. It is designed to shock the individual into acknowledging the nature of reality:

> Technically speaking, the *kōan* given to the uninitiated is intended to "destroy the root of life," "to make the calculating mind die," "to root out the entire mind that has been at work since eternity," etc. This may sound murderous, but the ultimate intent is to go beyond the limits of intellection, and these limits can be crossed over only by exhausting oneself once for all, by using up all the psychic powers at one's command. Logic then turns into psychology, intellection into conation and intuition. What could not be solved on the plane of empirical consciousness is now transferred to the deeper recesses of the mind.

Suzuki, D. T. (1956) *Zen Buddhism*, ed. W. Barrett, New York: Doubleday, p. 138

See also ENLIGHTENMENT, MEDITATION, ZEN

LANGUAGE

1 The nature of language was a constant point of controversy in Islamic philosophy and had significant theological consequences. Averroes argued that language is flexible and so there are many routes to the same truth, but al-Ghazali worked from the principle that meaning is simple and so only one route to the truth is feasible:

> Ghazali condemns the suggestion that equivocation is a feature of the relationship between our language describing God and our language describing the ordinary world. He sees this as an attack upon the notion of God as a powerful and all-encompassing individual. In his reply to Ghazali, Averroes argues that equivocation is an inevitable aspect of our language, since that language has to describe a wide gamut of views using the same name. We must respect the different uses of the same word because they represent different points of view, different points of view of the same thing. It is an error to represent some uses as essentially more accurate than others. At one time it was popular for philosophers to argue that, when a physicist and an ordinary person talk about a table, they have in mind different objects. The physicist knows that a table is 'really' a collection of immaterial atoms, while ordinary people think of it as something solid and stable. Averroes would argue that, when we talk about and observe a table, we are looking at one thing from a variety of points of view which are equally valid. The physicist is right because the table does have an atomic structure, and the ordinary person is right because he can eat his dinner on it. Our language is flexible enough to capture this diversity of view. In his philosophical methodology Averroes tries to show how it is possible for one thing to be described in a variety of ways. The arguments which have subsequently arisen concerning his 'real' views fail to grasp the philosophical approach he has constructed. When he tries to reconcile apparently contradictory views his strategy is to argue that all these views are acceptable as different aspects of one thing. The Averroist movement provides a useful focus for this idea, the precise nature of the apparent conflict between reason and religion. In his tentative remarks on language Averroes suggests that this conflict comes down to a stress upon different aspects of one thing, namely, the way the world really is. This is an intriguing interpretation of a longstanding philosophical dilemma, and may well be Averroes' most important contribution to philosophy itself.

Leaman, O. (1997) *Averroes and his Philosophy*, Richmond, Surrey: Curzon, pp. 195–6

See also GOD

According to Confucius, it is vital to use the right language in describing the   **2**
world. This led to a long tradition of analyzing the links between names and
reality, as with Hsun Tzu (Zunzi) here:

> Names have no correctness of their own. The correctness is
> given by convention. When the convention is established and
> the custom is formed, they are called correct names. If they are
> contrary to convention, they are called incorrect names. Names
> have no corresponding actualities by themselves. The actualities
> ascribed to them are given by convention. When the convention
> is established and the custom is formed, they are called names of
> such-and-such actualities. But some names are felicitous in
> themselves. When a name is direct, easy to understand, and self-
> consistent, it is called a felicitous name.

Chan, Wing-tsit (1972) *A Source Book in Chinese Philosophy*, Princeton, Princeton University Press, p. 126

See also CONFUCIANISM, HARMONY

Zunzi presents the Confucian Rectification of Names doctrine: **3**

> When sage-kings instituted names, the names were fixed and
> actualities distinguished. The sage-kings' principles were carried
> out and their wills understood. Then the people were carefully
> led and unified. Therefore, the practice of splitting terms and
> arbitrarily creating names to confuse correct names, thus causing
> much doubt in people's minds and bringing about much
> litigation, was called great wickedness. It was a crime, like private
> manufacturing of credentials and measurements and therefore
> the people dared not rely on strange terms created to confuse
> correct names. Hence the people were honest. Being honest,
> they were easily employed. Being easily employed, they achieved
> results. Since the people dared not rely on strange terms created
> to confuse correct names, they single-mindedly followed the
> law and carefully obeyed orders. In this way, the traces of

their accomplishments spread. The spreading of traces and the achievement of results are the highest point of good government. This is the result of careful abiding by the conventional meaning of names.

Ibid., p. 124

See also POLITICS AND POWER

4 Zhuangzi is critical of the Confucian notion of language, as are the Daoists generally:

Words exist to explicate forms. When one understands the forms, the words can be forgotten. Forms exist to embody the meaning. When one has the meaning, the forms can be forgotten. This is comparable to the snare existing for the sake of catching the rabbit. Having caught the rabbit, one can forget the snare. The trap is there to catch fish. Having caught the fish, one can forget the trap. . . . Therefore the one who can forget the words is the one who has understood the forms, and the one who can forget the forms is the one who has attained the meaning. Attaining the meaning lies in forgetting the form. Gaining the form lies in forgetting the words.

Fung Yu-Lan (1983) *A History of Chinese Philosophy*, trans. D. Bodde, Princeton: Princeton University Press, p. 184

See also DAOISM

5 Buddhism is suspicious of the idea that words stand for things which really exist:

The parable of the magician and the tiger's bone has been used in the Buddhist canons to show how proliferations of conceptual and linguistic snares capture man, who in fact is himself the creator of this labyrinth of concepts in the first place. Man objectifies the concepts only to be entangled by them. The story runs as follows: A magician found a bone, and claimed that he had some occult power which would enable him to collect all the other bones that went with that particular one, and form the complete skeleton of a dead animal. When this was done, it was found to be the skeleton of a huge creature. Blinded by success, the magician said he could even restore flesh, veins, etc. to that skeleton. When this was accomplished, to the utter astonishment of the spectators, it was found to be the dead body of a ferocious tiger. Then the magician said that he could even bring the carcass back to life. In spite of grave warnings from the spectators, the proud magician exercised his final occult power and so the tiger was brought back to life. The resurrected tiger instantly devoured up the magician.

The story undoubtedly has some soteriological significance, but that is not my concern here. The philosophical point of the story strikes a familiar note that seems closer to modern philosophic discussion. Language distorts reality by proliferating false concepts and images.

Matilal, B. (1986) *Perception: An Essay on Classical Indian Theories of Knowledge*, Oxford: Clarendon Press, p. 309

See also IMAGINATION

LEGALISM

An interesting link between Daoism and Legalism on the nature of action: **1**

"Doing nothing, yet there is nothing that is not done." This is the Taoist idea of *wu wei*, having-no-activity or non-action, but it is also a Legalist idea. According to Han Fei Tzu and the Legalists, the one great virtue required of a ruler is that he follow the course of non-action. He should do nothing himself but should merely let others do everything for him. Han Fei Tzu says: "Just as the sun and moon shine forth, the four seasons progress, the clouds spread, and the wind blows, so does the ruler not encumber his mind with knowledge, or himself with selfishness. He relies for good government or disorder upon laws and methods [*shu*]; leaves right and wrong to be dealt with through rewards and punishments; and refers lightness and heaviness to the balance of the scale." (*Hanfeizi* Ch. 29.) In other words, the ruler possesses the implements and mechanism through which government is conducted, and having these, does nothing, yet there is nothing that is not done.

Taoism and Legalism represent the two extremes of Chinese thought. The Taoists maintained that man originally is completely innocent; the Legalists, on the other hand, that he is completely evil. The Taoists stood for absolute individual freedom; the Legalists for absolute social control. Yet in the idea of non-action, the two extremes meet. That is to say, they had here some common ground.

Fung Yu-Lan (1948) *A Short History of Chinese Philosophy*, New York: Free Press, pp. 162–3

See also ACTION, DAOISM, EVIL, *FA*

LILA

1 Although the world may have been created through play or *lila*, this does not mean that it was created haphazardly or at random:

> The *līlā* theory of creation goes further than just regarding the world as 'given'. Not only does it regard the action by which God created the universe as bound by constitutive rule – it also regards the creator-God himself as so bound. This latter position is a bold one, certainly from the point of view of Western theologies, but it is not completely foreign to the world of Indian theology. (Intimations of it can be found, for example, in the polytheistic conception of the Vedas.) The relation between God and the world he created in accordance with a system of rules is not akin to the relation between a board-game and its inventor, but more like the relation between the board-game and one who is formally a player in it – a status the player holds by virtue of the rules of the game themselves. In other words, the Śaṅkaran God is totally bound by the constitutive rules of creation.

Biderman, S. (1982) 'A "constitutive" God – An Indian Suggestion', *Philosophy East and West*, 32, 425–37, pp. 431–2

See also CREATION, EMPTINESS

LOGIC

1 In Indian philosophy logic has far more than a technical role. It has an important part to play in the route to salvation:

Dignāga and Dharmakīrti are often presented as Buddhist logicians. This is not false, but it is bound to be misleading without some explanation. It wrongly suggests that these authors were interested primarily in the formal properties of reasoning. There is no denying that there is an important logical side to their works, but it must be understood that this logical side is always subordinate to pragmatic concerns. The primacy of the practical in the classical Indian study of reasoning is apparent in the origins of logic in India. These had to do with the validation of sacred texts. This emphasis on the practical is visible in the Nyāya school as well, where correct arguments, in conformity with the norms, free the soul.

Dreyfus, G. (1997) *Recognizing Reality: Dharmakirti's philosophy and its Tibetan Interpretations*, Albany: State University of New York Press, p. 16

See also ACTION, NYAYA

Gongsun Long produced this popular paradox in Chinese logic: 2

A. "Is it correct to say that a white horse is not a horse?"
B. "It is."
A. "Why?"
B. "Because 'horse' denotes the form and 'white' denotes the color. What denotes the color does not denote the form. Therefore we say that a white horse is not a horse."
A. "There being a horse, one cannot say that there is no horse. If one cannot say that there is no horse, then isn't [it] a horse? Since there being a white horse means that there is a horse, why does being white make it not a horse?"
B. "Ask for a horse, and either a yellow or a black one may answer. Ask for a white horse, and neither the yellow horse nor the black one may answer. If a white horse were a horse, then what is asked in both cases would be the same. If what is asked is the same, then a white horse would be no different from a horse. If what is asked is no different, then why is it that yellow and black horses may yet answer in the one case but not in the other? Clearly the two cases are incompatible. Now the yellow horse and the black horse remain the same. And yet they answer to a horse but not to a white horse. Obviously a white horse is not a horse."

A. "You consider a horse with color as not a horse. Since there is no horse in the world without color, is it all right [to say] that there is no horse in the world?"

B. "Horses of course have color. Therefore there are white horses. If horses had no color, there would be simply horses. Where do white horses come in? Therefore whiteness is different from horse. A white horse means a horse combined with whiteness. [Thus in one case it is] horse and [in the other it is] a white horse. Therefore we say that a white horse is not a horse."

A. [Since you say that] before the horse is combined with whiteness, it is simply a horse, before whiteness is combined with a horse it is simply whiteness, and when the horse and whiteness are combined they are collectively called a white horse, you are calling a combination by what is not a combination. This is incorrect. Therefore it is incorrect to say that a white horse is not a horse."

B. "If you regard a white horse as a horse, is it correct to say that a white horse is a yellow horse?"

A. "No."

B. "If you regard a white horse as different from a yellow horse, you are differentiating a yellow horse from a horse. To differentiate a yellow horse from a horse is to regard the yellow horse as not a horse. Now to regard a yellow horse as not a horse and yet to regard a white horse as a horse is like a bird flying into a pool or like the inner and outer coffins being in different places. This would be the most contradictory argument and the wildest talk."

A. "[When we say that] a white horse cannot be said to be not a horse, we are separating the whiteness from the horse. If [the whiteness] is not separated from [the horse], then there would be a white horse and we should not say that there is [just] a horse. Therefore when we say that there is a horse, we do so simply because it is a horse and not because it is a white horse. When we say that there is a horse, we do not mean that there are a horse [as such] and another horse [as the white horse]."

B. "It is all right to ignore the whiteness that is not fixed on any object. But in speaking of the white horse, we are talking about the whiteness that is fixed on the object. The object on which whiteness is fixed is not whiteness [itself]. The term 'horse' does not involve any choice of color and therefore either a yellow horse or a black one may answer. But the term 'white horse' does involve a choice of color. Both the yellow horse and the black one are excluded because of their color. Only a white horse may answer. What does not exclude [color] is not the same as what excludes [color]. Therefore we say that a white horse is not a horse."

Chan, Wing-tsit (1972) *A Source Book in Chinese Philosophy*, Princeton, Princeton University Press, pp. 235–7

LOTUS SUTRA

Nichiren characteristically argues that no-one (except himself) really **1** understands the *Lotus Sutra*:

Nowadays the followers of the Nembutsu address the "rulers, high ministers, Brahmans, and great patrons of Buddhism" who support the Tendai sect, saying, "The doctrines of the Lotus Sutra are so profound that we can barely comprehend them. The Dharma it teaches is extremely deep; our capabilities are extremely shallow." Just as the *Maka Shikan* says, "They object that it pertains to the lofty realm of the sages, something far beyond the capacity of their own wisdom to comprehend."

Again, the men of the Zen sect say: "The Lotus Sutra is a finger pointing at the moon, but the Zen sect is the moon itself. Once one has the moon, of what use is the finger? Zen is the mind of the Buddha. The Lotus Sutra is the word of the Buddha. After the Buddha had finished preaching the Lotus Sutra and all the other sutras, he took a single flower and gave it to Mahākāśyapa alone, [whereby the disciple understood its meaning]. As a symbol of this tacit communication, he also presented Mahākāśyapa with his own robe, which has been handed down from one to another by the twenty-eight patriarchs of Indian Zen and so on to the sixth patriarch of Chinese Zen." For many years now, the whole country has been intoxicated and deceived by this kind of absurd nonsense.

Again, the eminent monks of the Tendai and Shingon sects, though nominally representatives of their respective sects, are in fact quite ignorant of their teachings. In the depths of their greed and out of fear of the courtiers and warriors, they lend their support to the assertions of the Nembutsu and Zen followers and sing their praises. Long ago, Tahō Buddha and the various Buddhas who were emanations of Shakyamuni Buddha acknowledged their allegiance to the Lotus Sutra, saying, "We will make certain that the Law will long endure." But now the eminent leaders of the Tendai sect obsequiously testify that "the doctrines of the Lotus Sutra are profound but human understanding is slight." As a result, the Lotus Sutra exists in Japan today in name only – there is not a single person who actually practices it and attains enlightenment. Who can be called a votary of the Lotus Sutra? We see monks who burn down temples and pagodas and are exiled in numbers too great to count. And we see numerous eminent monks who fawn on the courtiers and warriors and are hated for it by the people. Can men such as these be called the votaries of the Lotus Sutra?

Nichiren (1990) *Selected Writings of Nichiren*, trans. B. Watson *et al.*, New York: Columbia University Press, pp. 133–4

See also AMIDA, ZEN

LOVE

1   Avicenna (ibn Sina) argues that love is linked with perfection:

We want to show in this chapter (i) that every single being loves the Absolute Good with an inborn love, and (ii) that the Absolute Good manifests Itself to all those that love It. However, the capacity of the latter to receive this manifestation differs in degree, and so does the connection they have with It. The highest degree of approximation to It is the reception of Its manifestations in its full reality, i.e., in the most perfect way possible, and this is what the Sufis call unification (*ittihâd*). In Its excellence It desires that Its manifestation should be received, and the existence of things depend on it.

Thus we say: since every being has a natural love for its perfection, – and "perfection" means the acquisition of its goodness – it is obvious that the term by reason which its goodness results to the thing – no matter what the situation and form of realization – should of necessity be loved as the source from which its goodness stems. But as far as this function is concerned, there is nothing more perfect than the First Cause and nothing prior to It. It follows that It is loved by all things. The fact that most things do not know It does not contradict the fact that love of It is inborn in them, – a love which is in these things directed toward their perfections. As far as Its essence is concerned, It is revealed and manifest to all beings. If It were in Its nature veiled from all things and not manifested to them, It could not be known and nothing could be obtained from It. If, on the other hand, It were manifested, but only under the influence of something else, there would have to be an external influence in Its essence which is too exalted to be subjected to such an influence; and this is impossible. [The truth is this]: as far as Its essence is concerned, It manifests Itself. If it appears veiled, this is due to the impotence of some things adequately to receive Its manifestation. Thus, in truth, the veil lies in those which are veiled, and this veil consists in impotence, weakness and defect.

Ibn Sina, "A Treatise on Love" trans. E. Fackenheim, *Mediaeval Studies,* (1945) 7, 221–8, p. 225

See also SUFISM

Mozi outlines the significance of general benevolence: 2

But what is the way of universal love and mutual aid?

Motse said: It is to regard the state of others as one's own, the houses of others as one's own, the persons of others as one's self. When feudal lords love one another there will be no more war; when heads of houses love one another there will be no more mutual usurpation; when individuals love one another there will be no more mutual injury. When ruler and ruled love each other they will be gracious and loyal; when father and son love each other they will be affectionate and filial; when elder and younger brothers love each other they will be harmonious. When all the people in the world love one another, then the strong will not overpower the weak, the many will not oppress the few, the wealthy will not mock the poor, the honoured will not disdain the humble, and the cunning will not deceive the simple. And it is all due to mutual love that calamities, strifes, complaints, and hatred are prevented from arising. Therefore the benevolent exalt it.

Mozi (1974) *The Ethical and Political Works of Motse,* trans. Yi-Pao Mei, Taipai: Ch'eng Wen Publishing Company, pp. 82–3

See also ETHICS

MADHYAMAKA/MADHYAMIKA

1   The Madhyamika conception of Philosophy as Prajñaparamita
(non-dual, content-less intuition) precludes progress and surprise.
Progress implies that the goal is reached successively by a series of
steps in an order, and that it could be measured in quantitative
terms. Prajña is knowledge of the entire reality once for all,
and it does not depend on contingent factors as a special faculty,
favourable circumstances, or previous information. . . . The
concept of progress is applicable to science, not to philosophy.
It is, however, possible to conceive of the progressive falling
away of the hindrances that obstruct our vision of the real.
But there is neither order nor addition in the content of our
knowledge of the real. The modern conception of philosophy
as a universal science, co-ordinating and weaving the findings of
the various sciences into a coherent system, is at variance with
the Madhyamika conception of philosophy as Prajñaparamita.

Murti, T. (1955) *The Central Philosophy of Buddhism*, London: George Allen
& Unwin, p. 220

See also PRAJNA

2   Madhyamaka thought often appears paradoxical since it stresses scepticism
in such a total manner:

That is the clue to Mādhyamika – it doesn't try to explain.
The challenge of explaining the world has been abandoned
as not worth attempting to meet. Nāgārjuna has no theory of
relations or of error – he has no theories at all. We may well ask,
then, what Nāgārjuna intends to do about the nagging doubts
that many serious would-be saints experience? Does Nāgārjuna
simply not believe in the occurrence of these doubts? Or is it
that he doesn't care? One might think that, although Nāgārjuna's
leap theory is not, properly speaking, skepticism, it nevertheless
comes to the same thing in that it breeds an irresponsibility about
moral endeavor. Nāgārjuna, however, is held up by Buddhists as
a venerable example of morality, and although his teaching is

negative with respect to reasoning it is quite positive on the moral side: Mādhyamika Buddhists, as all Buddhists, must respect the "three jewels" (the Buddha, the Law, and the monastic Order) and practice the five virtues of the *pañcaśīla* – giving, morality, patience, manliness, and meditation. If Nāgārjuna was teaching irresponsibility he covered it up well.

The answer is rather, I think, that Nāgārjuna quite appreciates the nature and force of the doubts and takes them very seriously indeed. Like many a Western sage, however, he does not believe in the power of the human mind to unravel the mysteries of the universe. That being the case, resolution to the doubts can only come when one becomes free. One does not (indeed cannot) first resolve the doubts and *then* achieve freedom. Obtaining freedom *is* the resolution of the doubts. Philosophy is not a movement of thought prior to our embarking on a path to freedom. It *is* the path. By applying the dialectic we follow the only path we can follow. We are forced to it by our predicament. And, since they signify a conscious awareness of the desirability of freedom on the pupil's part, doubts, far from being something to be explained away, are to be encouraged.

Potter, K. (1972) *Presuppositions of India's Philosophies*, Westport, Conn.: Greenwood Press, pp. 241–2

See also EMPTINESS

The nature of Madhyamaka thought was a constant topic of interest in 3 Tibetan philosophy. Dzong-ka-ba produces an interpretation which reduces its nihilist impact and links it with a common sense approach to reality:

By allowing conventional validity but refusing ultimate validity to things, Dzong-ka-ba proposes an interpretation of Madhyamaka thought that is realist but still maintains its liberational value. In an essenceless reality, the only possible ontology applies to conventions delineated through agreed upon practices. Practitioners must rely on these conventionalities in two ways. They must take them as the framework for practices other than the realization of emptiness. They must also consider conventionalities in understanding emptiness. In particular, this involves attending to the mind as it reaches beyond the objects agreed upon in our practice to cling to things as being more than convenient designations. By noticing what the mind grasps onto, practitioners identify the object of negation and become well positioned to understand its nonexistence. In this way it is possible to separate conventional from ultimate validity. Things do not have an intrinsic essence, but they do have a validity that is not the mere product of ignorance. This sifting through of appearances to eliminate reification yet preserve what is valid in common experience constitutes the essence of Dzong-ka-ba's philosophy. His approach is realist in that it attempts to preserve the reality implied by common sense. It is moderate in that it refuses to hypostatize commonsense intuitions: it takes them to be valid only within the critique of substance that runs throughout the Buddhist tradition. Now we can understand some of the more far-reaching implications of the moderate realism we have analyzed throughout this work. . . .

The Sa-gya approach . . . accentuates the antirealist character of Madhyamaka. This is hardly a surprise, for this emphasis is in harmony with this tradition's interpretation of Dharmakīrti's philosophy. Whereas the Ge-luk approach rests on a respect for common sense, the Sa-gya tradition sets forth a view that radically undermines common understanding, which is seen to consist of a network of reifications due to ignorance. Accordingly, the Sa-gya tradition insists that concepts apply only to conventional reality. Ultimate truth in Madhyamaka is completely beyond the reach of concepts. It is utterly ineffable, in the strong sense of the word. Hence for the Sa-gya tradition in general and Go-ram-ba in particular, the key concept in Madhyamaka philosophy is not the absence of real existence but freedom from elaborations (*prapañca, spros pa*). Ultimate truth is utterly beyond the reach of elaboration.

As its name indicates, Madhyamaka philosophy takes as its central and self-descriptive motive the idea of a middle ground avoiding extremes. There is nevertheless room for considerable disagreement among various interpreters on the exact way in which extremes are to be identified and rejected. Unsurprisingly, Ge-luk and Sa-gya traditions disagree on this topic. Both understand the Middle Way to be the emptiness of all phenomena; that is, that all phenomena lack essence. This essencelessness is understood differently by the two traditions, however.

For Dzong-ka-ba, all phenomena are essenceless in that they do not really exist, even though they exist conventionally. The meaning of the doctrine of the Middle Way reflects this understanding. Phenomena are said to abide in the middle, for they transcend the extremes of eternalism and nihilism. Phenomena transcend the extreme of eternalism inasmuch as they are devoid of real existence. They also transcend the extreme of nihilism inasmuch as they exist conventionally. Thus, for Dzong-ka-ba, the Middle Way is reached by negating real existence in a way that preserves the limited validity of conventional practices.

Dreyfus, G. (1997) *Recognizing Reality: Dharmakirti's Philosophy and its Tibetan Interpretations*, Albany: State University of New York Press, pp. 458–9

See also EMPTINESS, ENLIGHTENMENT

The Madhyamaka philosophy can be taken to challenge language itself as a   4
useful source of thought, which makes it appear paradoxical, since it is itself
expressed in language:

The Mādhymika school did not reject speech in order to affirm an absolute intuition. The followers of this school, for instance, used the discursive tool of negation – negation which did not admit (or affirm) the opposite of what was negated. They also used metaphors to suggest an approximation of things as they really are, i.e., "emptiness." This would suggest that no easy equation can be made between logical reasoning and mundane truth on the one hand, and intuition and Ultimate Truth on the other. The ability of Ultimate Truth to manifest itself through logical reasoning as well as intuition, furthermore, would be consistent with Nāgārjuna's recognition that "emptiness" applies both to mundane existence and to ultimate reality. This recognition does not deny that the Ultimate Truth is beyond all distinctions in the sense that no statement can reduce the vitality of what is actually real to a proposition. It does stress the fact that discursive reason can be illusory if one derives metaphysical content from the terms or logical structure of the discourse; or it can be revelatory if used in a critical dialectic to indicate the nonabsolute quality of any assertion.

Streng, F. (1967) *Emptiness: A Study in Religious Meaning*, Nashville: Abingdon Press, p. 94

See also EMPTINESS, LANGUAGE

MAHAYANA

1   What then were the main doctrinal innovations of the Mahāyāna? They can be summarized under five headings:

1. As concerns the goal there is a shift from the Arhat-ideal to the Bodhisattva-ideal;
2. A new way of salvation is worked out, in which compassion ranks equal with wisdom, and which is marked by the gradual advance through six "perfections" (pāramitā);
3. Faith is given a new range by being provided with a new pantheon of deities, or rather of persons more than divine;
4. "Skill in means" (upāyakauśalya), an entirely new virtue, becomes essential to the saint, and is placed even above wisdom, the highest virtue so far;
5. A coherent ontological doctrine is worked out, dealing with such items as "Emptiness", "Suchness', etc.

We will now consider these five points one by one.

1. The goal of Arhatship, which had motivated Buddhism in the first period, is now relegated to the second place. The Mahāyānistic saint strives to be a "Bodhisattva" – from bodhi, "enlightenment", and sattva, "being" or "essence". A Bodhisattva is distinguished by three features: (a) In his essential being he is actuated by the desire to win the full enlightenment of a Buddha, which, from this point of view, implies complete omniscience, i.e. the knowledge of all things at all times in all their details and aspects. (b) He is dominated by two forces, in equal proportion, i.e. by compassion and wisdom. From compassion he selflessly postpones his entrance into the bliss of Nirvana so as to help suffering creatures. From wisdom he attempts to win insight into the emptiness of all that is. He persists in his compassionate solidarity with all that lives although his wisdom shows him that living beings and all their woes are purely illusory. (c) Although intent on ultimate purity, a Bodhisattva remains in touch with ordinary people by having the same passions they have. His passions, however, do not either affect or pollute his mind.

2. A Bodhisattva's compassion is called "great", because it is boundless and makes no distinctions. A Bodhisattva resolves to become the saviour of all, whatever may be their worth or their

claim to his attention. In the first period the wisdom of the saints had been fully emphasized, but now their selfless desire to make others happy is said to rank equal in value with it. Enlightenment is the thorough and complete understanding of the nature and meaning of life, the forces which shape it, the method to end it, and the reality which lies beyond it. This enlightenment, the Mahāyānists agreed, does not automatically entail the desire to assist others. Among the enlightened they distinguished three types, two of them "selfish", one "unselfish". The "selfish" types are the Arhats and Pratyekabuddhas, who are said to represent the idea of the Hīnayāna, of the "inferior vehicle". They are described as aloof from the concerns of the world and intent on their own private salvation alone. The "unselfish" ones are the Buddhas, and the pursuit of the unselfish quest for enlightenment on the part of a Bodhisattva is called the "Buddha-vehicle", of the "Great Vehicle" (mahā-yāna).

A Bodhisattva must be a patient man. He wants to become a Buddha, but his distance from the transcendental perfection of a supreme Buddha, Who both knows and is everything, will obviously be nearly infinite. In one life it could not possibly be traversed. Countless lives would be needed and a Bodhisattva must be prepared to wait for acons and aeons before he can reach his goal. Yet, he is separated from Buddhahood only by one single small obstacle, i.e. his belief in a personal self, his assumption that he is a separate individual, his inveterate tendency towards "I-making and Mine-making" (ahamkāra-mamakāra). To get rid of himself is the Bodhisattva's supreme task. By two kinds of measures he tries to remove himself from himself – actively by self-sacrifice and selfless service, cognitively by insight into the objective non-existence of a self. The first is due to his compassion, the second to wisdom, defined as the ability to penetrate to the true reality, to the "own-being" of things, to what they are in and by themselves. It is believed that action and cognition must always go hand in hand to bring forth their spiritual fruits.

The unity of compassion and wisdom is acted out by the six "perfections", or *pāramitā*, the six "methods by which we go to the Beyond". A person turns into a Bodhisattva when he first resolves to win full enlightenment for the benefit of all beings. Thereafter, until his attainment of Buddhahood, aeons and aeons are devoted to the practice of the Pāramitās. So important is this concept that the Mahāyāna often refers to itself as the "Vehicle of the Pāramitās". The six are: the perfections of giving, morality, patience, vigour, meditation and wisdom. The first enjoins generosity, a willingness to give away all that one has, even one's own body, and the second the scrupulous observance of the moral precepts, even at the risk of one's own life. As for "patience", the Mahāyāna has much more to say about it than the Hīnayāna and it uses the word in a wider sense than is usual. As a moral virtue it means the patient endurance of all kinds of suffering and hostility and the absence of any feeling of anger or discontent when meeting with them. In addition, "patience" is here also considered as an intellectual virtue and as such it means the emotional acceptance, before one has fathomed the whole of their depth, of the more incredible and anxiety-producing ontological doctrines of the Mahāyāna, such as the non-existence of all things. Vigour means that the Bodhisattva indefatigably persists in his work over the ages and never feels discouraged; his perfection of meditation enables him to gain proficiency in trances "numerous as the sands of the Ganges". The perfection of wisdom finally is the ability to understand the essential properties of all processes and phenomena, their mutual relations, the conditions which bring about their rise and fall, and the ultimate unreality of their separate existence. At its highest point it leads right into the Emptiness which is the one and only reality.

3. Another distinctive contribution of the Mahāyāna is the distinction of ten stages which the Bodhisattva must traverse on his way to Buddhahood. This aspect of the doctrine reached its final formulation in the third century in the "Sūtra on the Ten Stages". The first six of these stages correspond to the six "perfections" and each of them is marked by the intensive practice of one of them. The sixth stage therefore corresponds to the perfection of wisdom and with it the Bodhisattva has by his understanding of emptiness come "face to face" (abhimukhī) with Reality itself. At that point he would be able to escape from the terrors of this world of birth-and-death and he could, if he wanted to, enter into Nirvana. Out of compassion he nevertheless makes no use of this possibility, but stays on in the world for a long time so as to help those in it. Although in the world, he now is no longer of it. During the last four stages a Bodhisattva gains what the texts call "sovereignty over the world", and he becomes a kind of supernatural being endowed

with miraculous powers of many kinds. From the ordinary Bodhisattvas as they exist on the first six stages, the "celestial Bodhisattvas" of the last four stages differ in that they were well suited to becoming objects of a religious cult.

Soon the faithful increasingly turned to all kinds of mythical Bodhisattvas, such as Avalokiteśvara, Mañjuśrī, Maitreya, Kshītigarbha, Samantabhadra and others. Though conceived in India some of these Bodhisattvas show strong non-Indian, and particularly Iranian, influences.

The development of mythical Bodhisattvas was accompanied, and even preceded by, that of mythical Buddhas, Who were held to reside in the heavens in all the ten directions. In the East lives Akshobhya, the "Imperturbable". In the West is the kingdom of the Buddha of "Infinite Light", Amitābha, not always clearly distinguished from Amitāyus, the Buddha who "has an infinite life-span". Amitāyus is a counterpart to the Iranian Zurvan Akaranak ("Unlimited Time"), just as the cult of Amitābha owed much to Iranian sun worship and probably originated in the Kushana Empire in the borderland between India and Iran. There are many other celestial Buddhas, in fact infinitely many, and most of them have a "kingdom" of their own, a world which is not of this world, a land which is "pure" because free from defilements and adverse conditions.

4. Next we must say a few words about the "skill in means", a virtue which is indispensable to a Bodhisattva at all times, but which he possesses in its fullness only late, on the seventh stage, after the "perfection of wisdom" has thoroughly shown him the emptiness of everything that seems to be. "Skill in means" is the ability to bring out the spiritual potentialities of different people, by statements or actions which are adjusted to their needs and adapted to their capacity for comprehension. If the truth be told, all that we have described so far as constituting the doctrine of the Mahāyāna is just "skill in means" and nothing more. It is a series of fictions elaborated to further the salvation of beings. In actual fact there are no Buddhas, no Bodhisattvas, no perfections, and no stages. All these are products of our imagination, just expedients, concessions to the needs of ignorant people, designed to ferry them across to the Beyond. Everything apart from the One, also called "Emptiness" or "Suchness", is devoid of real existence, and whatever may be said about it is ultimately untrue, false and nugatory. But nevertheless it is not only permissible, but even useful to say it, because the salvation of beings demands it.

5. So far we have spoken about the way to the Beyond. Now we come to the Beyond itself. Wisdom teachings about ontology, or the nature of reality, constitute the inner core of the Mahāyāna doctrine. These teachings are extremely subtle, abstruse and elusive and defy any attempt at summarizing them, because they are not meant as definite statements about definite facts and because it is said expressly that they do not explain anything, do not say anything in particular, for the ultimate transcendental reality is held to lie beyond the grasp of intellectual comprehension and verbal expression. Be that as it may, the peculiar ontological doctrines of the Mahayana developed logically from the philosophy of the Mahāsaṅghikas and in direct and conscious opposition to that of the Sarvāstivādins. Four basic propositions are common to all Mahāyānists:

1. All dharmas are "empty" in the sense that each one is nothing in and by itself. Any dharma is therefore indistinguishable from any other dharma. In consequence all dharmas are ultimately non-existent and the same.
2. This Emptiness can be called "Suchness", when one takes each thing "such as it is", without adding anything to it or subtracting anything from it. There can be only one Suchness and the multiple world is a construction of our imagination.
3. If all is one and the same, then also the Absolute will be identical with the Relative, the Unconditioned with the conditioned, Nirvana with Samsāra.
4. True Knowledge must rise above the duality of either subject and object, or of affirmation and negation.

These four propositions get near to the Beyond, but they do not quite reach it. The inmost sanctum of the whole doctrine is filled with nothing but silence.

We now come to the *systematized Mahāyāna*, which falls into two main philosophical schools, the Mādhyamikas and the Yogācārins.

The *Mādhyamika* school was founded by Nāgārjuna (*c* AD 150), a South Indian and one of the greatest minds India has produced. The school persisted for many centuries and has had a vigorous life also in China and Tibet. The Mādhyamika philosophy is primarily a logical doctrine which aims at an all-embracing scepticism by showing that all statements are equally untenable. This applies also to statements about the Absolute. They are all bound to be false and the Buddha's "thundering silence" alone can do justice to it. Soteriologically, everything must be dropped and given up, until absolute Emptiness alone remains, and then salvation is gained.

Conze, E. (1980) *A Short History of Buddhism*, London: George Allen & Unwin, pp. 46–51

See also BODHI, BODHISATTVA, EMPTINESS, SKILFUL MEANS

MANAS

The precise nature of the faculty of the mind was a topic of constant 1
interest in Indian thought:

Manas (which is often translated directly as 'mind', though it is only a single facet of the 'mental triplex') is viewed essentially as an organ, the special organ of cognition, just as the eyes are the special organs of sight. Indeed, *manas* is held to be intimately connected with perception, since the raw data supplied by the senses must be ordered and categorized with respect to a conceptual scheme before various objects can be perceived as members of their respective categories, and as inhabiting a world characterized by the systematic and distinguishable attributes normally perceived. This imposition of conceptual structure on the chaotic field of raw sensation is one of the basal activities of *manas*, and forms the distinction between brute sensation (*nirvikalpaka*) as opposed to differentiated perception (*savikalpaka*). Hence ordinary perceptual experience is already heavily conditioned by the activities of *manas*, and *manas* is thus sometimes referred to as the sixth organ of sensation.

Schweitzer, P. (1993) 'Mind/Consciousness Dualism in Sankhya-Yoga Philosophy', *Philosophy and Phenomenological Research*, LIII, 4, 845–59, p. 848

See also CONSCIOUSNESS

Here the mind is linked to a part of the body: 2

The nature of the self, as we have described it, is also attested by the verdict of the *Upaniṣads*. This self is directly revealed in its own notion as "I," and pleasure, pain, attachment, antipathy are but its states, which are also revealed along with the revelation of its own self as the "I." This self is not, however, perceived by any of the senses or even by the organ *manas*, as Kumārila supposed. For the question arises as to when, if the self is believed to be perceived by the *manas*, that takes place? It cannot take place precisely at the moment when the knowledge of an object arises; for then the notions of the self and the objects, as they occur at the same moment, could not so appear that one (the self) was the cognizer or determiner, and the others (the objects) were the cognized or the determined. If the knowledge of the objects and the self arose at two different moments as separate acts, it would be difficult to conceive how they could be related as cognizer and cognized. So it cannot be held that the self, though it always manifests itself to us in self-consciousness, could yet be perceived by any of the senses or the *manas*.

Dasgupta. S. (1940) *A History of Indian Philosophy*, III, Cambridge: Cambridge University Press, p. 148

See also ATMAN, UPANISHADS

MATERIALISM

1   There was a strong strand of materialism in Indian thought:

The Cārvākas had to contend on the one hand with those who admitted a permanent soul, such as the Jains, the Naiyāyikas, the Sāṃkhya-yoga and the Mīmāṃsā, and on the other hand with the idealistic Buddhists who believed in a permanent series of conscious states; for the Cārvākas denied all kinds of existence after death. Thus they say that since there is no permanent entity that abides after death, there is no existence after death. As the body, understanding and sense-functions, are continually changing, there cannot be any existence after death, and hence no separate soul can be admitted.

Dasgupta, S. (1940) *A History of Indian Philosophy*, III, Cambridge: Cambridge University Press, pp. 539–40

See   RLIFE, JAIN, MIMAMSA,
NY   HESHIKA, ORIENTALISM, SANKHYA-YOGA

The   restricted knowledge to what can be understood by   2
perc⌣⌣⌣⌣ ⌣ ⌣⌣

The Cārvākas admitted the validity only of perception. There is nothing else but what can be perceived by the five senses. No inference can be regarded as a valid means of knowledge, for inference is possible only when the universal concomitance of the reason (*hetus*) with the probandum is known, and such a reason is known to be existing in the object of the minor term (*vyāpti-pakṣa-dharmatā-śāli hi liṅgaṃ gamakam*). Such a concomitance is possible when it is known not only to be unconditional but when there is no doubt in the mind that it could be conditional. Such a concomitance must first be known before an inference is possible; but how can it be known? Not by perception, for concomitance is not an objective entity with which the senses can come in contact.

Ibid., pp. 532–5

See also INFERENCE, KNOWLEDGE

MAYA

The supreme Lord is but one – unchanging, eternal, absolute   1
Consciousness; but like a magician He appears diversely through Maya, otherwise known as *Avidya* (ignorance). (BSB I.iii. 19 p.195)

Shankara (1972) *Brahmasutrabhasya*, trans. S. Gamhirananda, Calcutta: Advaita Ashrama, p. 195

See also CONSCIOUSNESS

The illusory nature of the world is firmly disguised by our lack of   2
understanding of its real nature:

There was never a mother who did not think her child was a born genius, the most extraordinary child that was ever born; she dotes upon her child. Her whole soul is in the child. The child grows up, perhaps becomes a drunkard, a brute, ill-treats the mother, and the more he ill-treats her, the more her love increases. The world lauds it as the unselfish love of the mother, little dreaming that the mother is a born slave, she cannot help that. She would a thousand times rather throw off the burden, but she cannot. So she covers it with a mass of flowers, which she calls wonderful love. And this is Maya.

We are all like this in the world. A legend tells how once Nârada once said to Krishna, "Lord, show me Maya." A few days passed away, and Krishna asked Narada to make a trip with him towards a desert, and after walking for several miles, Krishna said, "Narada, I am thirsty; can you fetch some water for me?" "I will go at once, sir, and get you water." So Narada went. At a little distance there was a village; he entered the village in search of water and knocked at a door, which was opened by a most beautiful young girl. At the sight of her he immediately forgot that his Master was waiting for water, perhaps dying for the want of it. He forgot everything and began to talk with the girl. All that day he did not return to his Master. The next day, he was again at the house, talking to the girl. That talk ripened into love; he asked the father for the daughter, and they were married and lived there and had children. Thus twelve years passed. His father-in-law died, he inherited his property. He lived, as he seemed to think, a very happy life with his wife and children, his fields and his cattle, and so forth. Then came a flood. One night the river rose until it overflowed its banks and flooded the whole village. Houses fell, men and animals were swept away and drowned, and everything was floating in the rush of the stream. Narada had to escape. With one hand he held his wife, and with the other two of his children; another child was on his shoulders, and he was trying to ford this tremendous flood. After a few steps he found the current was too strong, and the child on his shoulders fell and was borne away. A cry of despair came from Narada. In trying to save that child, he lost his grasp upon one of the others, and it also was lost. At last his wife, whom he clasped with all his might, was torn away by the current, and he was thrown on the bank, weeping and wailing in bitter lamentation. Behind him there came a gentle voice, "My child, where is the water? You went to fetch a pitcher of water, and I am waiting for you; you have been gone for quite half an hour." "Half an hour!" Narada exclaimed. Twelve whole years had passed through his mind, and all these scenes had happened in half an hour! And this is Maya.

Vivekananda, S. (1961) *Jnana-Yoga*, Calcutta: Advaita Ashrama, pp. 100–3

See also IMAGINATION

MEDITATION

See also DHYANA

Meditation is a complex process, and very different from relaxation or **1**
following someone else:

Q: Is it good practice to meditate while listening to someone speak, you or someone else? Is meditating while listening a contradiction? How should one listen?

R: The traditional literature describes three types of listeners. In one case, one's mind is wandering so much that there's no room at all for anything that's being said. One is just there physically. This type is said to be like a pot turned upside-down. In another case, one's mind is relating somewhat to what's being said, but basically it is still wandering. The analogy is a pot with a hole in the bottom. Whatever you pour in leaks out underneath. In the third case, the listener's mind contains aggression, jealousy, destruction of all kinds. One has mixed feelings about what is being said and cannot really understand it. The pot is not turned upside-down, it doesn't have a hole in the bottom, but it has not been cleaned properly. It has poison in it.

The general recommendation for listening is to try to communicate with the intelligence of the speaker; you relate to the situation as the meeting of two minds. One doesn't particularly have to meditate at that point in the sense that meditation would become an extra occupation. But the speaker can become the meditation technique, taking the place of, let's say, identifying with the breath in sitting meditation. The voice of the speaker would be part of the identifying process, so one should be very close to it as a way of identifying with what the speaker is saying. . . .

Q: In meditation, can it be beneficial to try to relax?

R: From the Buddhist point of view, meditation is not intended to create relaxation or any other pleasurable condition, for that matter. Meditation is meant to be provocative. You sit and let things come up through you – tension, passion or aggression – all kinds of things come up. So Buddhist meditation is not the sort of mental gymnastic involved in getting yourself into a state of relaxation. It is quite a different attitude because there is no particular aim and object, no immediate demand to achieve something. It's more a question of being open.

Guenther, H. and Trungpa, C. (1975) *The Dawn of Tantra*, Berkeley: Shambhala, p. 83, 92

2 Meditation in Buddhism should be understood as part and parcel of correctly understanding the nature of reality. It is not just a way of achieving personal enlightenment:

But once the moral foundations are laid, the remainder of the Buddhist efforts consist in mental training, in *meditations* of various kinds. Meditation is a mental training which is carried out for three distinct, but interconnected, purposes:

1. It aims at a withdrawal of attention from its normal pre-occupation with constantly changing sensory stimuli and ideas centred on oneself.
2. It aims at effecting a shift of attention from the sensory world to another, subtler realm, thereby calming the turmoils of the mind. Sense-based knowledge is as inherently unsatisfactory as a sense-based life. Sensory and historical facts as such are uncertain, unfruitful, trivial, and largely a matter of indifference. Only that is worth knowing which is discovered in meditation, when the doors of the senses are closed. The truths of this holy religion must elude the average worldling with his sense-based knowledge, and his sense-bounded horizon.
3. It aims at penetrating into the suprasensory reality itself, at roaming about among the transcendental facts, and this quest leads it to Emptiness as the one ultimate reality.

In Buddhist terminology, the first preliminary step is known as "mindfulness" (*smṛti*), which is followed then by "ecstatic trance" (*samādhi*) and "wisdom" (*prajñā*). The relation of the three is indicated by the following diagram:

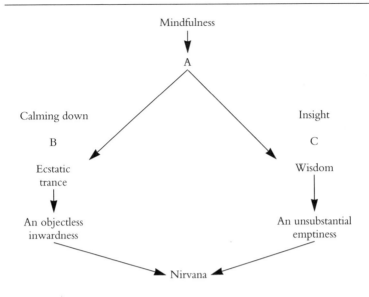

This is the classification of the meditations according to their purpose. From another point of view they can be classified according to their subjects or topics. A considerable number of such topics were offered to the aspirant, and his choice among them depends on his mental endowments and proclivities. So vast is the range of the possibilities offered that they cannot possibly be even enumerated here. There we have relatively simple breathing exercises of the Yogic type, a survey of the "thirty-two parts of the body", the contemplation of corpses in various degrees of decomposition, an introspective awareness of our mental processes as they go along, be they feelings, thoughts, or the hindrances to concentration, or the factors which make for enlightenment. Then there is the cultivation of the social emotions, such as friendliness and compassion, the recollection of the virtues of the three Jewels, the meditation on death and the aspiration for Nirvana. A favourite subject of meditation are the twelve links of the chain of conditioned co-production (*pratītya-samutpāda*), which shows how ignorance leads to the other factors of worldly existence ending in old age and death and how, conversely, the extinction of ignorance must lead to the extinction of all these factors. Other meditations again try to impress on our minds the facts of the impermanence of all conditioned things, to show up the full extent of suffering, demonstrate the inanity of the term "self", to foster insight into emptiness and to reveal the characteristic features of the path which leads to salvation. In fact, there seems to be almost no limit to the number of meditational devices which are attested for the first period of Buddhism, although it was apparently only in the second period that some systematic order was imposed upon them.

Conze, E. (1980) *A Short History of Buddhism*, London: George Allen & Unwin, pp. 23–5

See also CAUSATION, DEATH, DEPENDENT CO-ORIGINATION, ENLIGHTENMENT, *NIRVANA*, *PRAJNA*

3   Ashavaghosha in the 2nd century CE presents this advice to the Buddhist:

Then, my friend, you should find yourself a living-place which, to be suitable for Yoga, must be without noise and without people. First the body must be placed in seclusion; then detachment of the mind is easy to attain. But those who do not like to live in solitude, because their hearts are not at peace and because they are full of greed, they will hurt themselves there, like someone who walks on very thorny ground because he cannot find the proper road. It is no easier to deny the urges of a man who has not seen the real truth, and who finds himself standing in the fairground of the sensory world, fascinated by its brightness, than it is to deny those of a bull who is eating corn in the middle of a cornfield. A brightly shining fire, when not stirred by the wind, is soon appeased; so the unstimulated heart of those who live in seclusion wins peace without much effort. One who delights in solitude is content with his own company, eats wherever he may be, lodges anywhere, and wears just anything. To shun familiarity with others, as if they were a thorn in the flesh, shows a sound judgement, and helps to accomplish a useful purpose and to know the taste of a happy tranquillity. In a world which takes pleasure in worldly conditions and which is made unrestful by the sense-objects, he dwells in solitude indifferent to worldly conditions, as one who has attained his object, who is tranquil in his heart. The solitary man then drinks the nectar of the Deathless, he becomes content in his heart, and he grieves for the world made wretched by its attachment to sense-objects. If he is satisfied with living alone for a long time in an empty place, if he refrains from dallying with the agents of defilement, regarding them as bitter enemies, and if, content with his own company, he drinks the nectar of spiritual exultation, then he enjoys a happiness greater than that of paradise.

Conze. E. (1976) *Buddhist Scriptures*, Harmondsworth: Penguin, pp. 107–8

See also ASCETICISM

MOHISM

Mozi, the creator of Mohism, appears to be a more radical thinker than Confucius: 1

Mo Tzu was the founder of a school known after his name as the Mohist school. In ancient times his fame was as great as that of Confucius, and his teaching was no less influential. The contrast between the two men is interesting. Confucius felt a sympathetic understanding for the traditional institutions, rituals, music, and literature of the early Chou dynasty, and tried to rationalize and justify them in ethical terms; Mo Tzu, on the contrary, questioned their validity and usefulness, and tried to replace them with something that was simpler but, in his view, more useful. In short, Confucius was the rationalizer and justifier of the ancient civilization, while Mo Tzu was its critic. Confucius was a refined gentleman, while Mo Tzu was a militant preacher. A major aim of his preaching was to oppose both the traditional institutions and practices, and the theories of Confucius and the Confucianists. . . .

According to Mo Tzu, "the principles of the Confucianists ruin the whole world in four ways": (1) The Confucianists do not believe in the existence of God or of spirits, "with the result that God and the spirits are displeased." (2) The Confucianists insist on elaborate funerals and the practice of three years of mourning on the death of a parent, so that the wealth and energy of the people are thereby wasted. (3) The Confucianists lay stress on the practice of music, leading to an identical result. (4) The Confucianists believe in a predetermined fate, causing the people to be lazy and to resign themselves to this fate.

(The *Mo-tzu*, ch. 48.) In another chapter entitled "Anti-Confucianism," the *Mo-tzu* also says: "Even those with long life cannot exhaust the learning required for their [Confucianist] studies. Even people with the vigor of youth cannot perform all the ceremonial duties. And even those who have amassed wealth cannot afford music. They [the Confucianists] enhance the beauty of wicked arts and lead their sovereign astray. Their doctrine cannot meet the needs of the age, nor can their learning educate the people." (Ch. 39.) . . .

Mo Tzu makes no criticism of the Confucianists' central idea of *jen* (human-heartedness) and *yi* (righteousness); in the *Mo-tzu*, indeed, he speaks often of these two qualities and of the man of *jen* and man of *yi*. What he means by these terms, however, differs somewhat from the concept of them held by the Confucianists. For Mo Tzu, *jen* and *yi* signify an all-embracing love, and the man of *jen* and man of *yi* are persons who practice this all-embracing love. This concept is a central one in Mo Tzu's philosophy, and represents a logical extension of the professional ethics of the class of *hsieh* (knights-errant) from which Mo Tzu sprang. This ethics was, namely, that within their group the *hsieh* "enjoy equally and suffer equally." (This was a common saying of the *hsieh* of later times.) Taking this group concept as a basis, Mo Tzu tried to broaden it by preaching the doctrine that everyone in the world should love everyone else equally and without discrimination.

Fung Yu-Lan (1948) *A Short History of Chinese Philosophy*, New York: Free Press, pp. 49, 52, 53

See also CONFUCIANISM, ETHICS, HUMAN NATURE

2   Mozi presents criticisms of Confucianism, in particular of its support for rituals such as music and elaborate funerals:

Mo Tzu said: To levy heavy taxes on the people in order to produce the sounds of big bells, resounding drums, harps, and pipes does not help the promotion of benefits and the removal of harms in the world. Therefore Mo Tzu said: To engage in music is wrong. . . . To have men engage in music is to waste their time for ploughing and planting. To have women engage in music is to waste their effort for weaving and spinning.

Now, kings, dukes, and great officials engage in music. To strike musical instruments to produce music, they loot the people's resources for food and clothing to such an extent! Therefore Mo Tzu said: To engage in music is wrong. . . .

Now the gentlemen on the world still doubt whether elaborate funerals and extended mourning are right or wrong, beneficial or harmful. Therefore Mo Tzu said: I have inquired into the matter. If the doctrines of those who advocate elaborate funerals and extended mourning is followed in the affairs in the country, it will mean that whenever a king, duke, or great official dies, there would be layers of coffin, the burial would be deep, the shrouding would be plenty, the embroidery covering would be elaborate, and the grave mound would be massive. . . . Mourners would weep in a confused manner to the point of choking, wear sackcloth on the breast and flax on the head, keep the snivel dangling, live in a mourning hut, sleep on straw, and rest their heads on a lump of earth. . . . All this is to last for three years.

If such a doctrine is followed and such a principle is practiced, kings, dukes, and great officials practicing it cannot go to court early [and retire late to administer their government, and attend to the] five offices and six departments and develop agriculture and forestry and fill the granaries, farmers practicing it cannot start out early and return late to plough and plant, artisans practicing it cannot build vehicles and make utensils, and women practicing it cannot rise early and retire late to weave and spin. So, much wealth is buried in elaborate funerals and long periods of work are suspended in extended mourning. Wealth that is already produced is carried to be buried and wealth yet to be produced is long delayed. To seek wealth in this way is like seeking a harvest by stopping farming. . . .

Chan, Wing-tsit (1972) *A Source Book in Chinese Philosophy*, Princeton, Princeton University Press, pp. 228–9

See also ASCETICISM, DEATH

MOKSA/MOKSHA

The Indian notion of liberation is based on seeing the nature of reality correctly, and then acting appropriately, and so the question of knowledge has been of primary significance:

Mokṣa, therefore, in the perspective of Indian philosophy, is more talked about in the context of knowledge of what truth is, and knowledge in this case being of the self ensures or rather coincides with its own reality, that is, the real nature of the self.

Mokṣa then is not *dharma*, that is, it does not belong to the domain of moral action even though the latter may prepare the ground for the true knowledge of the self to arise and thus, in a sense, to also bring it into being. The central problem for the Indian philosophical reflection, therefore, has been that of error and not of evil as has been the case in the western tradition. And, depending on the way one conceives the true nature of the self to be, one also conceives of what the realization of *mokṣa* would consist of. But the acceptance of such an ideal would not necessarily make Indian philosophy spiritual, just as the acceptance of any other ideal, even with respect to the self, would make any philosophy spiritual or non-spiritual.

Krishna, D. (1991) *Indian Philosophy: A Counter Perspective*, Delhi: Oxford University Press, p. 39

See also DHARMA

NIRVANA

See also ENLIGHTENMENT

---

1   The Buddhist doctrine of *nirvana* often appears to be rather nihilist:

Nirvana is regarded as consummate salvation, supreme blessedness, the haven of peace and isle of deliverance. Could such figures be veils without substance, enshrouding nothingness? Or do they not rather conceal a positive core? Attention was called to this contradiction in the teachings of the Buddha, and he was asked whether the Perfected One would or would not exist beyond death. Buddha declined to answer this question, apparently because it is theoretical in nature and its solution is irrelevant to the one thing required, namely, the achievement of salvation. He was therefore accused of philosophical agnosticism. It is possible, however, that the Buddha did not wish to express himself regarding life in the beyond, since our conceptual language is not adequate to that purpose. Regarding the "other shore," the immortal sphere removed from death, nothing can be expressed with certainty in human words. That realm is accessible only in mystic ascent.

Dumoulin, H. (1963) *A History of Zen Buddhism*, London: Faber, p. 164

See also AFTERLIFE

How far the idea of *nirvana* is to be seen as more than an idea is a familiar issue of Buddhist controversy: 2

Nirvāṇa in life is the cessation of craving, alias greed-hatred-and-delusion and is indescribable because it is the opposite of the process of life as we know it; to discuss it in isolation is futile because you have to understand what, according to Buddhist ontology, is being negated. It is futile also for a more important reason: *nirvāṇa* is an experience, and all private experiences (e.g. falling in love) are ultimately beyond language (though they can to some extent be discussed with others who have had the experience). Experiences do have an objective facet. Objectively hunger is want of food, etc.; subjectively it is a kind of pain, imperfectly describable. My description of *nirvāṇa* as the cessation of craving is objective. As one cannot even fully describe the experience of the cessation of a toothache, the indescribability of *nirvāṇa* is unsurprising. For the convenience of discourse Buddhist saints did apply various kinds of epithets to it, and thus objectify and even reify what was for them the experience of the cessation of a process. Had they foreseen the confusion this would cause they might have kept silence.

Gombrich, R. (1972) Review, *Modern Asian Studies*, VI, p. 492. Reprinted by permission of Oxford University Press.

See also DUHKHA

Can *nirvana* be described in language? There seem to be significant problems in trying to undertake this: 3

Buddhism has always placed great emphasis on experience. The four basic axioms of Buddhism are highly experiential in character. The first is that everything is transitory; the second that everything is frustrating; the third that everything is without essence; the fourth that nirvana is bliss. These first three axioms relate very much to our actual way of going through life. We observe life and see that nothing lasts; we feel that being faced with trying to build something on this basis is very frustrating. Then we think and we ask ourselves, "How is this? Why is this?" We get the answer that if everything is transitory it cannot have an essence; because an essence is by definition the principle by which something is what it is. If we started reasoning from the idea of an essence, we could not account for transitoriness, nor could we account for the constant frustration which we experience.

Now the continual frustration makes us feel that some other mode of being must be possible. This is where we come to the fourth basic axiom, which says that nirvana is bliss. Buddha's disciple Ananda asked him how he could make such a statement, having said that feelings and all such forms are transitory. The Buddha replied that he had qualified nirvana as bliss only by way of language, that he did not thereby mean a judgment of feeling, such as when we call something pleasant. The term he used for bliss was *sukha*, which is very close to what we have referred to as the peak experience. This seems to be an experience in which all conceptions and judgments, even the idea of oneself, completely pass away. So what is referred to as bliss can be understood to transcend transitoriness or permanence or any other form.

Guenther, H. and Trungpa, C. (1975) *The Dawn of Tantra*, Berkeley: Shambhala, p. 13

See also LANGUAGE

---

4   The terms *nirvāṇa* (lit. "blowing out," i.e., elimination of attachment) and *tathāgatha* (lit. "thus gone" = the Buddha) are useful for indicating complete spiritual release, Nāgārjuna maintains, only if they do not refer to entities which become objects for "grasping." The first requirement for avoiding this subtle fabrication is to remember that there are no real ontological distinctions.

Streng, F. (1967) *Emptiness: A Study in Religious Meaning*, Nashville: Abingdon Press, pp. 69–70

See also EMPTINESS, *TATHAGATA*

Nagarjuna argues that the Abhidharma discussion of *nirvana* was too   5
abstract and impersonal:

We can come to grips with the meaning of *nirvāṇa* as empty of all
content by remembering that the purpose of the term was to
indicate "true freedom" – final release. It was first a soteriological
term – with metaphysical overtones. Nāgārjuna, following
the insights of the *Prajñāpāramitā* composers, held that the
Abhidharma literature became so "tied up" with explanations of
the nature and process of *nirvāṇa* that freedom from mental
fabrication could not be realized. Nāgārjuna attempted to
break the bonds which even such a "righteous concern" had by
subjecting the notions to a devastating dialectic. In destroying the
illusion of self-beings Nāgārjuna was establishing the freedom
which came from existing without attachment. It is this freedom
which applies both to existence and *nirvāṇa*; for it is *not* conceived
as a self-contained state of existence in the sense of a realm into
which one "enters."

Fundamental to an understanding of *nirvāṇa* is the perception
of the reality of "becoming" for which *nirvāṇa* is the answer.
If we see that the "becoming" is a fundamental ontological
category denying the static "being," then there is no need for
a static ontological substratum to undergird a "process of
becoming"; and the question of whether there "is" or "is not"
something remaining when there is no longer fabrication of
existence does not apply. For Nāgārjuna, common everyday
living more often than not imposed an illusory absolute character
on the everyday events and "things" of life. He claimed that
even the concern for spiritual insight could take on this
illusory absolute character if *nirvāṇa*, *tathāgata*, or "emptiness"
were regarded as self-existent realities. Another way of saying this
is that existence without a self-sufficient status is an *empty* relation
(or empty relations) which takes (take) on an illusory substantial
quality when "self-existence" (*sva-bhāva*) is emotionally and
perceptually attributed to it. *Nirvāṇa* is realizing the true, *empty*
structure of becoming, which then becomes religiously "more,"
but metaphysically "less" than "being" *or* "becoming."

Ibid., pp. 80–1

See also ABHIDHARMA, EMPTINESS, *TATHAGATA*

6   Rahulabhadra's account of *nirvana* in his *Prajnaparamitastotra* ('Hymn to Perfect Wisdom') draws on a familiar tradition of comparing it with a whole range of other phenomena:

4b. The nature of Nirvana

King Milinda said: 'I will grant you, Nagasena, that Nirvana is absolute Ease, and that nevertheless one cannot point to its form or shape, its duration or size, either by smile or explanation, by reason or by argument. But is there perhaps some quality of Nirvana which it shares with other things, and which lends itself to a metaphorical explanation?' – 'Its form, O king, cannot be elucidated by similes, but its qualities can.' – 'How good to hear that, Nagasena! Speak then, quickly, so that I may have an explanation of even one of the aspects of Nirvana! Appease the fever of my heart! Allay it with the cool sweet breezes of your words!'

'Nirvana shares one quality with the lotus, two with water, three with medicine, ten with space, three with the wishing jewel, and five with a mountain peak. As the lotus is unstained by water, so is Nirvana unstained by all the defilements. - As cool water allays feverish heat, so also Nirvana is cool and allays the fever of all the passions. Moreover, as water removes the thirst of men and beasts who are exhausted, parched, thirsty, and overpowered by heat, so also Nirvana removes the craving for sensuous enjoyments, the craving for further becoming, the craving for the cessation of becoming. As medicine protects from the torments of poison, so Nirvana from the torments of the poisonous passions. Moreover, as medicine puts an end to sickness, so Nirvana to all sufferings. Finally, Nirvana and medicine both give security. – And these are the ten qualities which Nirvana shares with space. Neither is born, grows old, dies, passes away, or is reborn; both are unconquerable, cannot be stolen, are unsupported, are roads respectively for birds and Arhats to journey on, are unobstructed and infinite. – Like the wishing jewel, Nirvana grants all one can desire, brings joy, and sheds light. – As a mountain peak is lofty and exalted, so is Nirvana. As a mountain peak is unshakeable, so is Nirvana. As a mountain peak is inaccessible, so is Nirvana inaccessible to all the passions. As no seeds can grow on a mountain peak, so the seeds of all the passions cannot grow in Nirvana. And finally, as a mountain peak is free from all desire to please or displease, so is Nirvana.' – 'Well said, Nagasena! So it is, and as such I accept it.'

Conze, E. (1976) *Buddhist Scriptures*, Harmondsworth: Penguin, pp. 156–7

See also BUDDHA NATURE

The emphasis on emptiness by Nagarjuna leads to the accusation that   7
he cannot provide an analysis of *nirvana* which does not identify it with
emptiness:

The *Śūnyatā*-doctrine of Nāgārjuna may seem incompatible with the doctrine of *nirvāṇa*. If everything be void and there be neither origination nor destruction, then by the destruction or arrest of what should we attain *nirvāṇa*? The reply of Nāgārjuna is that *nirvāṇa* is not something which is to be attained through the destruction or the arrest of anything whatsoever; it is but the complete cessation of all mental constructions. It has been described as the destruction of nothing, – the attainment of nothing, – it is neither annihilation, nor eternally existent ; – it is neither the arrested, nor the produced – this is the definition of *nirvāṇa*. Nothing is existent, – nothing is non-existent; so the question of annihilation or suppression does not arise at all. It is not the negation of any existence, – it is but the cessation of all notions of existence and non-existence. All consciousness vanishes in *nirvāṇa* like a lamp extinguished. *Nirvāṇa* is no Ens, neither non-Ens, it is like a knot entwined by the empty space (*ākāśa*) and untied again by that same empty space.

Dasgupta, S.B. (1974) *An Introduction to Tantric Buddhism*, Berkeley: Shambhala, p. 18

See also EMPTINESS, MADHYAMAKA

NYAYA-VAISHESHIKA

An account of the schools of Nyaya and Vaisheshika and why they are   1
generally linked:

The *Nyāya* deals mainly with logical methods and the *Vaiśeshika* mainly with the nature of the world, but each accepts the other's conclusions. The *Vaiśeshika* uses the analytical methods of the *Nyāya* and the latter accepts the former's thesis of an atomistic constitution of the world. There are four sources of knowledge, according to the *Nyāya* perception (*pratyaksha*), inference (*anumanā*), analogy (*upamāna*), and credible testimony (*śabda*). The principle of causation is accepted by the *Nyāya* school, but considerable attention is paid to problems arising from non-causal antecedents, plurality of causes, etc. The process of reasoning is discussed in detail and the analysis of the process remarkably resembles the syllogistic analysis of Aristotle. Some, for instance Max Müller, have considered this a coincidence, while others have treated it as an irrefutable proof of the Greeks borrowing from the Indians, or vice versa. In the absence of sufficient historical research on the subject, no very definite conclusion can be reached.

The first important exponent of the *Nyāya* was Gautama, who lived in the third century B.C.. His *Nyāya Sūtra* is the first systematic exposition of its approach. The history of the *Nyāya* is divided into two periods. The old *Nyāya* school ended with Gaṅgeśa (*c.* A.D. 1200) of Mithilā, the founder of the modern school. His *Tattvacintāmaṇi* is the standard text of the school in the second period. Partly inspired by the criticism of Śrīharsha, a member of the *Vedānta* school, who claimed that the *Nyāya* methods of dealing with knowledge of the external world were invalid and that it cannot really ever be proved whether a thing exists or not, Gaṅgeśa tried to build up a more rigorous structure for the discipline. There were various critics of the *Nyāya* school, but it is of interest to note that to debunk this discipline, the critics more often than not used the methods of reasoning of the *Nyāya* school. This really illustrates the importance of this school in Indian philosophical history.

The *Vaiśeshika* is more interested in cosmology. All material objects, it claims, are made of four kinds of atoms. Different combinations of these atoms of earth, water, fire, and air make different materials. But the substances of the world are not all material. There are in fact, it claims, nine substances; these include, apart from the four kinds of material atoms, space, time, ether (*ākāśa*), mind, and soul. It accepts a personal God. He created the world, but not out of nothing. The nine substances existed before the world was formed; He fashioned them into an ordered universe. God is thus the creator of the world, but not of its constituents. Therefore, the philosophy of the *Vaiśeshika*, while not atheistic, is different from that of most schools of traditional Hindu theology. In fact there were so many unorthodox thinkers in this school that Śaṃkara, the great champion of the *Vedānta*, described the followers of *Vaiśeshika* as *ardhavaināśikas*, i.e. half-nihilists.

The first notable member of the school was Kaṇāda (*c.* third century B.C.), whose *Vaiśeshika Sūtra* occupies in this system about the same place as the *Nyāya Sūtra* in the *Nyāya* school. Like the *Nyāya*, the *Vaiśeshika* too had two phases in its life. In fact the evolutions of the two systems have, throughout history, been very closely linked with each other. Together they represent the relatively analytical branch of Hindu philosophy.

Sen, K. (1973) *Hinduism*, Harmondsworth: Penguin, pp. 78–9

See also ADVAITA, INFERENCE

ONTOLOGY

Avicenna's (ibn Sina's) account of being makes an apparently sharp **1** distinction between the contingent and the necessary, which on closer examination does not appear to be very distinct at all:

So far we have been talking about three types of being. These are: (i) that which is necessarily existent in itself; (ii) that which is necessarily existent by reason of another but possibly existent by reason of itself; and (iii) that which is possibly existent by reason of itself without being necessarily existent by reason of another. As we have seen, members of the third class become rather difficult to distinguish from members of the second class. There is a class of things that are necessary without having a cause of their being necessary and another class of things which are necessary through a cause, this cause being a member of a former class. Examples of beings which are necessarily existent by reason of something else are 'combustion', which is 'necessarily existent . . . once contact is assumed to take place between fire and inflammable material', and 'four' which is 'necessarily existent . . . when we assume two plus two'. These examples suggest that the distinction between the kinds of being which we have called (ii) and (iii) above is rather artificial. One of the ways in which

Avicenna characterizes necessity is in terms of 'signifying certainty of existence'. The necessarily existent in itself is that which has certainty of existence by reason of itself, while the necessarily existent through another would be that which has certainty of existence through another. So in the end there is no real difference between necessary existence through another and actual existence for anything other than God. We might put Avicenna's argument in this way. So long as something is only possible, there is nothing in existence which can move it from non-existence to existence. The possibly existent can only become actually existent if something decides to shift it from the substitutes' bench to the playing area, as it were. Whenever that something is present and sets a series of events in train, the consequent existence of the possible being is inevitable. It will certainly exist and thus is necessary. So when the possibly existent actually exists, its existence is necessary, and when it does not exist, its existence is impossible. All that Avicenna can mean by talking about a class of things which are possibly existent without being necessarily existent is that, if we abstract from all external conditions, the class of possibly existent things can be *conceived* since they are always possibly existent. It we are to divide up the actual existents we need only two categories, that of the necessarily existent by reason of itself, where an impossibility results if we assume it not to exist by reason of itself, and the necessarily existent by reason of another, where an impossibility or contradiction also results if we assume it not to exist, but this time only because it is assumed that something else exists.

Leaman. O. (1985) *Introduction to Medieval Islamic Philosophy*, Cambridge: Cambridge University Press, pp. 31–2

See also EXISTENCE

ORIENTALISM

1   A defence of the idea that there is a basic opposition between the materialist West and the spiritual East:

The present era of the world is a stage of immense transformations. Not one but many radical ideas are at work in the mind of humanity and agitate its life with a vehement seeking and effort at change; and although the centre of the agitation is in progressive Europe, yet the East is being rapidly drawn into this churning of the sea of thought and this breaking up of old ideas and old institutions. No nation or community can any longer remain psychologically cloistered and apart in the unity of the modern world. It may even be said that the future of humanity depends most upon the answer that will be given to the modern riddle of the Sphinx by the East and especially by India, the hoary guardian of the Asiatic idea and its profound spiritual secrets. For the most vital issue of the age is whether the future progress of humanity is to be governed by the modern economic and materialistic mind of the West or by a nobler pragmatism guided, uplifted and enlightened by spiritual culture and knowledge. The West never really succeeded in spiritualising itself and latterly it has been habituated almost exclusively to an action in the external governed by political and economic ideals and necessities; in spite of the reawakening of the religious mind and the growth of a widespread but not yet profound or luminous spiritual and psychical curiosity and seeking, it has to act solely in the things of this world and to solve its problems by mechanical methods and as the thinking political and economic animal, simply because it knows no other standpoint and is accustomed to no other method. On the other hand the East, though it has allowed its spirituality to slumber too much in dead forms, has always been open to profound awakenings and preserves its spiritual capacity intact, even when it is actually inert and uncreative. Therefore the hope of the world lies in the re-arousing in the East of the old spiritual practicality and large and profound vision and power of organisation under the insistent contact of the West and in the flooding out of the light of Asia on the Occident, no longer in forms that are now static, effete, unadaptive, but in new forms stirred, dynamic and effective.

Aurobindo (1987) *The Essential Aurobindo*, ed. R. McDermott, Great Barrington, MA: Lindisfarne Press, pp. 188–9

A critique of the above view, pointing to the important aspects of Indian   **2**
culture which are far from predominantly spiritual:

The internal identities of Indians draw on different parts of India's diverse traditions. The observational leanings of Western approaches have had quite a major impact – positively and negatively – on what contributes to the Indian self-image that emerged in the colonial period and survives today. The relationship has several dialectical aspects, connected to the sensitivity towards selective admirations and dismissals from the cosmopolitan West as well as to the mechanics of colonial confrontations.

The differences between the curatorial, magisterial, and exoticist approaches to Western understanding of Indian intellectual traditions lie, to a great extent, in the varying observational positions from which India has been examined and its overall images drawn. The dependence on perspective is not a special characterisitic of the imaging of India alone. It is, in fact, a pervasive general feature in description and identification. "What is India really like?" is a good question for a foreign tourist's handbook precisely because the description there may sensibly be presented from the particular position of being a foreign tourist in India. But there are other positions, other contexts, other concerns.

The three approaches investigated here have produced quite distinct views of Indian intellectual history, but their overall impact has been to exaggerate the nonmaterial and arcane aspects of Indian traditions compared to its more rationalistic and analytical elements. While the curatorial approaches have been less guilty of this, their focus on what is really different in India has, to some extent, also contributed to it. But the bulk of the contribution has come from the *exoticist admiration* of India (particularly of its spiritual wonders) and the *magisterial dismissals* (particularly of its claims in mathematics, science, and analytical pursuits).

The nature of these slanted emphases has tended to undermine an adequately pluralist understanding of Indian intellectual traditions. While India has inherited a vast religious literature, a large wealth of mystical poetry, grand speculation on transcendental issues, and so on, there is also a huge – and often pioneering – literature, stretching over two and a half millennia, on mathematics, logic, epistemology, astronomy, physiology, linguistics, phonetics, economics, political science, and psychology, among other subjects concerned with the here and now.

Even on religious subjects, the only world religion that is firmly agnostic (Buddhism) is of Indian origin, and, furthermore, the atheistic schools of Carvaka and Lokayata have generated extensive arguments that have been seriously studied by Indian religious scholars themselves. Heterodoxy runs throughout the early documents, and even the ancient epic *Ramayana*, which is often cited by contemporary Hindu activists as the holy book of the divine Rama's life, contains dissenting characters. For example, Rama is lectured to by a wordly pundit called Javali on the folly of his religious beliefs: "O Rama, be wise, there exists no world but this, that is certain! Enjoy that which is present and cast behind thee that which is unpleasant."

What is in dispute here is not the recognition of mysticism and religious initiatives in India, which are certainly plentiful, but the overlooking of all the other intellectual activities that are also abundantly present.

Sen. A. (1997) "Indian traditions and the Western imagination", *Daedalus* 126, 2, 1–26. Reprinted by permission of Daedalus, Journal of the American Academy of Arts and Sciences, from the issue entitled "Human Diversity", Spring 1997, vol. 126, No 2., pp. 21–2

See also MATERIALISM

POLITICS AND POWER

Political science is the knowledge of things through which those **1** who live in political groups attain happiness, each in proportion to his natural capacity. It will be obvious . . . that the political group and the larger organization which comes about through the association of the citizens in the cities is like the association of bodies in the universe itself. It will become clear that everything which the state and the country possess has an equivalent in what the universe as a whole contains.

Al-Farabi (1890) *Alfarabi's philosophische Abhandlungen*, Leiden: Brill, p. 16

A Legalist account of power which brings out nicely the links with Daoist **2** language:

The Way lies in what cannot be seen, its function in what cannot be known. Be empty, still, and idle, and from your place of darkness observe the defects of others. See but do not appear to see; listen but do not seem to listen; know but do not let it be known that you know. When you perceive the trend of a man's words, do not change them, do not correct them, but examine them and compare them with the results. Assign one man to each office and do not let men talk to each other, and then all will do their utmost. Hide your tracks, conceal your sources, so that your subordinates cannot trace the springs of your action. Discard wisdom, forswear ability, so that your subordinates cannot guess what you are about. Stick to your objectives and examine the results to see how they match; take hold of the handles of government carefully and grip them tightly. Destroy all hope, smash all intention of wresting them from you; allow no man to covet them. . . .

The way of the ruler of men is to treasure stillness and reserve. Without handling affairs himself, he can recognize clumsiness or skill in others; without laying plans of his own, he knows what will bring fortune or misfortune. Hence he need speak no word, but good answers will be given him; he need exact no promises, but good works will increase. When proposals have been brought before him, he takes careful note of their content; when undertakings are well on their way, he takes careful note of the result; and from the degree to which proposals and results tally, rewards and punishments are born. Thus the ruler assigns undertakings to his various ministers on the basis of the words they speak, and assesses their accomplishments according to the way they have carried out the undertaking. When accomplishments match the undertaking, and the undertaking matches what was said about it, then he rewards the man; when these things do not match, he punishes the man. It is the way of the enlightened ruler never to allow his ministers to speak words that cannot be matched by results. . . .

Though a skilled carpenter is capable of judging a straight line with his eye alone, he will always take his measurements with a rule; though a man of superior wisdom is capable of handling affairs by native wit alone, he will always look to the laws of the former kings for guidance. Stretch the plumb line, and crooked wood can be planed straight; apply the level, and bumps and hollows can be shaved away; balance the scales, and heavy and light can be adjusted; get out the measuring jars, and discrepancies of quantity can be corrected. In the same way one should use laws to govern the state, disposing of all matters on their basis alone. . . .

Do not let your power be seen; be blank and actionless. Government reaches to the four quarters, but its source is in the center. The sage holds to the source and the four quarters come to serve him. In emptiness he awaits them, and they spontaneously do what is needed. When all within the four seas have been put in their proper places, he sits in darkness to observe the light. When those to his left and right have taken their places, he opens the gate to face the world. He changes nothing, alters nothing, but acts with the two handles of reward and punishment, acts and never ceases: this is what is called walking the path of principle.

Things have their proper place, talents their proper use. When all are in their proper place, then superior and inferior may be free from action. Let the cock herald the dawn, let the cat catch rats. When each exercises his ability, the ruler need do nothing. If the ruler tries to excel, then nothing will go right. If he boasts of an eye for the abilities of others, he will invite deceit among his subordinates. If he is lenient and fond of sparing lives, his subordinates will impose upon his kind nature. If superior and inferior try to change roles, the state will never be ordered. . . .

The ruler of men must prune his trees from time to time and not let them grow too thick for, if they do, they will block his gate; while the gates of private men are crowded with visitors, the ruler's courts will stand empty, and he will be shut in and encircled. He must prune his trees from time to time and not let them obstruct the path for, if they do, they will impinge upon his dwelling. He must prune his trees from time to time and not let the branches grow larger than the trunk for, if they do, they will not be able to bear up under the spring wind, and will do injury to the heart of the tree. When cadet houses become too numerous, the royal family will face anxiety and grief. The way to prevent this is to prune your trees from time to time and not let the branches grow too luxurious. If the trees are pruned from time to time, cliques and parties will be broken up. Dig them up from the roots, and then the trees cannot spread. Fill up the pools and do not let water collect in them. Search out the hearts of others, seize their power from them. The ruler himself should possess the power, wielding it like lightning or like thunder.

Han Fei Tzu (1964) *Han Fei Tzu: Basic Writings*, trans. B. Watson, New York: Columbia University Press, pp. 17–18, 19, 28, 35–6, 41–2

See also DAOISM, *FA*, HARMONY, LEGALISM

3   Mohism is more pessimistic about the possibility of using power properly:

> Among the five weapons the sharpest will be broken first. Among the five swords the keenest will be first worn out. The sweet wells become sooner dry and the elegant trees are oftener felled. The tortoises that are more responsive are oftener burned and the snakes that show more magic power are more sacrificed. Thus, Pi Kan died of his uprightness ; Meng Fen perished by his strength ; Hsi Shih paid with her life for her beauty ; and Wu Ch'i was torn alive for his achievement. This shows that there are but few who excel other people and do not perish on account of it. Hence the saying : Position of the supreme is hard to keep.

Mozi (1974) *The Ethical and Political Works of Motse*, trans. Yi-Pao Mei, Taipai: Ch'eng Wen Publishing Company, pp. 3–4

See also MOHISM

---

4   A plea for gentlemanly behaviour in politics:

> Motse said: He who rules a large state does not attack small states: he who rules a large house does not molest small houses. The strong does not plunder the weak. The honoured does not disdain the humble. The clever does not deceive the stupid. This is beneficial to Heaven above, beneficial to the spirits in the middle sphere, and beneficial to the people below. Being beneficial to these three it is beneficial to all. So the most excellent name is attributed to such a man and he is called sage-king. . . .
>
> Motse said: The will of Heaven to me is like the compasses to the wheelwright and the square to the carpenter. The wheelwright and the carpenter measure all the square and circular objects with their square and compasses and accept those that fit as correct and reject those that do not fit as incorrect. The writings of the gentlemen of the world of the present day cannot be all loaded (in a cart), and their doctrines cannot be exhaustively enumerated. They endeavour to convince the feudal lords on the one hand and the scholars on the other. But from magnanimity and righteousness they are far off. How do we know? Because I have the most competent standard in the world to measure them with.

Ibid., 139, 140

See also HEAVEN, MOHISM

Daoism seeks to demystify power: 5

Ruling a large state is like cooking small fish.

When you use the Way to govern the world, evil spirits won't
have godlike power.
Actually, it's not that evil spirits won't have godlike power,
It's that their power will not harm men.
But it's not just that *their* power won't harm men,
The Sage, also, will not harm them.
Since these two do not harm others,
Therefore their Virtues intermingle and return to them.

Laozi (1989) *Te-Tao Ching*, trans. R. Henricks, New York: Ballantine Books,
Ch. 60 p. 29

See also ACTION, DAOISM, EVIL

PRAJNA

The links between knowledge and salvation are a key aspect of Indian and 1
Tibetan thought:

The perception of shunyata as openness is connected with the
development of what is known as *prajna*. Because there are some
very fantastic translations in vogue of this term prajna, it is
worthwhile having a good look at what the term means. There
are various words in Sanskrit which refer to the cognitive process.
Two most frequently used ones are prajna and jnana. If we
look at the words, we immediately notice that both contain the
root *jña*, which signifies the cognitive potentiality. Jnana is the
primary formation from this root in the Sanskrit language; in
prajna, the same root *jña* is there with the prefix *pra*.

If we look at the Tibetan translations for these terms, we
find that the very same root connection has been preserved.
The Tibetan for prajna is *shes-rab*, and for jnana it is *ye-shes*. In
both cases, the *shes*, the cognitive potentiality, is there. *Ye* means
"primordial" or "original." Thus ye-shes refers to primordial
awareness. The Sanskrit prefix *pra* and the Tibetan particle *rab*

have the sense of "heightening" or "intensification." Therefore, shes-rab or prajna refers to an intensification or heightening of the cognitive processes. The cognitive potentiality that is present in everyone is to be developed, intensified, and brought to its highest pitch. To bring this potentiality to its highest pitch means to release it, to free it from all the extraneous material that has accumulated. . . .

Freedom is inherent in all the cognitive processes. Here it helps to see that the opposite of freedom is not determination but compulsion. One is quite free to determine one's way of life, free to determine whether to look at things in a categorical way or an aesthetic way. That is, we can look at things relative to a set of goals to be achieved, or can simply appreciate them, and recognize their intrinsic value. So we must understand that freedom is a basic phenomenon and not some end-product of getting rid of something or subjecting oneself to some transcendental nebulosity, as it would seem that Western philosophy has generally approached it.

Prajna or shes-rab as the heightening of the cognitive capacity, also means a weakening of the network of relative considerations in which, ordinarily, it is embedded. The weakening of this network permits the emergence of the cognitive capacity in its original freedom.

Prajna operates on different levels. It is operative when we listen to someone merely on a rudimentary level, when we merely hear something that the person we are listening to says. Just to hear what someone is saying, some understanding must be there. Prajna can be present on a more significant level. For instance, we can go beyond the mere momentary taking in of what someone says, to the point where we retain it and think about it. This may lead us to weigh seriously what we have heard and to try implementing our conclusions such that we embody them in our lives.

Prajna can operate on a still further level. Instead of attending to what we perceive, hear or think about, in terms of categories related to the narrow limits of self-preservation or personal ends, we can come to appreciate things as values in themselves. When we come to this point there is a sort of a release, since there is no longer a need to manipulate our perceptions – we can let things be as they are. In speaking of arriving at this point it is possible to speak of freedom as an achievement, but we must see that this freedom has been there all the time. However, we have lost sight of this freedom through being involved with all sorts of unnecessary constructions – constantly seeing things as means in relation to our personal orientation. Having come to this basic appreciation and openness, we have the possibility of staying with it and seeing things as valuable, or we can fall back to seeing things as means for further means *ad infinitum*.

It is at this crucial point that shunyata comes in. Shunyata is the objective correlate of this heightened or opened state of awareness. In this state, we do not see different things but we do see things differently. When I meet someone, I can immediately snap into a state of mind where I am asking myself what I have to gain or lose from meeting this person and I can then involve myself in the appropriate strategy. Or, I can merely take in the impression of this person and relate to him without preconception. Very likely if I do the latter, a very satisfactory meeting will ensue. I have related to this open dimension of my impression. Now this is a very simple thing, there is nothing special about it and anybody can do it. But, as I have said, the simplest things are often the most difficult. Probably one of the most difficult things is for a person to do without his fixations and preconceptions.

Guenther, H. and Trungpa, C. (1975) *The Dawn of Tantra*, Berkeley: Shambhala, pp. 27–9

See also EMPTINESS

Wisdom is a "means of knowing" which releases a person from 2
the attachment to things. Within the context of our discussion regarding emptiness, wisdom is the presupposition for, and the culmination of, the negation of self-sufficient entities. The aim of wisdom is to melt the chains of greed and thirst for possession of "things." Or to state the same thing from the viewpoint of a religious goal, its aim is to relate oneself to all "things" in an *empty* relationship, i.e., in total freedom. . . .

Prajna (wisdom), which permitted one "to see things as they really are," was significant from a religious point of view since one "became" what one knew. In summary we would say that the insight into the emptiness of all things destroyed illusion; for this illusion was created by positing self-existence on "things" distinguished by perception or imagination. Wisdom was not itself an ultimate view, nor was it an assertion about an absolute being. Wisdom was the practice (*carya*) of dissolving the grasping-after-hoped-for-ultimates either in the phenomenal world or the realm of ideas. To know "emptiness" was to realize emptiness.

Streng, F. (1967) *Emptiness: A Study in Religious Meaning*, Nashville: Abingdon Press, pp. 82, 98

See also EMPTINESS, MADHYAMAKA

3   The source of the wisdom which leads to enlightenment is difficult to determine:

Buddhist logic assumes that the world of efficient causality, of things which exert force and constitute reality, is made up of momentary but completely distinct events. These events are taken to be, in themselves, completely different from one another; they have nothing in common, they share no qualities. But as we saw, it is difficult to explain, on this basis, how our mental activities fit into the series of events about which we care – or indeed to explain anything whatsoever, since explanation itself presupposes recognizable or repeated characters shared by several things. In particular, insight (*prajñā*), which is held to destroy ignorance, does not seem to be a forceful element in the external world but to belong to a different chain, a chain of non-forceful elements, if you will. Thus the Buddhists develop a mind-body dualism, and co-ordination is the relation which is supposed to span the gap. But just because it is a relation one of whose terms is nonforceful and the other of which is forceful, its *own* status becomes dubious. Moreover, we can't say that the mind exerts force and orders the elements in the world, since this contradicts the presupposed character of the mind and the world; nor can we say that the world exerts force on the mind but not vice-versa, since this removes freedom from our control.

Potter, K. (1972) *Presuppositions of India's Philosophies*, Westport, Conn.: Greenwood Press, pp. 187–8

See also ANALYSIS, CAUSATION, INFERENCE, LOGIC

PRAKRITI

The material aspect of the universe is described in the *Gita* in complex ways: **1**

Prakṛti is called *mahad brahma* (the great Brahma or the great multiplier as procreatress) in the *Gītā*, XIV. 3. It is said there that this *prakṛti* is described as being like the female part, which God charges with His energy for the creation of the universe. Wherever any living beings may be born, the great Brahman or *prakṛti* is to be considered as the female part and God as the father and fertilizer. Three types of qualities are supposed to be produced from *prakṛti* (*guṇāḥ prakṛti-sambhavāḥ*). These are *sattva, rajas* and *tamas*, which bind the immortal self in its corporeal body. Of these, *sattva*, on account of its purity, is illuminating and untroubling (*anāmayam*, which Śrīdhara explains as *nirupadravam śāntam*), and consequently, on account of these two qualities, binds the self with the attachment for knowledge (*jñāna-saṅgena*) and the attachment for pleasure (*sukha-saṅgena*). It is said that there are no living beings on earth, or gods in the heavens, who are not pervaded by the three *guṇas* produced from the *prakṛti*. Since the *guṇas* are produced from the *prakṛti* through the fertilization of God's energy in *prakṛti*, they may be said to be produced by God, though God always transcends them. The quality of *sattva*, as has been said above, associates the self with the attachments for pleasure and knowledge. The quality of *rajas* moves to action and arises from desire and attachment (*tṛṣṇā-saṅga-samudbhavam*), through which it binds the self with egoistic attachments for action. The quality of *tamas* overcomes the illumination of knowledge and leads to many errors. *Tamas*, being a product of ignorance, blinds all living beings and binds them down with carelessness, idleness and sleep. These three qualities predominate differently at different times. Thus, sometimes the quality of *sattva* predominates over *rajas* and *tamas*, and such a time is characterized by the rise of knowledge in the mind through all the different sense-gates; when *rajas* dominates *sattva* and *tamas*, the mind is characterized by greed, efforts and endeavours for different kinds of action and the rise of passions, emotions and desires; when *tamas* predominates over *sattva* and *rajas*, there is ignorance, lethargy, errors, delusions and false beliefs.

Dasgupta, S. (1932) *A History of Indian Philosophy*, II, Cambridge: Cambridge University Press, p. 462

See also GUNAS

2   The material has to be sharply distinguished from the mental, according to the Sankhya-Yoga theory:

On the Sāṅkhya-Yoga account, the realm of *prakṛti* or matter is held to be inherently unconscious, and is thereby incapable of producing consciousness as an effect. The manifestations of *prakṛti* are always objects, and it is argued that objects can never transform themselves into subjects. Thus at the heart of this dualistic position is the notion that mind–material is not capable of *generating* consciousness out of unconscious ingredients. Subjective awareness is a distinct ontological category, and in principle it cannot be derived from the stuff of which objects are made. So, in sharp contrast to the western approach, the mind and the cognitive activities it sustains are held to be intrinsically unconscious, since *manas, buddhi* and *ahamkāra* are all manifestations of *prakṛti*.

According to the ancient view, the dynamics of *prakṛti* are governed by the interactions of the three *guṇas*, which are the basic types of constituent of physical substance. The three *guṇas* are *sattva, rajas* and *tamas*, which correspond roughly with 'transparency and buoyancy,' 'energy and activity,' and 'inertia and obstruction.' All physical phenomena are believed to consist of unstable mixtures of these three types of constituent, and the instability of these mixtures is responsible for the evolution and transformations of the material world. Thus the conceptual processes sustained by the mind are governed by the mechanical and unconscious interplay of the *guṇas*, and to this extent, mental phenomena are viewed in purely 'physicalistic' or mechanical terms. The unfolding of thought-forms is an integral part of the evolution of *prakṛti*, and mental processes are simply the result of appropriate transformations of unconscious material substance. It is worth noting at this point that the Sāṅkhya-Yoga view thereby avoids one of the most serious pitfalls of Cartesian dualism, since on the Indian account, mental causation does not violate physical conservation laws. By including the mind in the realm of matter, mental events are granted causal efficacy, and are therefore able to directly initiate bodily motions.

Schweitzer, P. (1993) 'Mind/Consciousness Dualism in Sankhya-Yoga Philosophy', *Philosophy and Phenomenological Research*, LIII, 4, 845–59, pp. 848–9

See also BUDDHI, GUNAS, MANAS, SANKHYA-YOGA

The most frequent use of the notion of matter in Indian thought lies in its 3
relationship with spirit (*purusha*):

> The difference which the structure of apprehension makes
> in attaining liberation can be seen, for instance, by comparing
> one of the ontological presuppositions of Sāṃkhya-Yoga with
> the denial of this presupposition by Nāgārjuna. In the former
> view both "substance" (*prakṛti*) and spirit (*puruṣa*) are considered
> to be real and eternal. Liberation is achieved in realizing the
> pure *puruṣa* as distinct from the complex of psycho-mental
> experiences which forms the notion of the ego and which
> resulted from the confusion of *puruṣa* with *prakṛti*. Nāgārjuna, on
> the other hand, maintains that such realization does not effect
> release, for both a phenomenal and a transcendental entity are
> empty of self-existence.

Streng, F. (1967) *Emptiness: A Study in Religious Meaning*, Nashville:
Abingdon Press, p. 145

See also MOKSHA

PURVA-MIMAMSA AND VEDANTA

We may now have a look at the last group, that of the *Pūrva-* 1
Mīmāṃsā and the *Vedānta*. The main text of the first system is the
Pūrva-Mīmāṃsā Sūtra by Jaimini (*c.* 400 B.C.). It is a scholastic
piece of work and confines itself almost entirely to the interpretation of the *Vedas*. This school of philosophy is interested mainly
in inquiring into the nature of *dharma* (right action), and since
it accepts the *Vedas* to be both infallible and the sole authority
on *dharma*, one can call it a fairly orthodox school. Its interest
is more practical than speculative and its importance is less as a
school of philosophy than as a useful system of interpreting the
Vedas.

Perhaps the most influential of the philosophical systems has
been, and still is, the *Vedānta*. It springs from the *Upanishads* and
its central thesis is the Upanishadic doctrine of the *Brahman*. Its
founder was Bādarāyaṇa, whose *Brahma Sūtra* (also called the

Uttar-Mīmāṃsā) makes up, along with the *Upanishads* and the *Bhagavad-Gītā*, the foundation of the *Vedānta* system. The most famous exponent of the *Vedānta* was undoubtedly Śaṃkara, who lived in South India in the eighth century A.D. There are two main divisions in the *Vedānta* school, one rigidly non-dualistic (*advaita*) in its outlook and the other tolerating various degrees of dualism (*dvaita*). Śaṃkara was the champion of the former branch of the school.

Śaṃkara was preceded by Gauḍapāda, a believer in a very strict form of monism. He asserted categorically that the external world was unreal, the only reality being the *Brahman*. Outer objects are purely subjective, and dreams are hardly different from our experiences while we are awake. The whole world is a vast illusion and nothing exists other than the *Brahman*. Like the Buddhist spiritual absolutist Nāgārjuna, Gauḍapāda denies the possibility of change or the validity of causation. 'There is no destruction, no creation, none in bondage, none endeavouring [for release], none desirous of liberation, none liberated; this is the absolute truth.'

Śaṃkara's position is less extreme. While asserting the identity of the *Brahman* with the *Ātman*, and denying that the world was outside the Supreme, he did not accept the description of the world as a pure illusion. Waking experiences are different from dreams and external objects are not merely forms of personal consciousness. Śaṃkara explains the appearance of the world with an analogy. A person may mistake a rope for a serpent. The serpent is not there, but it is not entirely an illusion, for there is the rope. The appearance of the serpent lasts until the rope is closely examined. The world can be compared with the serpent and the *Brahman* with the rope. When we acquire true knowledge we recognize that the world is only a manifestation of the *Brahman*. The world is neither real nor quite unreal; it is an appearance based on the existence of the *Brahman*. The precise relationship between the *Brahman* and the world is inexpressible and is sometimes referred to as *māyā*.

Statements about *Brahman*, to be intelligible, must use empirical forms. The wise recognize these forms to be necessities of concrete thought, but fools take them to be the real truth. One must also recognize that the relationship between the *Brahman* and the world is not reversible. There will be no world without the *Brahman*, but the existence of the *Brahman* does not depend on the appearance of the world, just as the appearance of the serpent depends on the existence of the rope but not vice versa.

The *jīva*, or the individual soul, is a particular manifestation of the *Brahman*. Because of *avidyā* (ignorance), the root of all troubles, the ego-feeling exists. The end is liberation, and that is achieved through a practical realization (not merely a theoretical acceptance) of the oneness of the self with the Absolute. If a person reaches this state he becomes *jīvan-mukta*, i.e. liberated while alive. Realizing the oneness of all, his life becomes one of unselfish service. At death his freedom from bondage is complete. Casting off the physical body, the soul becomes completely free.

Somewhat different interpretations of the *Upanishads* were put forward by some later Vedāntists. Two *Vaishṇava* scholars, Rāmānuja and Madhva, were prominent among the branch of the *Vedānta* that is sometimes called dualistic (*dvaita*). Rāmānuja's philosophy was in fact a different version of the *advaita* doctrine. To put it in a few words, he claimed that the world, the *Ātman* and God (*Īśvara*) are distinct though not separate. The individual souls and the concrete world are like the body of God, and *Īśvara* possessed of the two is the *Brahman*. Thus, everything is within the *Brahman*, but still individual souls are different from *Īśvara*. The thesis, as we shall see later, helped the intellectual acceptance of the *Bhakti* movement, i.e. the approach to God through devotion rather than through knowledge.

Rāmānuja belonged to the eleventh century. Madhva came in the thirteenth. He believed in the dualism of the *Brahman* and the *jīva* (the individual souls). His philosophy is, thus, called *Dvaita*. In fact he also accepted the existence of the physical world, thereby introducing a third entity. *Brahman*, or God (*Vishṇu*), is of course complete, perfect, and the highest reality, but the world too is real. The differences between Śaṃkara's philosophy and that of Madhva can be readily noticed. The *Vaishṇava* movement, as one might imagine, owed much to the contribution of Madhva.

Sen, K. (1973) *Hinduism*, Harmondsworth: Penguin, pp. 82–5

See also ATMAN, BHAGAVAD GITA, BRAHMAN, DHARMA, GOD, JIVA, MAYA, UPANISHADS

SAMSARA

1   The cycle of death and rebirth is a central idea in Indian philosophies:

The going from birth to death, this travelling, is what is called Samsâra in Sanskrit, the round of birth and death literally. All creation, passing through this round, will sooner or later become free. The question may be raised that if we all shall come to freedom, why should we *struggle* to attain it? If every one is going to be free, we will sit down and wait. It is true that every being will become free, sooner or later; no one can be lost. Nothing can come to destruction; everything must come up. If that is so, what is the use of our struggling? In the first place, the struggle is the only means that will bring us to the centre, and in the second place, we do not know why we struggle. We have to. "Of thousands of men some are awakened to the idea that they will become free." The vast masses of mankind are content with material things, but there are some who awake, and want to get back, who have had enough of this playing down here. These struggle consciously while the rest do it unconsciously.

Vivekananda, S. (1961) *Jnana-Yoga*, Calcutta: Advaita Ashrama, pp. 325–6

See also AFTERLIFE, DEATH, *JIVANMUKTI*

SAMKHYA/SANKHYA-YOGA

1   The Sāṅkhya school, or *darśana*, is one of the oldest philosophical traditions of India, and many of its ideas are traceable to the Ṛgveda and the early Upaniṣads. Its historical founder is Kapila, though the original *Sāṅkhyasūtras* (aphorisms) he is said to have written during the 6th or 7th century B.C. are now lost, and the most important of the existing texts is the *Sāṅkhyakārikā* (explanatory verses) of Īśvarakṛṣṇa, from around the 3rd century A.D. The Sāṅkhya tradition has a great many theoretical points in common with the classical Yoga *darśana* as expounded in Patañjali's *Yogasūtra*, probably written somewhere from the 4th to the 2nd century B.C., and the metaphysical position discussed in the present paper is part of their shared philosophical framework. Thus the basic dualism between consciousness and matter, as well

as more specific allied points, will henceforth be referred to, somewhat generically, as the 'Sāṅkhya-Yoga view.'

According to the Sāṅkhya-Yoga view, the ultimate principle underlying matter is *prakṛti*, the metaphysical substrate supporting all material phenomena. The mind is deemed to be part of the material world, and hence to be metaphysically grounded in *prakṛti*.

Schweitzer, P. (1993) 'Mind/Consciousness Dualism in Sankhya-Yoga Philosophy', *Philosophy and Phenomenological Research*, LIII, 4, 845–59, p. 847

See also PRAKRITI, UPANISHADS

Although the Sankhya and the Yoga schools are distinct, they are often linked into one common theory: 2

The *Sāṃkhya* school was founded by Kapila, who lived probably in the seventh century B.C. The system is in one sense dualistic, since it recognizes two basic categories in the universe – the *purusha* and the *prakṛiti*. The *purusha* consists of selves or spirits, eternal entities of consciousness. The *prakṛiti* represents the potentiality of nature, the basis of all objective existence. It does not consist of matter alone and includes all resources of nature, material and psychical. The *prakṛiti* is thus the fundamental substance out of which, the *Sāṃkhya* claims, the world evolves. This evolution of the *prakṛiti* is possible only under the influence of the *purusha*, and the history of the world is the history of this evolution.

The *Sāṃkhya* believes very strongly in the principle of causation, and in fact uses this to show the necessity of assuming the eternal existence of *prakṛiti*, for something cannot come out of nothing. But, claims the *Sāṃkhya* school, while the cause and the effect are different things distinct from each other, the effect is always present in the cause. The former is just a different arrangement of the latter, both consisting of the same substance. A jar is *not* a lump of clay from which it is made, but they consist of the same substance. There is an underlying assumption of the indestructibility of substance. This view of causality has been strongly criticized by the *Nyayā-Vaiśeshika* school. A part of the difference between the two is verbal, but there is also a more real element in the difference between their respective views of causality and, hence, of evolution.

Another important *Sāṃkhya* contribution to Hindu thought is the doctrine of *triguṇa*, the three qualities of nature. The three qualities are *sattva* (light, purity, harmonious existence), *rajas* (energy, passion), and *tamas* (inertia, darkness). These three conflicting aspects of *prakṛiti* play different parts in its evolution. *Sattva* is primarily responsible for the manifestations of *prakṛiti* and the maintenance of its evolution. *Rajas* causes all activity and *tamas* is responsible for inertia and restraint. While these qualities conflict with each other, they all have their part in the evolution. Evolution proceeds through various stages. There is first the development of *buddhi* (intellect), described as the *mahat* (great). Then evolves the self-sense, the feeling of ego. Gradually develop the five cognitive organs, the five motor organs, and the disciplined mind.

For emancipation from the bondage of one's body, what is needed is the knowledge of the distinction between the *purusha* and the *prakṛiti*, the self and non-self. The self tends to confuse itself with *buddhi*, the intellect. When the knowledge of the distinction is achieved, the soul is no longer bound by the *prakṛiti*. The person becomes a disinterested spectator of the happenings in the world. At death the bond between the *purusha* and the *prakṛiti* is completely dissolved and the emancipated soul, unlike other souls is free from rebirth. Bondage, according to this philosophy, is due to ignorance, and emancipation comes through knowledge.

The *Saṃkhya* has been described as an atheistic philosophy, though this is not entirely correct. The *Sāṃkhya-pravacana Sūtra* (attributed to Kapila) finds it unnecessary to make the assumption of the existence of God, though it does not deny it either. It maintains that the existence of God cannot be *proved* by evidence. The later *Sāṃkhya* philosophers seem to abandon this agnostic position and the existence of God is later accepted. Vijñānabhikshu even tries to reconcile the *Sāṃkhya* views with those of the *Vedānta*

The philosophical basis of the *Yoga* is the same as that of the *Sāṃkhya*, except that a personal God is introduced into the system. God controls the process of evolution and is, as one might expect, Omniscient and Omnipotent. Periodically He dissolves the cosmos and then initiates the process of evolution again.

In practice, the *Yoga* system of discipline consists of exercises of the mind and the body, including the very difficult exercise of not exercising them *at all*. In addition to making us healthier in mind and body in this world, these exercises are supposed to facilitate emancipation. Unlike the *Sāṃkhya* system, the *Yoga* school does not believe that freedom comes only from knowledge; the discipline of the mind and the body is supposed to contribute to the process. Various methods of concentration are recommended, as well as methods of suppressing those mental activities that increase our bondage by making us more dependent on *prakṛti*.

Sen, K. (1973) *Hinduism*, Harmondsworth: Penguin, pp. 80–2

See also GOD, *GUNAS, PRAKRITI*

The Sāṃkhya-Yoga is usually classed as one of the six schools of Indian philosophy. This may lead to misunderstanding; for in so far as the Sāṃkhya analyses the nature of the universe, it falls more properly within the sphere of cosmology, and in so far as it concerns itself with the nature of human personality, it must be classed as a branch of psychology. Indeed the whole idea of the 'self' as distinct from the 'ego' (*puruṣa* and *ahaṃkāra* in the Sāṃkhya system) has now received the blessing of C. G. Jung and the whole school of psychology to which he has given his name. There is, of course, a fundamental difference between Jung and the Sāṃkhya-Yoga since, in Jung's sense of the word, the 'self' is seen indeed as the immortal centre of the human personality, but the aim of his psychological method is not only to bring the self to light and enable it to displace the ego as the directing principle of the total psyche, but also to harmonize the rest of the psyche around this new centre, whereas the aim of the Sāṃkhya-Yoga is to divorce for ever the immortal self from all purely spatio-temporal elements in the psyche. Jung sees the process as 'individuation' or 'integration of the personality': the Sāṃkhya-Yogin sees it as the 'isolation' of the 'person' – for that is what *puruṣa* means – from the psycho-physical envelope which surrounds him.

Zaehner, R. (1958) *At Sundry Times: An Essay in the Comparison of Religions*, London: Faber, p. 42

See also SELF

SELF

1 Buddhism is fascinated with the notion of the self:

> For Buddhism categorically to assert the distinction between
> conventional and ultimate truth is, of course, not enough. The
> questions which arise from its acceptance of the *saṃsāra/karma*
> belief system, and its simultaneous denial of a permanent self
> or person are legion, and King Milinda asks many of them, for
> example 'Who is reborn?' Nāgasena replies 'name-and-form';
> not in the sense that it is reborn unchanged, but in the sense that
> 'one does a good or evil deed with (one) name-and-form, and
> because [or "by means"] of this deed [instrumental case] another
> name-and-form is reborn'. If any 'individual' needs to be
> identified as the subject of the first verb here, it is the illusory and
> impermanent 'I' of each lifetime, the *attabhāva*. Each lifetime,
> delimited by the birth and death of the physical element, is a
> collection of impersonal elements – summarised here as 'name-
> and-form'. From this collection, with the help of 'the conceit "I
> am"', arises the phenomenological *sense* of personal agency
> which, in Buddhist eyes, is the only truth corresponding to the
> linguistic usage of active verbs with an implied subject. The
> monk continues by adducing a number of comparisons: a man
> who has stolen some mangoes claims himself to be innocent of
> theft, on the grounds that the mangoes he stole were different
> from the mangoes the owner had planted. A man lit a fire to
> warm himself, and left it alight when he went away; it burned a
> neighbour's field, but the man claims himself to be innocent on
> the grounds that the fire he failed to put out was different from
> the fire which burned the field. Similar defences are given by a
> man whose lamp set fire first to a house then to a whole village;
> and by a man who married a girl who had previously, as a child,
> been betrothed to another (along with the bride-price).

Collins, S. (1982) *Selfless Persons: Imagery and Thought in Theravada Buddhism*,
Cambridge: Cambridge University Press, p. 185

See also ANATMAN, ATMAN, CONSCIOUSNESS, *KARMA*,
SAMSARA

2 The Personalist controversy discussed how far Buddhists are allowed to
talk of selves. Some Buddhists accepted the critique of the permanent self

but nonetheless argued that there remains a sort of ephemeral self. Vasubandhu, the Indian 5th century CE thinker, reported the issue in his *Abhidharmakosha* thus:

> Is final deliverance then possible outside this Dharma, and can it be won on the basis of non-Buddhist doctrines? – No, it cannot, for all other teachings are corrupted by false ideas about a 'self'. Instead of taking it as a mere conventional term applied to a series of impersonal processes, they believe in a self which is a substance independent of the Skandhas. But the mere belief in such a self must of necessity generate defilements. Those who hold it will be forced to pursue life in the Samsaric world, and will be unable to free themselves completely from it.
>
> *The Personalist thesis, first part:* But is it not true that a Buddhist school, the Personalists, speak of a Person who is neither identical with the Skandhas, nor different from them? And is not this Person a kind of self? And yet, as Buddhists they should be able to win deliverance! – We must ask ourselves whether this Person exists as a real entity, i.e. as one of the separate elements of existence, like the elementary sight-objects, sounds, and so on, which careful analysis reveals; or whether it has a merely nominal existence, which denotes a combination of simple elements, as 'milk' is a combination of sights, smells, tastes and touchables.
>
> *The Personalist:* Why should not either assumption be true? – *Vasubandhu:* If the Person is a real entity with a nature of its own, it must be different from the elementary data, just as these are different from one another. It must then be either produced by causes, or unconditioned. In the first case it is not eternal, as you maintain, and you must be able to state its conditions in detail. In the second case you adopt a clearly non-Buddhistic doctrine, and, in addition, your Person could not do anything, and would be a rather useless hypothesis. The Person is therefore unlikely to be a real entity. But if you regard it as a mere designation, then your view does not differ in the least from ours. – *The Personalist:* We claim that there is a Person; but we do not say that he is an entity. Nor do we believe that he exists merely as a designation for the Skandhas. What we say is that the word 'Person' denotes a kind of structural unity which is found in correlation with the Skandhas of one individual, i.e. with those elements which are actually present, internal to him, and appropriated by him.

The Personalist thesis, second part: The Personalist also teaches that the Person is 'ineffable', that his relation to the elements cannot be defined, that he is neither identical nor non-identical with them. He distinguishes five kinds of cognizable things – the first three are the conditioned dharmas, i.e. those past, future and present; the fourth is the Unconditioned; and the fifth is the 'ineffable', and refers to the Person. – But if the Person were quite ineffable, if nothing at all could be stated about it, then one could also not say of it either that it is the fifth category or that it is not!

Conze, E. (1976) *Buddhist Scriptures*, Harmondsworth: Penguin, pp. 192–3

See also ANATMAN, CAUSATION, CONSCIOUSNESS

SKILFUL MEANS

1   Although the doctrine of skilful means is typically regarded as Buddhist, and is discussed in the section on Mahayana, it is interesting to note a very similar idea in Islamic philosophy, as presented here by Avicenna (ibn Sina):

As for religious law, one general principle is important, namely that religions and their laws, produced by a prophet, seek to communicate with the masses as a whole. It is obvious that the deeper truths concerning the real unity, that there is one maker who is exalted above quantity, quality, place, time, position and change, which lead to the belief that God is one without anyone sharing his species, that he contains no parts . . . that he cannot be pointed to as existing in a particular place, it is obvious that these deeper truths cannot be passed on to the multitude. For if this had been communicated in its true form to the bedouin Arabs and the crude Hebrews, they would have immediately refused to believe and would have unanimously declared that the belief which it was proposed they accept was belief in an absolute nonentity.

Rahman, F. (1958) *Prophecy in Islam*, London: George Allen & Unwin, p. 42

See also MAHAYANA

SUFISM

Mysticism has difficulties with expressing itself in language: **1**

> The scientific observation of Nature keeps us in close contact with the behaviour of Reality, and thus sharpens our inner perception for a deeper vision of it. I cannot help quoting here a beautiful passage from the mystic poet Rumi in which he describes the mystic quest after Reality:
>
> > The Sufi's book is not composed of ink and letters: it is not but a heart white as snow. The scholar's possession is pen-marks. What is the Sufi's possession? – foot-marks. The Sufi stalks the game like a hunter: he sees the musk-deer's track and follows the footprints. For some while the track of the deer is the proper clue for him, but afterwards it is the musk-gland of the deer that is his guide. To go one stage guided by the scent of the musk-gland is better than a hundred stages of following the track and roaming about.
>
> The truth is that all search for knowledge is essentially a form of prayer. The scientific observer of Nature is a kind of mystic seeker in the act of prayer. Although at present he follows only the footprints of the musk-deer, and thus modestly limits the method of his quest, his thirst for knowledge is eventually sure to lead him to the point where the scent of the musk-gland is a better guide than the footprints of the deer. This alone will add to his power over Nature and give him that vision of the total-infinite which philosophy seeks but cannot find. Vision without power does bring moral elevation but cannot give a lasting culture. Power without vision tends to become destructive and inhuman. Both must combine for the spiritual expansion of humanity.

Iqbal, M. (1934) *The Reconstruction of Religious Thought in Islam*, London: Oxford University Press, pp. 86–7

See also LANGUAGE

TANTRA

Tantric Buddhism argues in favour of the transformation of physical **1**
processes into salvific experiences:

According to all schools of Tantra, bliss is the nature of the Absolute, which is conceived both positively and negatively. The Absolute is realised by us when we realise our self as perfect bliss. The ultimate aim is, therefore, to attain a state of perfect bliss. In all our ordinary experiences of pleasure we have but a momentary glimpse of the same bliss as constitutes the ultimate nature of our self. But these experiences of pleasure, because of their extremely limited and defiled nature, bind us to a lower plane of life, instead of contributing to our advancement towards self-realisation. Herein comes the question of Sādhanā which may transform even gross sense-pleasure into the boundless serenity of perfect bliss.

In our ordinary life we have the experience of the most intense pleasure in our sex-experiences. Wide is the difference between this sex-pleasure and perfect bliss which is the ultimate nature of the self and the not-self; yet the distinction can be wholly removed by a total change of perspective and process. The sexo-yogic Sādhanā of the Tāntrikas is a Sādhanā for transforming this sex-pleasure into a realisation of infinite bliss in which the self and the world around are lost in an all-pervading oneness. This immersion of the self and the not-self in the all-pervading oneness of bliss is what is conceived as Nirvāṇa by the Tāntric Buddhists.

Dasgupta, S. B. (1974) *An Introduction to Tantric Buddhism*, Berkeley: Shambhala, pp. 145–6

See also NIRVANA, SELF

TATHATA / TATHAGATA

1   Fundamental to the notion of Buddhism is the idea of suchness, of how things really are:

When the mind of all creatures, which in its own nature is pure and clear, is stirred up by the wind of ignorance (*avidyā*), the waves of mentality (*vijñāna*) make their appearance'. So the external world, with all its variety and complexity, has no real existence and as such the fundamental nature of things is neither namable nor explicable. Things have no signs of distinction, they possess absolute sameness (*samatā*). But how can all beings conform to and have an insight into suchness? The answer is, – 'As soon as you understand that when the totality of existence is spoken of, or thought of, there is neither that which speaks, nor that which is spoken of, there is neither that which thinks nor that which is thought of; then you conform to suchness; and when your subjectivity is thus completely obliterated, it is said to have the insight'.

This 'suchness' of things may be viewed under two aspects, negative and positive. On its negative side (*śūnyatā*) it asserts the complete negation of all the attributes of all things; in its metaphysical origin it has nothing to do with things defiled, which are conditional or relative by nature, – it is free from all signs of distinction existing among phenomenal objects, – it is independent of unreal, particularising consciousness. The suchness is 'neither that which is existence, nor that which is non-existence, nor that which is at once existence and non-existence, nor that which is not at once existence and non-existence; it is neither that which is unity, nor that which is plurality, nor that which is at once unity and plurality, nor that which is not at once unity and plurality'. In a word, as suchness cannot be comprehended by the particularising consciousness of all beings, we call it the negation (*śūnyatā*). The 'tathatā' is *śūnya* (void) for two reasons, – firstly, there is no content in it, it being the oneness of the totality of things; secondly, there is neither any subject to comprehend it; so that its nature involves the denial of both the subject and the object; there is neither that which is negated, nor that which negates – both being absorbed in the nature of the 'tathatā'.

But this 'tathatā' may also be viewed as something positive (*aśūnyatā*) in the sense that it contains infinite merits, that it is self-existent. By the non-void nature of the 'tathatā' should never be meant any sort of affirmation on it, – we can have only a glimpse of the truth by transcending our subjective categories.

The quintessence of all things is one and the same, perfectly calm and tranquil, and shows no sign of becoming; ignorance, however, is in its blindness and delusion oblivious of enlightenment and on that account cannot recognise truthfully all those conditions, differences and activities which characterise the phenomena of the universe. The annihilation of ignorance is, therefore, the only way of liberation from the cycle of birth and death. But it should also be remembered that the mere eradication of ignorance is not sufficient to guarantee liberation, for, so long as there will remain a mind, ignorance may recur at any time; so the total extinction of mind is the safest course for attaining eternal liberation.

Dasgupta, S. B. (1974) *An Introduction to Tantric Buddhism*, Berkeley: Shambhala, pp. 20–1

See also *MOKSHA*

2   The account of suchness or thusness in the Tian Tai school is of something which does not change:

This mind is the same as the Mind of Pure Self-nature, True Thusness, Buddha-nature, Dharma-body, the Storehouse of the Thus-come (Tathāgata), the Realm of Dharmas, and Dharma-nature. . . .

Question: Why is it called the Mind of Pure Self-nature?

Answer: Although this mind has been obscured from time immemorial by contaminating dharmas based on ignorance, yet its nature of purity has never changed. Hence it is called pure. Why? Because contaminating dharmas based on ignorance are from the beginning separated from the mind. Why do we say that they are separated? Because dharmas with ignorance as their substance are nonexistent dharmas. Their existence is the same as nonexistence. Since they are nonexistent, they cannot be associated with the mind. Therefore we say they are separated. Since there are no contaminating dharmas based on ignorance to be associated with it, therefore it is called pure in nature. Being central (without going to the extreme) and real, it is originally awakened. It is therefore called the mind. For these reasons it is called the Mind of Pure self-nature.

Question: Why is it called True Thusness (True Reality)?

Answer: All dharmas depend on this mind for their being and take the mind as their substance. When it is compared with dharmas all of them are unreal and imaginary, and their existence is the same as non-existence. Contrasted with these unreal and false dharmas, the mind is regarded as true.

Furthermore, although dharmas are really nonexistent, because they are caused by illusion and imagination, they have the character of coming into and going out of existence. When unreal dharmas come into existence, this mind does not come into existence, and when the dharmas go out of existence, this mind does not go out of existence. Not coming into existence, it is therefore not increased, and not going out of existence, it is therefore not decreased. Because it neither comes into nor goes out of existence and is neither increased nor decreased, it is called true. The Buddhas of the three ages (past, present, and future) and all sentient beings have this one Pure Mind as their substance. All ordinary and saintly beings and dharmas each have their own differences and differentiated characters. But this True Mind has neither differentiation nor characters. It is therefore called Thusness.

Chan, Wing-Tsit (1963) *A Source Book in Chinese Philosophy*, Princeton: Princeton University Press, pp. 399–400

See also DHARMA, TIAN TAI

TENDAI

Japanese version of Tian Tai

TIAN TAI

This school is to be distinguished from the Yogachara school. For Tian Tai, the world is not solely the product of consciousness: 1

> The central doctrines of the T'ien-t'ai School may be summed up in its three common sayings, namely, "the true nature of all dharmas (elements of existence)"; "the perfect harmony of the Three Levels of Truth;" and "the three thousand worlds immanent in an instance of thought." By the perfect harmony of the Three Levels of Truth is meant that all dharmas are empty because they have no nature of their own but depend on causes for their production. This is the Truth of Emptiness. But dharmas *are* produced and do possess temporary and dependent existence. This is Temporary Truth. Being both empty and temporary is the very nature of dharmas. This is the Truth of the Mean. The three involve each other, for Emptiness renders dharmas really empty, dependent existence makes them relatively real, and the Mean embraces both. Consequently the three are one and one is three. This mutual identity is the true state of all dharmas.

In the realm of Temporary Truth, that is, the phenomenal world, there are ten realms: Buddhas, bodhisattvas, buddhas-for-themselves, direct disciples of the Buddha, heavenly beings, spirits, human beings, departed beings, beasts, and depraved men. Since each of these involves the others, there are thus one hundred realms. Each of these in turn possesses the Ten Characters of Thusness: character, nature, substance, energy, activity, cause, condition, effect, retribution, and being ultimate from beginning to end, that is, each is "thus-caused," "thus-natured," and so forth. Each of these consists of living beings, of space, and of aggregates (matter, sensation, thought, disposition, and consciousness). The result is three thousand worlds, which is the totality of manifested reality.

This does not mean a pluralistic universe but one in which one is all and all is one. The worlds are so interpenetrated that they are said to be "immanent in a single instant of thought." This is not to say that they are produced by any mind, for production implies a sequence in time. Nor are they to be thought of as being included in an instant of thought, for inclusion implies space. Rather, it means that all the possible worlds are so much identified that they are involved in every moment of thought. In other words, all phenomena are manifestations of the Mind of Pure Nature and each manifestation is the Mind in its totality.

This Mind is to be carefully differentiated from that of the Consciousness-Only School. The world is not consciousness itself but the manifestation of the Mind. It is not in constant transformation as is the Mind of the Consciousness-Only School. Instead, it does not change. Since it involves all, it cannot, like the Consciousness-Only School, exclude a certain group of people from salvation. In fact, one of the outstanding features of T'ien-t'ai is the doctrine of universal salvation. Since everything involves everything else, it follows that all beings possess Buddha-nature and are therefore capable of salvation. The logical position of the T'ien-t'ai School cannot tolerate any different position, although the Confucian doctrine that everyone can become a sage definitely prepared for it. As to methods for salvation, the school lays dual emphasis on concentration and insight.

Chan, Wing-tsit (1963) *A Source Book in Chinese Philosophy*, Princeton: Princeton University Press, pp. 396–7

See also CONFUCIANISM, ENLIGHTENMENT, *TATHAGATA*, YOGACHARA

TIME

In the Warring States period (476–221 B.C.) the Mohist school 1 gave a relatively scientific definition of time: "'Jiu' includes all the various units of time." In other words, 'jiu' is the sum of all the different moments and periods, such as antiquity, the present, sunrise, and sunset. It represents the continuity of the processes of matter. "Time possesses both 'jiu' and the absence of 'jiu'. . . . 'Jiu' is both finite and infinite." Here "the absence of 'jiu'" refers to situations where the continuous time interval approaches zero, such as the instant when motion begins. (The beginning should be "the absence of 'jiu'" or timeless.) 'Finite' means that the continuing time of any change in the motion of an object is limited. But this is neither the beginning nor the end of time itself because other things are still in motion. Only when all things stop moving can we say that 'jiu' has ended. ("'jin,' or exhaustion, means motion has stopped.") As a matter of fact, while motion continues, time is infinite. This shows that the Mohists had already recognized the inseparability of time and the motion of things and, further, that they regarded time as the unity of the finite and the infinite. The Mohists also emphasized the abstractness of the concept of time. ("'Jiu' cannot be seen with the eyes. . . . Knowledge does not come from the five senses.") They believed that the concept of time is an abstraction which lies beyond the perceptions of the five sense organs and specific forms of motion and reflects the generality and universality of the motion of things.

The Mohist concept of time is the product of an awakening awareness of time which occurred after the Spring and Autumn Period. Confucius compared time to a river, sighing, "time is just like this flowing river." This is an emotional description of such an awakening. Rapid changes in the world make people hold time in awe. No wonder the story of the origin of the world in *The Book of Master Zhuang (Zhuang Zi)* refers to fast-moving time ('shu' and 'hu') as the active force which motivates the creation of heaven and earth. This means that time is neither generated nor finite. Master Zhuang not only described the infinity of time, noting that "'zhou' is something which grows yet has no origin" but also logically proved that "everything that has a beginning must be preceded by another beginning which in turn must be preceded by yet another and so on to infinity." Thus it's natural that Zhang Hen of the Han Dynasty should conclude that "the beginning of the universe is infinite."

Luo Jiachang (1996) "Time: A Philosophical Survey" in F. Dainian and R. Cohen (eds) *History and Philosophy of Science and Technology*, Dordrecht: Kluwer, 77–94, p. 78

See also CONFUCIANISM, DAOISM, MOHISM

---

2   Time and space, in both the special theory of relativity and the modern model of the universe, together form a unified whole. This is an important characteristic of Einstein's concept of time and space and differs from Newton's absolute time and absolute space which are separate.

During the Warring States period, Shi Jiao gave a profound definition of the 'cosmos' ('yu zhou'), "Yu means the four directions and up and down, and zhou includes the past and the present." In fact, this understanding was not confined to isolated individuals. A similar discussion appears in the *Mohist Canon (Mo Jing)*, "Yu incorporates different places . . . jiu [zhou] is composed of different times." *Jing Shuo* also explains that "'yu' embodies east, west, south and north . . . and 'jiu' encompasses past and present, dawn and dusk." It can be seen that 'yu' refers to space and 'zhou' to time. 'Yuzhou' is thus the unity of space and time. This is very clear.

The Mohist Canon describes how time and space are unified. "'Yu' moves or stops in 'jiu.'" The *Jing Shuo* explains that "'Yu' moves or stops, from north to south, from dawn to dusk: in all 'yu' there is floating 'jiu.'" That is to say, the movement of things must pass through a certain space and time, from this place at this time to that place at that time. For instance, from south to north, from dawn to dusk. The passing of time and changes in space are closely interrelated. Space and time are unified in the motion of matter.

Lishi, F. and Youyuan, Z. (1996) "Concepts of Space and Time in Ancient China and in Modern Cosmology", in Ibid., Dainian and Cohen, pp. 56–7

See also MOHISM

Classical Confucians did not engage in much metaphysical   **3**
metaphorizing like their Daoist contemporaries. That they did
not feel the need to do so may have come in part from their
appreciation of the Daoist formulation of the common Chinese
heritage; but it also came from their immanent concerns with
social and personal life. Nevertheless, like the Daoists, the
Confucians assumed an ontological asymmetry of genesis as
a vertical dimension within the horizontal dimension of time.
As to time, the Confucians were extraordinarily subtle in their
theories of education and character development; moreover,
they understood units of passage of time on the model of the
paradigmatic changes in the *Yijing*. But at any moment of time
there operates a vertical asymmetry uniting the incipience of
affairs with the co-temporal outcome. Confucius argued, for
instance, that it takes a long while to learn the rules of propriety.
But 'humanity', that which gives authenticity to proper actions,
can be touched in the depths of the situation at any moment.
Even more directly, Mengzi illustrated the ontological asymmetry
in his remarks about the 'Four Beginnings'. Each of the beginnings is an incipience of a virtue that can be expressed in the
proper medium, or inhibited in its expression. The beginning has
no special shape of its own, but is known by its unfolded
expressions. In the example of the start of alarm and distress
caused by the sight of a child about to fall into a well, Mengzi was
not speaking about a baby's condition, but a condition that
permanently remains with people throughout their lives,
however much they may cover it over and block its expression
with selfishness. The point of his moral claim that human nature
is innately good is that the ontological underpinnings of overt
action, no matter how evil, corrupted, or depraved, include the
incipiently virtuous responses of the four beginnings.

Neville, R. (1989) 'The Chinese Case in a Philosophy of World Religions',
in Allinson, R. (ed.) (1989) *Understanding the Chinese Mind*, Hong Kong:
Oxford University Press, 48–74, pp. 63–4

See also BOOK OF CHANGES, CONFUCIANISM, DAOISM,
ETHICS, EVIL, ONTOLOGY

Zoroastrians linked time with good and evil:

4   (5) The creator Ohrmazd dyed Time with colour – with good because in substance the benefit accruing to creatures is from the good and the evil of the Aggressor which is from an evil origin is vanquished by the good – and with evil because the evil of the Aggressor comes upon creation from without to confound it. From a single inconsistency which exists in potency (and entered) into creation during the millennia (times) between the original creation and the final rehabilitation during which time there is dissipation of energy, proceeds the restoring of the balance which consists in continuity and the restoration of creation at the rehabilitation, which means the destruction of evil by the power of the good (accumulated) throughout the millennia. In times which are mainly coloured with evil, evil will exceed the good: but after the passage of such periods comes complete victory, that is the time of the rehabilitation (brought about) by the power of good (which means) the complete defeat of the evil (which had come into being) throughout the millennia. That is the moment of the rehabilitation when good is established in its pure state: through it will come the annihilation of the Destructive Spirit and the triumph of creation, the Final Body, immortality, ecstasy for all the good creation through the Creator's wise design, will and power.

'Texts other than the Avesta', Zaehner, R. (1955) *Zurvan: A Zoroastrian Dilemma* NY: Biblio & Tanven, p. 381

See also CREATION, EVIL

UNIVERSALS

1   Given their suspicion of the existence of essences, it is hardly surprising that Buddhists should be concerned at the status of universals, i.e. general terms:

Bhartṛhari would therefore consider it a confusion to think that at least some words (for instance, proper names), directly *mean* i.e. refer to, concrete things such as a man. For no word *directly* means the external reality. Words directly refer to, i.e. mean, metaphorically existent entities, which are then rightly or wrongly identified with external realities. Notice also that the ordinarily understood concrete entity such as a man or a table is, for Bhartṛhari, already an abstraction, for it is severed from the total reality and is being considered in isolation. This apparently fosters the metaphorical identification of the intentional with the so-called extensional or external.

Apoha *and Natural Kinds*

Our brief survey of the problem of universals in classical India cannot be complete without a reference to Diṅnāga's *apoha* doctrine. Diṅnāga agreed with what we may call the Bhartṛhari thesis: the ultimate (real) object never appears without any guise or *vikalpa*, and is invariably grasped under some guise or mode of presentation. But the major disagreement with Bhartṛhari probably lies in Diṅnāga's view that the *naked* object can be grasped or is grasped by our purely sensory awareness, and the pure percept is therefore ineffable (*anirdeśya*) and self-cognized (*sva-saṃvedya*). In this respect Diṅnāga was closer to the sense-datum philosophers. For him, the percepts are pure data free from any *vikalpa* or conception, while the guises or the words/concepts are extraneous to the pure data. Diṅnāga was an atomist while Bhartṛhari was a holist.

In Diṅnāga's phenomenalism objects are in fact unique particulars which are infinitely propertied. But these properties or guises are not ontological; they are not resident in the object but superimposed by the mind on the object or conceptually constructed. For example, a particular comes to be recognized as blue only when it is excluded from non-blue things, and this process of exclusion is certainly a contribution of the mind or thought which we call *vikalpa* or conceptual construction. In the same manner, the same particular may be recognized as being of round shape or as being P or Q according as it is excluded from non-round-shaped things, or non-Ps, non-Qs, etc. This is how the particular appears as infinitely propertied or under infinitely many guises. If, as Bhartṛhari has argued, the concepts or universals are only superimposed guises or cloaks on the object, then Diṅnāga offers here an explication of the guise or *vikalpa*. The guises are all *apoha*. 'The word means a concept or a universal' would in Diṅnāga's language be read as 'the word *excludes*'. By using the word 'pain' or 'cow', the speaker does not say, in this theory, 'What X is like' or even, 'What sort of thing an X is', but only 'What sorts of things the X is not', or 'What X is not like.'

The usual question 'What is the meaning of "cow"?' may cause us to suppose that there is some entity which answers to the description, 'the meaning of "cow"'. This is highly misleading. A satisfactory theory of meaning should be able to explain how we are able to apply the term 'cow' to just those things which are cows. According to the Buddhists, the *apoha* theory can do just this without admitting real universals in their ontology.

Matilal, B. (1986) *Perception: An Essay on Classical Indian Theories of Knowledge*, Oxford: Clarendon Press, pp. 398–9

See also ATOMISM, IMAGINATION, LANGUAGE

2   Universals as imaginative representations in our way of thinking and talking:

For what we are aware of from hearing the words 'Fire is hot' is very different from what we are aware of when we *see* or perceive that fire is hot. In the latter case, fire feels hot and removes my cold instantly, but no verbal knowledge derived from the sentence 'Fire is hot' is going to work the same way. Language-meanings and inferences, therefore, deal with the universals or concepts, not the actual object. Perception deals with the actual object, the exclusive particular.

The point of the above example 'Fire is hot' seems to be obscure. Nobody imagines the perceptual awareness to be equivalent to the knowledge derived from the sentence or utterances of words. But the point is probably this. The actual object is present in the perceptual situation, whereas our knowledge of 'meaning' from the word-utterances has very little to do with the actual object. 'Meanings' that we understand from words are like *shadows* of the objects. Thus, the actual presence of the object might not occasion the utterance of such words. Therefore our awareness through word-utterances is invariably conditioned by these *shadow* entities, which markedly distinguish it from perceptual awareness. In short, word-utterance is possible even in the absence of the object but perception cannot arise when the object is not there. This suggestion comes from Udayana.

The universals, the attributes, and other abstractions – all these are theoretical constructs for the Buddhist. For even ordinary language, as I have already noted, mirrors a *theory* of reality, according to the Buddhist. It does not mirror reality as such. Therefore, the ordinary distinction between a description and an interpretation does not exist for the Buddhist. The actual objects, the particulars, are real or existent as Dharmakīrti asserts, mainly because they have what may be called 'causal efficacy' (*arthakriyāsāmarthya*). Only a particular fire can cook my food or even burn it. But the concept *fire* or firehood does not burn or do anything. The particulars are real also because they can fulfil the purpose (*artha*) of humans. This is the second sense of the cryptic term *arthakriyā*, as Udayana clearly notes. The human purpose can take a million forms depending upon the object, time, place and person. Fire will serve the purpose of removing cold. A thorn pricks. And so on. But the humans cannot *do* anything with the abstractions, firehood, pitcherhood, snakeness, thornhood, etc. Therefore they are said to be unreal in the ultimate sense. In other words, their usefulness is only theoretical. They cannot themselves *force* a perceptual awareness of them on us, as a particular object can. No (perceptual) awareness, therefore, can represent them in the way a perception of fire, being forced into existence by fire, represents fire. The abstractions are therefore non-perceptual in every way. This is in brief the Buddhist position about universals. They are like theoretical constructs, useful for language and communication, shadow entities construed as meanings of words, but they are never present in the object we see.

Ibid., pp. 320–1

See also KNOWLEDGE, LANGUAGE

The Nyaya response to Buddhism on universals is to suggest that since universals are different from particulars, it is hardly surprising that there is a difference between them: **3**

The particular is said to 'manifest' or 'reveal' the universal. All universals are regarded as distinct realities having spatial manifestations at different places at the same time. The familiar Buddhist critique of such real universals is absorbed into the system by claiming that the so-called problems are not problems at all but rather answer to the relevant questions. For example, it is pointed out that cowness as an objective universal has to be related to the particular object as soon as a calf is born, and has to disappear from the spatial location as soon as an old cow dies. The well-known verse of Dharmakīrti says that it (cowhood) cannot travel from the former cow to the latter cow, for then the former would not be a cow any longer; nor can it remain stationary, for then the latter cow would not even be a cow ('*Aho vyasana-santatih*' 'And how disastrous the consequences are!'). Nyāya in reply says not without a touch of irony, that these are not problems for they simply describe the nature of the universals. They show only that universals are not particulars; they are universals!

Ibid., p. 382

See also LANGUAGE

4   Even the Hindu philosopher Ramanuja was suspicious of the existence of universals:

> In the case of things such as generic characteristics, because they are the mode of an entity in that they express the generic configuration [of that entity] – here the mode [i.e. the generic characteristic] and the mode-possessor [i.e. the individual entity] are different kinds of being – the mode is incapable of being realised apart from [the mode-possessor] and indeed of being rendered intelligible apart from [the latter]. . . .

Rāmānuja is here considering the ontological dependence of such things as generic or class characteristics (which he calls the modes of the individual entities instantiating them) on the latter entities. For him a class-characteristic (or *jāti*, such as 'cowness'), like the Cheshire cat's grin, cannot exist *in abstracto*, as it were; it is realised in and through the individual (cows). *Mutatis mutandis*, the same observation applies for properties (or *guṇas*) such as 'white', 'brown' and so on. Modes such as properties and class-characteristics, which for Rāmānuja have a tenuous reality-status, essentially have a borrowed being: they exist as the things they are by inhering in their ontological supports. In other words, from the point of view of their being they 'are incapable of being realised apart from' their ontological supports.

Lipner, J. (1986) *The Face of Truth: A Study of Meaning and Metaphysics in the Vedantic Theology of Ramanuja*, Basingstoke: Macmillan, p. 125

See also GUNAS

UPANISHADS 1

The Rig-Veda is the oldest portion of the whole corpus of sacred literature which goes by the name of Veda. Beside it there exist three other Vedas; and to each of the four are attached later writings known as Brāhmaṇas, Āraṇyakas, and Upanishads. The first two we can safely ignore since they deal almost exclusively with the sacrificial ritual, the incredibly complex theories that purport to explain it, and the sympathetic magic attached to it. Moreover, these documents, whatever they may have meant to their original authors, are wholly incomprehensible to the modern mind. The Upanishads, however, we cannot ignore; for when the Hindus speak of the Vedas, it is primarily the Upanishads that they mean. The Upanishads constitute the *Vedānta* or 'end of the Veda': they are the basis on which almost all subsequent Indian religious thought is built up.

Unlike the Rig-Veda the Upanishads are philosophical in content, but they do not form a single 'system': they neither give a single consistent interpretation of the universe, nor do they claim to do so. They are rather the first gropings of the Indian mind in its attempt to find the ultimate ground of the universe. This simple fact has been obscured by the medieval Indian philosophers, each of whom has tried to force consistency on to the Upanishads – a consistency that is always the philosopher's own and into which he vainly tries to force the unwilling texts. It is then refreshing that Professor Surendranath Dasgupta, the foremost authority on Indian philosophy today, has expressed the following view. 'It is necessary,' he writes, 'that a modern interpreter of the Upanishads should turn a deaf ear to the absolute claims of these [ancient] exponents, and look upon the Upanishads not as a systematic treatise but as a depository of diverse currents of thought – the melting-pot in which all later philosophic ideas were still in a state of fusion.'[1] No one who has made a study of the Upanishads without reference to the later commentaries which so obviously distort them, is likely to quarrel with this eminently sound judgement. It is, however, encouraging that India's foremost scholar should state the case so plainly; for the Indian tendency which we have already noticed, to regard different interpretations of reality merely as aspects of one 'truth', has in recent times monopolized Indian thinking in so far as it is popularly presented to the West.[2]

The Upanishads themselves are the reverse of dogmatic, and in them we find the first strivings of the Indian mind towards the formulation of metaphysical concepts. In the history of Indian thought they correspond to the phase represented by Hesiod and the pre-Socratics among the Greeks. The difference, which is enormous, is that the Upanishads became a sacred book, whereas the pre-Socratics did not. One can, however, imagine how great the confusion would have been if the pre-Socratics had been anonymous and if their joint productions had been gathered up into a sacred canon in which Heraclitus and Parmenides, for instance, would enjoy an equally infallible authority.

The Upanishads, then, can be regarded as the beginning of Indian philosophy.

1 Surendranath Dasgupta, *A History of Indian Philosophy*, Cambridge, 1951, vol. i, p. 42.
2 This is equally true of the Neo-Vedāntins who derive from Vivekananda, of Coomaraswamy and his disciples Guénon and Schuon, and of Radhakrishnan.

Zaehner, R. (1958) *At Sundry Times: An Essay in the Comparison of Religions*, London: Faber, pp. 35–7

VEDANTA

See PURVA MIMANSA AND VEDANTA

WAR

1 There is an inconsistency in our treatment of occasional murder and mass murder in war:

The murder of one person is called unrighteous and incurs one death penalty. Following this argument, the murder of ten persons will be ten times as unrighteous and there should be ten death penalties; the murder of a hundred persons will be a hundred times as unrighteous and there should be a hundred death penalties. All the gentlemen of the world know that they should condemn these things, calling them unrighteous. But when it comes to the great unrighteousness of attacking states, they do not know that they should condemn it. On the contrary, they applaud it, calling it righteous. And they are really ignorant of it being unrighteous. Hence they have recorded their judgment to bequeath to their posterity. If they did know that it is unrighteous, then why would they record their false judgment to bequeath to posterity?

Mozi (1974) *The Ethical and Political Works of Motse*, trans. Yi-Pao Mei, Taipai: Ch'eng Wen Publishing Company, p. 99

See also ETHICS

WORK

If work is done as though it were religious duty, it will lead to   1
enlightenment:

The only way to rise is by doing the duty next to us, and thus we go on gathering strength until we reach the highest state. A young Sannyasin went to a forest; there he meditated, worshipped, and practised Yoga for a long time. After years of hard work and practice, he was one day sitting under a tree, when some dry leaves fell upon his head. He looked up and saw a crow and a crane fighting on the top of the tree, which made him very angry. He said, "What! Dare you throw these dry leaves upon my head!" As with these words he angrily glanced at them, a flash of fire went out of his head – such was the Yogi's power – and burnt the birds to ashes. He was very glad, almost overjoyed at this development of power – he could burn the crow and the crane by a look. After a time he had to go to the town to beg his bread. He went, stood at a door, and said, "Mother, give me food." A voice came from inside the house: "Wait a little, my son." The young man thought: "You wretched woman, how dare you make me wait! You do not know my power yet." While he was thinking thus the voice came again: "Boy, don't be thinking too much of yourself. Here is neither crow nor crane." He was astonished; still he had to wait. At last the woman came, and he fell at her feet and said, "Mother, how did you know

275

that?" She said, "My boy, I do not know your Yoga or your practices. I am a common everyday woman. I made you wait because my husband is ill, and I was nursing him. All my life I have struggled to do my duty. When I was unmarried, I did my duty to my parents; now that I am married, I do my duty to my husband; that is all the Yoga I practise. But by doing my duty I have become illumined; thus I could read your thoughts and know what you had done in the forest. If you want to know something higher than this, go to the market of such and such a town where you will find a Vyâdha who will tell you something that you will be very glad to learn." The Sannyasin thought: "Why should I go to that town and to a Vyadha!" But after what he had seen, his mind opened a little, so he went. When he came near the town, he found the market and there saw at a distance a big fat Vyadha cutting meat with big knives, talking and bargaining with different people. The young man said, "Lord help me! Is this the man from whom I am going to learn? He is the incarnation of a demon, if he is anything." In the mean time this man looked up and said, "O Swami, did that lady send you here? Take a seat until I have done my business." The Sannyasin thought, "What comes to me here?" He took his seat; the man went on with his work, and after he had finished he took his money and said to the Sannyasin, "Come, sir, come to my home." On reaching home the Vyadha gave him a seat, saying, "Wait here", and went into the house. He then washed his old father and mother, fed them, and did all he could to please them, after which he came to the Sannyasin and said, "Now, sir, you have come here to see me; what can I do for you?" The Sannyasin asked him a few questions about soul and about God, and the Vyadha gave him a lecture which forms a part of the Mahâbhârata, called the Vyâdha-Gitâ. It contains one of the highest flights of the Vedanta. When the Vyadha finished his teaching, the Sannyasin felt astonished. He said, "Why are you in that body? With such knowledge as yours why are you in a Vyadha's body and doing such filthy, ugly work?" "My son," replied the Vyadha, "no duty is ugly, no duty is impure. My birth placed me in these circumstances and environments. In my boyhood I learnt the trade; I am unattached and I try to do my duty well. I try to do my duty as a householder, and I try to do all I can to make my father and mother happy. I neither know your Yoga, nor have I become a Sannyasin, nor did I go out of the world into a forest; nevertheless, all that you have heard and seen has come to me through the unattached doing of the duty which belongs to my position."

There is a sage in India, a great Yogi, one of the most wonderful men I have ever seen in my life. He is a peculiar man, he will not teach any one; if you ask him a question, he will not answer. It is too much for him to take up the position of a teacher, he will not do it. If you ask a question, and wait for some days, in the course of conversation he will bring up the subject, and wonderful light will he throw on it. He told me once the secret of work, "Let the end and the means be joined into one." When you are doing any work, do not think of anything beyond. Do it as worship, as the highest worship, and devote your whole life to it for the time being. Thus, in the story, the Vyadha and the woman did their duty with cheerfulness and whole-heartedness; and the result was that they became illuminated; clearly showing that the right performance of the duties of any station in life, without attachment to results, leads us to the highest realisation of the perfection of the soul.

It is the worker who is attached to results that grumbles about the nature of the duty which has fallen to his lot; to the unattached worker all duties are equally good and form efficient instruments with which selfishness and sensuality may be killed and the freedom of the soul secured. We are all apt to think too highly of ourselves. Our duties are determined by our deserts to a much larger extent than we are willing to grant. Competition rouses envy, and it kills the kindliness of the heart. To the grumbler all duties are distasteful; nothing will ever satisfy him, and his whole life is doomed to prove a failure. Let us work on, doing as we go whatever happens to be our duty and being ever ready to put our shoulders to the wheel. Then surely shall we see the Light!

Vivekananda, S. (1960) *Karma-Yoga*, Calcutta: Advaita Ashrama, pp. 64–9

See also ACTION, *KARMA*

YIN-YANG

See also BOOK OF CHANGES

1   Chinese and Indian (*Ayurveda*) medicine are both linked with philosophical and cosmological principles:

India's neighbor, China, was to develop a medical system no less efficacious and in a sense more remarkable in both its practice and results. The medicine based on acupuncture and acupressure, which developed in China and later spread to Japan, Korea, and Indo-China, is as closely related to the cosmological principles of the Chinese tradition as the *Ayurveda* is to the Indian. Chinese medicine is based on the basic Chinese doctrine of the masculine-feminine principles of *Yin* and *Yang*, two principles which are opposite yet complementary, the five elements also found in traditional Chinese cosmology and physics, and the ether sometimes translated as energy or the principle of life (*ch'i*) which pervades the human microcosm. Centers of the psychic body which facilitate the flow of life energy and connect the psychic and physical elements of the human microcosm have been discovered by Chinese medicine in a most accurate fashion and a treatment is applied which deals directly with the principle of the physical body rather than the physical body itself. If there were any need of empirical proof of the validity of the Chinese cosmology which underlies acupuncture, one would only need to observe the remarkable results of treating certain types of illnesses through the methods of Chinese medicine. The revival of this school even in the modern West and in a context in which this medicine is often practiced in forgetfulness of its cosmological and metaphysical background is proof of the powerful means it has developed to deal with human illness by considering man in his total relationship with the cosmos about him, although the efficacy of this medicine cannot be total if it is severed from its cosmological principles.

Nasr, S. H. (1993) *The Need for a Sacred Science*, Albany: State University of New York Press, p. 108–9

See also HARMONY

2   Zunzi argues that there is no point in regretting the working of *yin* and *yang*:

When stars fall or trees make a [strange] noise, all people in the state are afraid and ask, "Why?" I reply: There is no need to ask why. These are changes of heaven and earth, the transformation of yin and yang, and rare occurrences. It is all right to marvel at them, but wrong to fear them. For there has been no age that has not had the experience of eclipses of the sun and moon, unreasonable rain or wind, or occasional appearance of strange stars. If the ruler is enlightened and the government peaceful, even if all of these things happen at the same time, they would do no harm. If the ruler is unenlightened and the government follows a dangerous course, even if [only] one of them occurs, it would do no good. For the falling of stars and the noise of trees are the changes of heaven and earth, the transformations of yin and yang, and rare occurrences. It is all right to marvel at them, but wrong to fear them.

Chan, Wing-Tsit (1963) *A Source Book in Chinese Philosophy*, Princeton: Princeton University Press, p. 120

See also FATALISM

YOGA

Although there are obvious similarities between yoga and Buddhism, there are important differences: 1

It is easy to see that, though Patañjali's *yoga* is under a deep debt of obligation to this Buddhist *yoga*, the *yoga* of the *Gītā* is unacquainted therewith. The pessimism which fills the Buddhist *yoga* is seen to affect not only the outlook of Patañjali's *yoga*, but also most of the later Hindu modes of thought in the form of the advisability of reflecting on the repulsive sides of things (*pratipakṣa-bhāvanā*) which are seemingly attractive. The ideas of universal friendship, etc. were also taken over by Patañjali and later on passed into Hindu works. The methods of concentration on various ordinary objects also seem to be quite unlike what we find in the *Gītā*. The *Gītā* is devoid of any tinge of pessimism such as we find in the Buddhist *yoga*. It does not anywhere recommend the habit of brooding over the repulsive aspects of all things, so as to fill our minds with a feeling of disgust for all worldly things. It does not rise to the ideal of regarding all beings as friends or to that of universal compassion. Its sole aim is to teach the way of reaching the state of equanimity, in which the saint has no preferences, likes and dislikes – where the difference between the sinner and the virtuous, the self and the not-self has vanished. The idea of *yoga* as self-surrendering union with God and self-surrendering performance of one's duties is the special feature which is absent in Buddhism. This self-surrender in God, however, occurs in Patañjali's *yoga*, but it is hardly in keeping with the technical meaning of the word *yoga*, as the suspension of all mental states. The idea appears only once in Patañjali's *sūtras*, and the entire method of *yoga* practices, as described in the later chapters, seems to take no notice of it. It seems highly probable, therefore, that in Patañjali's *sūtras* the idea was borrowed from the *Gītā*, where this self-surrender to God and union with Him is defined as *yoga* and is the central idea which the *Gītā* is not tired of repeating again and again.

Dasgupta, S. (1932) *A History of Indian Philosophy*, II, Cambridge: Cambridge University Press, pp. 460–1

See also BHAGAVAD-GITA, GOD

---

2   The notion of yoga came to change its meaning in the variety of texts and systems in which it came to be used:

The *Mahā-bhārata* also refers to *sāṃkhya* and *yoga* in several places. But in almost all places *sāṃkhya* means either the traditional school of Kapila-Sāṃkhya or some other school of Sāṃkhya, more or less similar to it: *yoga* also most often refers either to the *yoga* of Patañjali or some earlier forms of it. In one place are found passages identifying *sāṃkhya* and *yoga*, which agree almost word for word with similar passages of the *Gītā*. But it does not seem that the *sāṃkhya* or the *yoga* referred to in the *Mahā-bhārata* has anything to do with the idea of Sāṃkhya or *yoga* in the *Gītā*. As has already been pointed out, the *yoga* in the *Gītā* means the dedication to God and renunciation of the fruits of one's *karma* and being in communion with Him as the supreme Lord pervading the universe. The chapter of the *Mahā-bhārata* just referred to speaks of turning back the senses into the *manas* and of turning the *manas* into *ahaṃkāra* and *ahaṃkāra* into *buddhi* and *buddhi* into *prakṛti*, thus finishing with *prakṛti* and its evolutes and meditating upon pure *puruṣa*. It is clear that this system of *yoga* is definitely associated with the Kapila school of Sāṃkhya.

In the *Mahā-bhārata*, XII. 306, the predominant feature of *yoga* is said to be *dhyāna*, and the latter is said to consist of concentration of mind (*ekāgratā ca manasaḥ*) and breath-control (*prāṇāyāma*). It is said that the *yogin* should stop the functions of his senses by his mind, and the movement of his mind by his reason (*buddhi*), and in this stage he is said to be linked up (*yukta*) and is like a motionless flame in a still place. This passage naturally reminds one of the description of *dhyāna-yoga* in the *Gītā*, VI. 11–13, 16–19 and 25, 26; but the fundamental idea of *yoga*, as the dedication of the fruits of actions to God and communion with Him, is absent here.

Ibid., pp. 458–9

See also BUDDHI, DHYANA, MANAS, MEDITATION, PRAKRITI, SANKHYA-YOGA

The notion of yoga was originally psychological, and came to be used   3
metaphysically in later systems:

The practice of Yoga most probably preceded the Aryan invasion of India, for among the recent discoveries at Mohenjo Daro there are figurines of a deity sitting in the Yoga position of meditation, reminiscent of later statues of Śiva as the great ascetic. The existence of Yoga as a technique is therefore indisputably very ancient, and although it is rarely mentioned in the Upanishads themselves, it forms, from the beginning, part and parcel of the technique of salvation practised by both the Buddhists and Jains whose philosophy of existence differed substantially from that of the Upanishads. Thus it would appear that Yoga techniques were current in India from the earliest times and were practised by all religious sects. Philosophy took due account of the transformation of consciousness that Yoga could produce and pressed Yoga experience into its service; and the Yogins themselves evolved an empirical philosophy of their own which was far different from that of the Upanishads and runs directly counter to many of their more extravagant conclusions. But basically the aims of Yoga and Upanishadic speculation are poles apart. The one is a psychological technique, the other metaphysical inquiry.

In the Upanishads we have a quasi-rational investigation into the nature of things, the search for the eternal ground of the universe. Simultaneously, in Yoga, we have the search of man for the eternal essence of his own soul, which, it is claimed, can be and actually is experienced by the Yogin in trance. It seems to have been the combination of a rational and reverent inquiry on the one hand and the experiences of Yoga on the other that led to the ultimate conclusion, which is undoubtedly the purport of a majority of Upanishadic texts, that the eternal element in the human soul at its deepest level is identical with the ground and origin of the universe. God is man; and man is God, and between the two, as they are in their essence and when stripped of all that is accidental, there is no difference at all. This is the basic conclusion of the Vedānta philosophy in its extreme non-dualist form as interpreted by Śankara in the ninth century A.D.; and this absolute monism is regarded by many in India as being the bald statement of absolute truth. It is as foreign to the Judaic conception of deity as it is possible to be.

In ancient India nothing is datable; nor is it possible to judge the comparative age of a given doctrine even from an approximate dating. Thus we cannot be sure what philosophical system, if any, the Yoga technique was originally designed to serve. We do know, however, that from the earliest times both the Buddhists and Jains made use of this technique, and that within orthodox Hinduism it came to be so closely linked with the Sāmkhya philosophy that the two were normally classed together as the Sāmkhya-Yoga. This is significant: for all three systems – Buddhist, Jain, and Sāmkhya – are atheistical; and for all of them *mokṣa*, 'deliverance', 'emancipation', or 'release' consists simply and solely in freeing the soul from all its physiological and psychological adjuncts. Primitive Buddhism has no metaphysics, and the Buddha therefore refused to speculate on the nature of the released state though he let it be understood that it partook of immortality. Neither the Jains nor the Sāmkhya-Yogins, however, were so non-committal. For both of them 'release' constituted the release of the individual soul, which was regarded as an eternal monad, having its being outside space and time, from all that is not eternal, that is, from body, emotion, and discursive thought. The bliss of release, then, consisted in isolation (*kaivalyam*), the isolation and insulation of the soul within itself, a timeless enjoyment of a timeless essence. Yoga, then, seems originally to have been a psychological technique for uncovering the immortality of one's own soul in distinction and separation from both the empirical 'ego' and the objective world.

Zaehner, R. (1958) *At Sundry Times: An Essay in the Comparison of Religions*, London: Faber, pp. 38–40

See also JAINISM, *MOKSHA*, SANKHYA-YOGA, *UPANISHADS*

Yoga is a process: 4

> Yoga-siddhi, the perfection that comes from the practice of Yoga, can be best attained by the combined working of four great instruments. There is, first, the knowledge of the truths, principles, powers and processes that govern the realisation – *śāstra*. Next comes a patient and persistent action on the lines laid down by the knowledge, the force of our personal effort – *utsāha*. There intervenes, third, uplifting our knowledge and effort into the domain of spiritual experience, the direct suggestion, example and influence of the Teacher – *guru*. Last comes the instrumentality of Time – *kāla*; for in all things there is a cycle of their action and a period of the divine movement.

Aurobindo (1987) *The Essential Aurobindo*, ed. R. McDermott, Great Barrington, MA: Lindisfarne Press, p. 141

See also ACTION, *GURU*, TIME

The idea here is that there is a type of yoga appropriate for each   5
individual:

> Vivekananda, pointing out that the unity of all religions must necessarily express itself by an increasing richness of variety in its forms, said once that the perfect state of that essential unity would come when each man had his own religion, when not bound by sect or traditional form he followed the free self-adaptation of his nature in its relations with the Supreme. So also one may say that the perfection of the integral Yoga will come when each man is able to follow his own path of Yoga, pursuing the development of his own nature in its upsurging towards that which transcends the nature. For freedom is the final law and the last consummation.

Ibid., p. 145

6 The *sadhaka* is the person who submerges his individuality in what is higher:

The process of the integral Yoga has three stages, not indeed sharply distinguished or separate, but in a certain measure successive. There must be, first, the effort towards at least an initial and enabling self-transcendence and contact with the Divine; next, the reception of that which transcends, that with which we have gained communion, into ourselves for the transformation of our whole conscious being; last, the utilisation of our transformed humanity as a divine centre in the world. So long as the contact with the Divine is not in some considerable degree established, so long as there is not some measure of sustained identity, *sāyujya*, the element of personal effort must normally predominate. But in proportion as this contact establishes itself, the Sadhaka must become conscious that a force other than his own, a force transcending his egoistic endeavour and capacity, is at work in him and to this Power he learns progressively to submit himself and delivers up to it the charge of his Yoga. In the end his own will and force become one with the higher Power; he merges them in the divine Will and its transcendent and universal Force. He finds it thenceforward presiding over the necessary transformation of his mental, vital and physical being with an impartial wisdom and provident effectivity of which the eager and interested ego is not capable. It is when this identification and this self-merging are complete that the divine centre in the world is ready. Purified, liberated, plastic, illumined, it can begin to serve as a means for the direct action of a supreme Power in the larger Yoga of humanity or superhumanity, of the earth's spiritual progression or its transformation.

Ibid., pp. 146–7

YOGACHARA

1 Vasubandhu explores the central idea of Buddhism that there is no acceptable dualism between our mind and anything else:

Vasubandhu tries to justify one of the most important claims of the Mahāyānists. He points out that reality was analyzed by the Buddha into twelve 'gateways' (*āyatana*) of cognition in order to eliminate the belief in an eternal and unchanging 'self' (*ātman*). This is the theory of the nonsubstantiality of the individual (*pudgala-nairātmya*), which was upheld by the Hīnayānists. But by denying the reality of the external object, the Mahāyānists claimed that they supersede the Hīnayānists because they advocate the nonsubstantiality of the *dharmas* (*dharma-nairātmya*) as well. This criticism of the Mahāyānists may be considered valid as far as some of the later schools of Buddhism are concerned, for the Sarvâstivādins as well as the post-Buddhaghosa Theravādins, in a sense, accepted the substantiality of the *dharmas*.

Next, Vasubandhu takes up the different atomic theories presented by the realist schools. In the Abhidharma schools as well as in some of the Hindu schools, the external object was analyzed in terms of material atoms. Vasubandhu adduced dialectical arguments to refute these atomic theories.

The net result of all these speculations was the view that perception cannot guarantee the existence of external objects, because the awareness of them does not seem to be very different from that of dream experience. Memory, too, is not helpful in that it implies the perception of consciousness itself, or rather what is found in the stream of consciousness. Anticipating objections from the opponent, Vasubandhu maintains that before we are fully awake we cannot know that dream objects are unreal. Things seen in a dream are as real to the dreamer as any object is to a person who is awake. The unreality of dream objects is realized only when a person is awake. The difference between dream consciousness and waking consciousness is that in the former, a person's mind is overwhelmed by torpor (*middha*). Similarly, compared with a person in the highest state of yogic concentration, worldly people are slumbering in ignorance. So long as they remain in this state of ignorance they do not realize that the world of sense experience does not exist in reality. Highest knowledge yields the realization that reality is pure and undiscriminated consciousness. This, of course, leads Vasubandhu to deny not only the validity and possibility of sense perception, but also of extrasensory perception. For example, in telepathy one is said to perceive the nature and functioning of another's mind (*para-citta*). If this is possible, here again there will be dichotomy of subject (i.e., one's own mind, *sva-citta*) and object (i.e., another's mind, *para-citta*), and this dichotomy is false. This is absolute Idealism. And like Nāgârjuna, Vasubandhu, with the intention of justifying the Mahāyāna doctrine of 'one vehicle' (*eka-yāna*), insisted that this highest knowledge is attained with the realization of Buddhahood.

Kalupahana, D. (1996) *Buddhist Philosophy: A Historical Analysis*, Honolulu: University Press of Hawaii, pp. 146–7

See also ABHIDHARMA, *ATMAN*, ATOMISM, CONSCIOUSNESS, *DHARMA*, ENLIGHTENMENT, SELF, TIAN TAI

ZEN

1   The Chan notion of enlightenment is linked with non-Buddhist Chinese ideas:

The seemingly naive faith of Ch'an (Zen) practitioners in East Asia that one can achieve enlightenment in one's own lifetime through one's own effort is perhaps unique in human salvific history. Particularly intriguing, in a comparative religious perspective, is that this premium on self-reliance is predicated on the paradox that the total annihilation of the self is synonymous with the complete affirmation of the self through ultimate self-transformation. No reference is made to a transcendent reality that provides a real fiat for this incredible human capacity. Rather, the enlightening process occurs in the structure of the self in this world in common activities such as eating, walking, and resting. The highest achievement of personal knowledge is not separable from what we normally do in our practical daily living.

This Ch'an approach to enlightenment obviously has deep roots in indigenous Chinese cosmological thinking. Take, for example, the veneration of the person as a co-creator of the universe. If humans are the most sentient of all the beings in the world, the human body is intrinsically spiritual. Since there are no standards of human perfection outside the human community except the natural transformation of the cosmic order of which the human body is a microcosm, the spiritual resources inherent in human nature are sufficient for self-transformation. We might ask, why is there any need for self-transformation if human nature is already endowed with sufficient spirituality? The answer could be that the person, who is not only the body but also mind-heart, soul, and spirit, is a process of becoming rather than a static structure. To the extent that the person is becoming, and thus an activity, a path for self-transformation is necessarily involved. A person cannot but transform. Any static notion of the self, as in the case of an unchanging selfhood fails to accommodate the dynamic process of growth as a defining characteristic of the person.

Tu-Wei Ming 'Afterword' in Gregory, P. (ed.) (1987) *Sudden and Gradual: Approaches to Enlightenment in Chinese Thought*, Honolulu: University of Hawaii Press, pp. 448–9

Zen philosophy has to deal with an important controversy, viz. whether 2
enlightenment can be attained suddenly or gradually:

Unlike the Buddha who could reject the pre-Buddhist doctrines and modes of life if they did not conform to his philosophy, the Zen masters were restricted by their Mahāyāna background and had to achieve the two goals, namely, rejection of speculation and restriction of the use of meditation, within the Mahāyāna framework. While the Buddha could reject the non-Buddhist metaphysical speculations regarding the nature of Ultimate Reality and adopt the powers gained by mind control for regulating his life, the Zen masters had to grapple with the metaphysical speculations of the Mahāyānists, especially of the Mādhyamika-Yogâcāra syncretism, for they could not abandon this framework, it being Buddhist and not non-Buddhist. It is evident that the conception of an underlying reality, an Absolute, indescribable and indefinable, is at the back of all Zen practices. The nature of the *kōan* explicates this concept.

It has been mentioned that Zen represents the culimination of two trends, the Mādhymika and the Yogâcāra. In spite of reciprocal influences, the two trends appear to have retained their salient features, thus giving rise to two different forms of Zen. The school of Zen which emphasized 'gradual enlightenment' was perhaps inspired by the Yogâcāra tradition with its emphasis on the gradualness of the path of meditation aimed at developing the highest form of illumination. The Zen school upholding 'sudden illumination' seems to have been influenced by the Mādhyamika conception of 'emptiness' (*śūnyatā*). These two trends may be traced back to the two disciples of the Fifth Patriarch, Hung-jên. Hung-jên had two disciples, Shên-hsiu and

Hui-neng. According to the *Platform Sūtra* of Hui-neng, Hung-jên ordered his disciples each to compose a verse in order to reveal to the master their degree of enlightenment. His purpose was to find a successor to whom he could entrust the patriarchal insignia. Shen-hsiu composed the following verse and wrote it on the wall of the pillared hall of the monastery:

> The body is the Bodhi-tree,
> The mind is like a clear mirror.
> At all times we must strive to polish it,
> And must not let the dust collect.

This verse, no doubt, presents the Yogâcāra philosophy in a nutshell. The mind is pure by nature (*prabhāśvara*) and is defiled by the inflowing cankers (*āśrava*). Therefore, it should be constantly cleaned by wiping off the particles of dust settling on it. And this is achieved through constant meditation.

The legend says that the other disciples read these lines with admiration and believed that the question of succession was thereby settled. But the Fifth Patriarch, Hung-jên, was not completely satisfied and privately informed Shen-hsiu that the verse showed no sign of enlightenment. Should this be taken as a hint that Hung-jên did not favor the Yogâcāra teachings on which the theory of gradual enlightenment was based?

The legend continues: At this time, a boy of little or no education named Hui-neng was living in the monastery. He had come from South China, having heard of the fame of Hung-jên, and begged the master to accept him as a disciple. Although Hung-jên recognized this boy's extraordinary intuitive and intellectual capacities, he did not admit him to the circle of disciples. Instead, he was allowed to work in the monastery splitting firewood and grinding rice. The boy heard of Shên-hsiu's verse, and, because he was illiterate, he asked to have it read for him twice. Thereupon, he composed another verse and had it written on the wall:

> The *bodhi* originally has no tree.
> The clear mirror also has no stand.
> From the beginning not a thing is.
> Where is there room for dust?

Compared with the earlier verse, this one shows definite traces of Mādhyamika thought, especially the doctrine of 'emptiness' (*śūnyatā*). The fact that Hung-jên may have been well disposed toward Mādhyamika rather than Yogâcāra thought is further suggested by the fact that he secretly summoned Hui-neng to his room by night and conferred upon him the patriarchal insignia; but he ordered Hui-neng to flee south across the Yangtse, for he feared the envy of Shên-hsiu and other disciples.

Kalupahana, D. (1996) *Buddhist Philosophy: A Historical Analysis*, Honolulu: University Press of Hawaii, pp. 172–3

See also BODHI, DHYANA, EMPTINESS, ENLIGHTENMENT, EVIL, *KOAN*, MADHYAMAKA, MEDITATION, YOGACHARA

Although there is an important tradition of zen in Korean philosophy, there have been critics. This modern Korean thinker points out that there is a tendency for the ritual which has grown up with zen to overwhelm the meaning of zen itself:

> I find the practitioners of Zen very strange indeed. The meditators in the past tried to keep their minds quiet, but the meditators of today keep their dwelling places quiet. The meditators of the past kept their minds static, but the meditators of today keep their bodies static. If one keeps one's dwelling place quiet, one cannot but become misanthropic, and if one keeps one's body static, one cannot but become self-righteous. Buddhism is a teaching of salvationism and the leadership of the masses. Then, how can it but be wrong for a follower of Buddha to pass into misanthropy and self-righteousness?

Han Yong-woon, tr. Y. Mu-woong, in Shin-Yong, C. (ed.) (1974) *Buddhist Culture in Korea*, Seoul: International Cultural Foundation, p. 104

REFERENCES

Abe, M. (1985) *Zen and Western Thought*, Basingstoke: Macmillan.

Allinson, R. (ed.) (1989) *Understanding the Chinese Mind*, Hong Kong: Oxford University Press.

Aurobindo (1987) *The Essential Aurobindo*, ed. R. McDermott, Great Barrington, MA: Lindisfarne Press.

Averroes (1978), *Averroes' Tahafut al-Tahafut* (The Incoherence of the Incoherence) trans. S. Van Den Bergh, London: Luzac.

—— (1976) *On the Harmony of Religion and Philosophy* trans. G. Hourani, London: Luzac.

Basham, A. (1951) *History and Doctrines of the Ajivikas: A Vanished Indian Religion*, Delhi: Motilal Banarsidass.

Biderman, S. (1982) 'A "constitutive" God – an Indian suggestion', *Philosophy East and West*, 32, 425–37.

Boyce, M. (1984) *Textual Sources for the Study of Zoroastrianism*, ed. and trans. M. Boyce, Manchester: Manchester University Press.

Carr, D. (1997) "Sankaracarya" Companion Encyclopedia of Asian Philosophy, ed. I. Mahalingam and B. Carr, London: Routledge, 189–210: 198–9.

Chan, Wing-tsit (1963; 1972) *A Source Book in Chinese Philosophy*, Princeton: Princeton University Press.

Cheng, Chung-Ying (1989) 'Chinese Metaphysics as Non-Metaphysics: Confucian and Daoist Insights into the Nature of Reality', in Allinson *op. cit.* 167–208.

Chuang Tzu (1968) *The Complete Works of Chuang Tzu*, trans. B. Watson, New York: Columbia University Press.

Collins, S. (1982) *Selfless Persons: Imagery and Thought in Theravada Buddhism*, Cambridge: Cambridge University Press.

Confucius, trans. R. Dawson (1993) *The Analects*, Oxford: Oxford University Press.

Conze, E. (1976) *Buddhist Scriptures*, Harmondsworth: Penguin.

—— (1980) *A Short History of Buddhism*, London: George Allen & Unwin.

Dainian, F. and Cohen, R. (eds) (1996) *History and Philosophy of Science and Technology*, Dordrecht: Kluwer.

Dasgupta, S. (1932) *A History of Indian Philosophy*, II, Cambridge: Cambridge University Press.

—— (1940) *A History of Indian Philosophy*, III, Cambridge: Cambridge University Press.

Dasgupta, S. B. (1974) *An Introduction to Tantric Buddhism*, Berkeley: Shambhala.

de Bary, W. T. (1991) *The Trouble with Confucianism*, Cambridge, Mass.: Harvard University Press.

—— (1958) (ed.) *Sources of Japanese Tradition*, II, New York: Columbia University Press.

Dreyfus, G. (1997) *Recognizing Reality: Dharmakirti's Philosophy and its Tibetan Interpretations*, Albany: State University of New York Press.

Dumoulin, H. (1963) *A History of Zen Buddhism*, London: Faber.

Al-Farabi (1961) *The fusul al-madani of al-Farabi* (Aphorisms of the statesman, ed. and trans. D. Dunlop, Cambridge: Cambridge University Press.

—— (1974) 'Book of Letters', trans. L. Berman, 'Maimonides, the disciple of Alfarabi', *Israel Oriental Studies*, 4.

—— (1890) *Alfarabi's philosophische Abhandlungen*, ed. F. Dietrici, Leiden: Brill.

Feuerstein, G. (1980) *The Philosophy of Classical Yoga*, Manchester: Manchester University Press.

Gandhi, M. (1958) *Hindu Dharma*, Ahmedabad: Navajivan Publishing House.

al-Ghazali, *Incoherence of the Philosophers* see Averroes (1978).

Gombrich, R. (1972) Review, *Modern Asian Studies*, VI, 492.

Gregory, P. (ed.) (1987) *Sudden and Gradual: Approaches to Enlightenment in Chinese Thought*, Honolulu: University of Hawaii Press.

Guenther, H. and Trungpa, C. (1975) *The Dawn of Tantra*, ed. G. Eddy, Shambhala: Berkeley

Ha'iri Yazdi, M. (1992) *The Principles of Epistemology in Islamic Philosophy: Knowledge by presence*, Albany: State University of New York Press.

Han Fei Tzu (1964) *Han Fei Tzu: Basic Writings*, trans. B. Watson, New York: Columbia University Press.

Hansen, C. (1989) 'Language in the Heart-mind' in Allinson *op. cit.* 75–124.

Hoshino, K. (ed.) (1997) *Japanese and Western Bioethics*, Dordrecht: Kluwer.

Ibn Sina (1945) "A Treatise on Love" trans. E. Fackenheim, *Mediaeval Studies*, 7, pp. 221–8: p. 225.

Iqbal, M. (1934) *The Reconstruction of Religious Thought in Islam*, London: Oxford University Press pp. 86–7.

Jiachang, L. (1996) 'Time: A Philosophical Survey', in Dainian and Cohen *op. cit.* 77–94.

Kalupahana, D. (1996) *Buddhist Philosophy: A Historical Analysis*, Honolulu: University Press of Hawaii.

Krishna, D. (1991) *Indian Philosophy: A Counter Perspective*, Delhi: Oxford University Press.

Kukai (1972) *Kukai: Major Works*, trans. Y. Hakeda, New York: Columbia University Press.

Laozi (1989) *Te-Tao Ching*, trans. R. Henricks, New York: Ballantine Books.

—— (1997) "'Power and Paradox': Selections from a New Translation of the Tao Te Ching" *Parabola* Summer 1997 trans. U. K. Le Guin.

Leaman, O. (1985) *An Introduction to Medieval Islamic Philosophy*, Cambridge: Cambridge University Press.

—— (ed.) (1996) *Friendship East and West: Philosophical Perspectives*, Richmond: Curzon.

—— (1997) *Averroes and his Philosophy*, Richmond: Curzon.

Lipner, J. (1986) *The Face of Truth: A Study of Meaning and Metaphysics in the Vedantic Theology of Ramanuja*, Basingstoke: Macmillan.

Lishi, F. and Youyuan, Z. (1996) 'Concepts of Space and Time in Ancient China and in Modern Cosmology', in Dainian and Cohen *op. cit.* 55–60.

Malalaseekara, G. (1957) *The Buddha and his teachings*, The Buddhist Council of Ceylon.

Mao (1967) *Selected Works of Mao Tse-Tung*, Beijing: Foreign Languages Press, I, 308.

Matilal, B. (1986) *Perception: An Essay on Classical Indian Theories of Knowledge*, Oxford: Clarendon Press.

Mohanty, J. (1992) *Reason and Tradition in Indian Thought: An Essay on the Nature of Indian Philosophical Thinking*, Oxford: Clarendon Press.

Mozi (1974) *The Ethical and Political Works of Motse*, trans. Yi-Pao Mei, Taipai: Ch'eng Wen Publishing Company.

Murti, T. (1955) *The Central Philosophy of Buddhism*, London: George Allen & Unwin.

Nasr, S. (1993) *The Need for a Sacred Science*, Albany: State University of New York Press.

Neville, R. (1989) 'The Chinese Case in a Philosophy of World Religions', in Allinson *op. cit.* 48–74.

Nichiren (1990) *Selected Writings of Nichiren*, trans. B. Watson et al., New York: Columbia University Press.

Nyanatiloka, M. (1973) *Impermanence*, Buddhist Publication Society, Wheel no. 186–7, Ceylon.

Otani, K. (1957) *Sermons on Shin Buddhism*.

Parrinder, G. (1997) *Avatar and Incarnation*, Oxford: Oneworld.

Potter, K. (1972) *Presuppositions of India's Philosophies*, Westport, Conn., Greenwood Press.

Rahman, F. (1958) *Prophecy in Islam*, London: George Allen & Unwin, 41.

Sambhava, P. (1994) *The Tibetan Book of the Dead*, trans. R. Thurman, Aquarian/Thorsons: London.

Schweitzer, P. (1993) 'Mind/Consciousness Dualism in Sankhya-Yoga Philosophy', *Philosophy and Phenomenological Research*, LIII, 4, 845–59.

Sen, A. (1997) 'Indian Traditions and the Western Imagination', *Daedalus* 126, 2, 1–26.

Sen, K. (1973) *Hinduism*, Harmondsworth: Penguin.

Shankara (1972) *Brahmasutrabhasya*, trans. S. Gamhirananda, Calcutta: Advaita Ashrama.

Shin-Yong, C. (ed.) (1974) *Buddhist Culture in Korea*, Seoul: International Cultural Foundation.

Simmer-Brown, J. (1997) "Inviting the Demon": *Parabola, The Magazine of Myth and Tradition*, XXII, No. 2 Summer, 12, 16–17.

Stafford, Betty L. (1983) 'Nagarjuna's masterpiece – logical, mystical, both, or neither?', *Philosophy East and West*, 33, 123–38.

Streng, F. (1967) *Emptiness: A Study in Religious Meaning*, Nashville: Abingdon Press.

Suzuki, D. (1973) *Zen and Japanese Culture*, Princeton: Princeton University Press.

—— *Zen Buddhism*, ed. W. Barrett, NY, Doubleday, 1956.

Sze-Kwang, Lao (1989) 'On Understanding Chinese Philosophy: An Inquiry and a Proposal' in Allinson *op. cit.* 265–93.

Tai Chen (1990) *Tai Chen on Mencius: Explorations in Word and Meaning*, trans. Ann-ping Chin and M. Freeman, New Haven: Yale University Press.

Tsunoda, R. de Bary, W. T. and Keene, D. et al. (1964) *Sources of Japanese Tradition*, New York: Columbia University Press.

Tu Wei-Ming *Centrality and Commonality: An Essay on Confucian Religiousness*, Albany: State University of New York Press, 1988.

Vivekananda, S. (1959) *Bhakti-Yoga*, Advaita Ashrama: Calcutta.

—— (1960) *Karma-Yoga*, Advaita Ashrama: Calcutta.

—— (1961) *Jnana-Yoga*, Advaita Ashrama: Calcutta.

Yoshida Kenko (1967) *Tsurezure-gusa, Essays in Idleness*, trans. D. Keene, New York: Columbia University Press.

—— (1948) *A Short History of Chinese Philosophy*, New York: Free Press.

Yu-Lan, F. (1952; 1983) *A History of Chinese Philosophy*, trans. D. Bodde, Princeton: Princeton University Press.

Zaehner, R. (1958) *At Sundry Times: An Essay in the Comparison of Religions*, London: Faber.

—— (1955) *Zurvan: A Zoroastrian Dilemma* NY, Biblio & Tanven.

Zhuangzi (1968) *The Complete Works of Chang Tzu*, trans. B. Watson, New York: Columbia University Press, pp. 112–13.

GLOSSARY

This is a list of concepts and thinkers which appear in the texts themselves, or who are frequently authors, and which are not always explained there. On the whole where a technical expression is used just once and its meaning is explained in the extract it has not been listed here. Most foreign terms except names are italicized, with the exception of some which have become well-known in English such as zen and yoga.

In parentheses are details of the relevant language:

a = Arabic
c = Chinese
j = Japanese
p = Pali
s = Sanskrit
WG = Wade–Giles (Chinese)

Transliteration

Occasionally where the correct pronunciation is rather different from the transliterated version I have placed the former after the identity sign ("="). The point of transliteration is to enable readers to understand precisely how the term in English can be reconstructed in the original language, but this is not relevant to our purposes here in an introductory text. It is important that readers become familiar with the various kinds of transliteration, since they will find them all in the relevant books. I have in the Glossary reproduced the transliterated terms not explained in the texts themselves without the macrons and diacritical marks which are often used.

Chinese terms are transliterated in either the older Wade–Giles system (WG), or the modern pinyin system (c), and it is important that readers are relatively familiar with both, since both are used today.

Terms from Indian philosophy are represented in either Sanskrit (s) or Pali (p).

More detailed information about many of the terms in this glossary are to be found in my *Key Concepts in Eastern Philosophy*, London: Routledge, 1999.

Dates

These are often only approximate when far in the past, and are CE unless otherwise specified as BCE.

Abhidhamma (p), Abhidharma (s) higher teaching, a Buddhist school of thought

abhimukhi (s) the stage where the *boddhisattva* is almost in contact with the highest level of knowledge, i.e. face to face

Abu Hamid see al-Ghazali

acala (s) immovable

Advaita, Advaita Vedanta a school of Indian philosophy, whose main thinker is Shankara, which emphasizes the non-duality of reality

advaitin follower of Advaita Vedanta

ahamkara (s) phenomenal self

ahimsa, ahinsa (s) non-violence, non-injury

Ahriman source of evil in Zoroastrianism

Ajivika materialist philosophy committed to atomism and fatalism

akara (s) formless

akasa (s) = *akasha* empty space, ether

alambana-pratyaya (s) causal basis of human experience

alayavijnana (s) unconscious; source of consciousness

Amida (j) "boundless light" of the pure land of the Buddha

anabhidhya (s) absence of selfishness

anatman (s) *anatta* (p) absence of self

aneka (s) collection of atoms

anitya (s) *anicca* (p) impermanence

antahkarana (s) inner instrument i.e. mind

anumana (s) inference, syllogism

apoha (s) elimination

arahat (s) *arhat* (p) an enlightened Buddhist saint/perfected individual

arcismati(s) full of flames (of enlightenment)

arjava(s) sincerity

Arjuna one of the main characters in the *Bhagavad Gita,*

artha (s) meaning (language), material wealth, purpose

asadhya (s) incurable

asat (s) unreal

atma, atman (s) *atta* (p) self, essence

see *atman*

attha (p) meaning

Aurobindo 1870–1950 Advaita thinker

avatara (s) incarnation of the divine

avayavin (s) whole

Averroes 1126–98 latin name of ibn Rushd, Islamic philosopher

Avicenna 980–1037 latin name of ibn Sina, Persian philosopher and physician *avidya* (s) *avijja* (p)   ignorance

Ayurveda   Indian traditional medicine, 'health knowledge'

Badarayana   probably *c.* 1st or 2nd century, mentioned in *Brahmasutra*, possibly its author

Bhagavadgita = *Bhagavad Gita*   Part of the *Mahabharata*, 'Song of the Lord', key Hindu text

bhakta (s)   devotee of the Lord

bhakti (s)   worship, devotion

Bhartrhari/Bhartrihari   early 5th century Indian grammarian and philosopher

bodhi(s)   enlightenment, perfect wisdom

bodhi-paksikas (s)   the virtues leading to enlightenment

bodhicitta (s) = *bodhichitta*   the awakened or enlightened mind

bodhisatta (p) *bodhisattva* (s)   someone about to be enlightened, someone who leads others to enlightenment

boddhisattva-bhumi(s)   stages of *bodhisattva*

brahma (s)   Hindu God linked with creation

brahmacarin (s) = *brahmacharin*   religious disciple or student

brahman (s)   reality, what sustains the universe, ritual

brahmasahavyataya (s)   union with Brahma

Brahmasutra (s)   theological text dealing with nature of *brahman*

brahmin (s)   control over mind, caste role, reciter of Vedic hymns

Buddha   the highest level of enlightenment; the person who has achieved it; Siddhartha Gautama (s) Siddhatha Gotama (p)

Buddhaghosa   5th century commentator and compiler of Pali texts, part of the Theravada school

buddhi (s)   intellect, reason

bushido (j)   the way of the warrior

Carvaka (s) = Charvaka   a school of materialists, Charvaka being the legendary founder; see also Lokayata

catu-patisambhida (p)   types of logical analysis

Chan (c)   meditation, school of Buddhism in China which later went on to create zen in Japan

chan (c) *ch'an* (WG)   meditation

chen (WG) *zhen* (c)   activity

cheng (WG) *zheng* (c)   correct, proper

ch'i (WG) *qi* (c)   energy

ch'ien (WG) *tian* (c)   heaven

chih (WG) *zhi* (c)   straightforwardness, knowledge, intelligence

chitta (s)   mind

Chou, see Zhou

Chou I, see *Zhouyi*

Chuang Tzu, see Zhuangzi

chueh (WG) *jue* (c)   enlightening

chun-tzu (WG) *junzi* (c)   gentleman

chung(WG) *zhong* (c)   the mean, middle, loyalty, centrality
cin-matram (s)   pure intelligence
citta (s) = *chitta*   mind
Confucius   latinized version of Master Kong 551–479 BCE

daiva (s)   God
dao (c) *tao* (WG)   the way
Dao dejing (c)   main Daoist text, the "Classic of the Way and its Virtue"
    350–250 BCE
Daoism   philosophy based on the *Dao dejing*
darsana (s) = *darshana*   school (of thought); perception, vision
daya (s)   selfless right action
de (c)   virtue
dhamma (p) see *dharma*
dharana (s)   concentrating the mind, stabilization
dharma (s) *dhamma* (p)   aspects of life, factors of existence, teaching
Dharmakirti   7th century Buddhist thinker
dharma-megha (s)   clouds of *dharma*, last state of progress to become a perfect
    Buddha
dharmata (s)   the truth
dhyana (s)   meditation
Dignaga, Dinnaga   6th century Indian Buddhist thinker
do (j)   the way
dosa (s) = *dosha*   defect, malice
dravya (s)   substance
drsti (s)   views, vision
dukkha (p) *duhkha* (s)   suffering
durangama (s)   gone far away i.e. where the *boddhisattva* acquires knowledge
    of what will lead to *bodhichitta*
Dvaita (s)   duality, main philosophical thinker is Madhva
Dzong-ka-ba   Tibetan Madhyamaka philosopher 1357–1419

eka (s)   whole

fa (c)   law
al-Farabi   *c.* 870–950 Islamic thinker

Gaudapada   *c.* 5/6th century Sankhya thinker; early exponent of Advaita
Gautama, see Buddha
Ge-luk   Tibetan school, generally aligned with the Madhyamaka
al-Ghazali   Abu Hamid al-Ghazali, Persian philosopher 1058–1111
Gita see *Bhagavad Gita*
Gongsun Long   *c.* 325–260 Chinese logician
guna (s) *gunas*   qualities of basic matter
Guo Xiang (c) Kuo Hsiang (WG)   Chinese thinker d. *c.* 312
guru (s)   teacher

Han Fei Tzu, Han Fei Zi legalist thinker d. 233 BCE
Han Fei Tzu, Han Fei Zi legalist text
hetu (s) reason
himsa (s) violence, harm, injury
Hinayana lesser vehicle, reference by Mahayana tradition to the Theravada
Hsiang-Kuo, see Guo Xiang
hsieh (WG) *xie* (c) knights
hsin (WG) *xin* (c) confidence
hsueh (WG) *xue* (c) learning
Hsun-Tzu (WG) Xunzi (c) *c.* 325–238 BCE Confucian thinker
Hua Yan, Hua-yen Flower Garland form of Buddhism

i (WG) *yi* (c) change
I Ching, Yijing 'Book of Changes'
ibn Abbas figure in the *hadith* literature, i.e. in the traditional accounts of the
    sayings of the Prophet and his Companions
ibn al-`Arabi 1165–1240 Islamic mystical philosopher
ibn Rushd, see Averroes
ibn Sina, see Avicenna
Iqbal, Muhammad Iqbal 1877–1938 Indian Islamic thinker
`*irfan* (a) mystical knowledge
isvara (s) = *ishvara* the Lord
ittihad (a) unification (with God)

Jainism Indian philosophy, linked with Ajıvika
jen (WG) *ren* (c) humanity, human being
jiu (c) time
jiva(s) soul
jivanmukta (s) living enlightened being
jivanmukti (s) the state of being enlightened while alive
jnana (s) knowledge
jnana-yoga (s) the route to salvation through knowledge
jue (c) *chueh* (WG) enlightening
junzi (c) *chun-tzu* (WG) gentleman

kalpana (s) imaginative construction
kamma (p) *karma* (s) action
k'an (WG) *kan* (c) pit
Kapila *c.* 100 BCE–200 CE, legendary founder of the Sankhya school
Karikas, see *Madhyamakakarikas*
karma (s) action
karma yoga (s) the route to salvation through action
karuna (s) compassion
ken (c) to stop
klesa (s) = *klesha* fruits of action
koan (j) riddle, paradox

Kongzi, see Confucius

Krsna = Krishna, *avatara* of Vishnu, popular deity

ksatriya (s) = *kshatriya* warrior caste

Kukai 774–835 Japanese Shingon Buddhist philosopher

Kumarila early Mimamsa thinker *c.* 8th century

k'un (WG) kun (c) earth

K'ung see Confucius

Kung Sun Lung, see Gongsun Long

Kuo Hsiang, see Guo Xiang

Laozi (abo Lao Dan, Lao Tan, Lao Tzu) *c.* 580–480 BCE "Old Master", the legendary founder of Daoism

Legalism social philosophy based on law

li (c) rules of propriety, ritual

li (c) principle

lila (s) play, recreation

Lokayata materialist Indian philosophy

lokayatika (s) materialist

Lotus sutra Mahayana sutra emphasizing the view that there is only one route to becoming perfectly enlightened

Madhva 13th century Indian Dvaita Vedanta philosopher

Madhyamaka/Madhyamika Middle Way, Buddhist school whose main thinker is Nagarjuna

Madhyamakakarikas 'Verses on the Middle' by Nagarjuna

Madhyamaka-sastra = Madhyamaka-shastra 'Textbook about the Madhyamaka'

Mahabharata epic poem and Hindu text *c.* 500–100 BCE

mahakaruna(s) the greatest compassion

maha-sukha supreme bliss

Mahayana (s) Great Way, offering a route to enlightenment for everyone

manas (s) mind

mantra (s) 'hymn' or 'spell', used in some forms of Buddhism to help visualization, and in various tantric practices

Mao Zedong, Mao Tse Tung 1893–1976 Chinese political leader and thinker

Master Kong, see Confucius

maya(s) illusion

Mencius, Mengzi Chinese philosopher 371–289 BCE

see Mencius

Milarepa 1040–1123 Tibetan Buddhist thinker

Milinda Bactrian Greek king who had a famous conversation with the monk Nagasena, mainly on the topic of Buddhist understandings of the notion of the self

Mimamsa (s) philosophical school based on exegesis of the Vedas, outlining the principles of dharma or correct action

Mimamsaka follower of Mimamsa school

ming (c)   fate, destiny

ming-chiao (WG) *ming jiao* (c)   institutions

Mohism   established by Mozi, philosophy based on the notion of general benevolence

Mojing (c)   the Mohist canons

moksa (s) = *moksha*   liberation, salvation

moksha, see *moksa*

Motoori, Motoori Noringa   1730–1801 Japanese Shinto philosopher

Mozi (Motse, Mo Tzu)   5th century BCE Chinese philosopher, founder of Mohism

Muhyi al-Din ibn al-`Arabi, see ibn al-`Arabi

mukti (s)   release

Nagarjuna   2nd Century Buddhist thinker, see *Madhyamaka*

Nagasena   see Milinda

Naiyayikas   follower of Nyaya school

nembutsu (j)   calling on the Amida Buddha

nibbana (p) *nirvana* (s)   ultimate liberation

Nichiren   1222–82 Japanese Buddhist thinker

nirantara (s)   gap between atoms

nirguna (s)   unqualified i.e. indescribable

nirutti (p)   grammar, definitions

nirvana (s) *nibbana* (p)   ultimate liberation

nishta (s)   attachment

Nyaya   largely realist and logical philosophical system, often linked with the Vaisheshika approach

Nyaya-Vaisesika = Nyaya-Vaisheshika, see Nyaya

Ohrmazd   Ahura Mazda, the "Wise Lord" of Zoroastrian philosophy

pancasila (s)   charity, morality, patience, humanity, meditation

paramartha (s)   ultimate reality

paramita (s)   perfections

paramanu (s)   atom

parapeksa (s) = *parapeksha*   mutual dependence

Patanjali   *c.* 200 BCE 400 CE legendary Indian founder of the Yoga school

patibhana (p)   analysis of knowing

paticcasamuppada (p)   causation, dependent co-origination

paudgalika (s)   material

phala (s)   fruits (of action), results

prabhakari (s)   that which illuminates

prajna (s)   knowledge

prakriti, prakrti (s)   basic matter

Prajnaparamita (s)   "Perfection of Wisdom", a Mahayana Buddhist collection of texts

pramana (s)   knowledge

pramudita (s) stage to delight

prapanca (s) material extension

Prasastapada = Prashastapada early 6th Century Vaisheshika thinker

pratitya-samutpada (s) dependent origination

pratyaksha (s) perception

pudgala (s) matter in Jainism, the individual self in Hinduism and Buddhism

Pure Land School of Buddhism according to which there is a pure land where salvation lies and which may be gained by reciting the Buddha's name

purusa (s) = purusha spirit, thought, person

Purva-Mimamsa school of Vedic analysis, based on analysis of *dharma*

qi (c) *ch'i* (WG) energy

rajas (s) energy, passion

Ramanuja 1017–1137 Indian founder of the Vishistadvaita school

Ramayana 'Story of Rama', Hindu text exploring a variety of key philosophical and theological concepts such as *dharma*, loyalty, trust etc.

ren (c) *jen* (WG) humanity

Rgveda = Rig Veda the earliest of the Vedas

rupaslesa (s) = *rupashlesha* combination of atoms leading to appearance of colour

sabda (s) testimony

sadasadvilaksana (s) neither real nor unreal

sadhana (s) reaching perfection

sadhumati (s) good will

saguna (s) qualified

saguna brahman (s) qualified notion of the absolute, equivalent to the idea of a personal deity

Sa-gya Tibetan school of philosophy, emphasizing in particular logic and epistemology

sakara (s) formed

samadhi (s) bliss, trance

Samkara see Sankara

Samkhya-Yoga = Sankhya-Yoga

samsara (s) transmigration

sangha (s) the community, religious order in Buddhism

Sankara = Shankara 788–820 Advaita Vedanta thinker

sannyasin (s) someone who renounces the material world

santara (s) space (between atoms)

Sarvastivada/Sarvastivadin the Buddhist school based on the thesis that 'all exists'

sat (s) real, being, existent

satori (j) enlightenment, awakening

satta (s) being, existence

sattva (s)   transparency/a being

satya (s)   truthfulness

Sautrantika   'follower of the sutras', someone who opposes the Sarvastivadin Abhidharma

shi (c) *shih* (WG)   power

Shingon   Japanese Buddhist philosophy based on the *mantra*

shu (c)   methods of government, empathy, mutuality

Siddhartha, see Buddha

skandha (s)   groups, molecules, aggregates

smrti (s)   mindfulness/sacred texts

subitism   sudden enlightenment

sudra (s) = *shudra*   agriculture, tending of cattle and trade caste, servants

sudurjaya (s)   stage where the *bodhisattva* is almost invincible

sufi (a)   mystical school in Islam

sukha (s)   bliss

sun (c)   bending

sunyata (s) = *shunyata*   emptiness

sutra (s)   a report of the Buddha's words, discourse, literally 'thread'

svadharma (s)   intrinsic nature, duty linked to caste

tamas (s)   inertia, darkness, non-being

tantra (s), tantric   a procedure designed to lead to enlightenment along an esoteric route

tao, (WG) *dao* (c)   the way

Tao te ching (WG), see *Dao dejing*

tapas (s)   austerity

tathagata, tathagatha (s)   enlightened being, 'thus gone'

tathata (s)   thusness

tathyam (s)   actual, truth

tattva (s)   reality

te (WG) *de* (c)   virtue

Tendai (j)   see Tian Tai

Theravada   A Buddhist school, literally 'teaching of the elders'

tian (c) *ch'ien*, (WG)   heaven

Tian Tai (c) Tendai (j) T'ien-t'ai   "Heavenly Platform' school of Buddhism, which places particular emphasis on the *Lotus Sutra*

trikalabadhya (s)   unsublated through the three times (past, present and future)

triratna (s)   the Three Jewels

trsna (c) = *trishna* (s)   desire, craving

tui (c)   pleasure

tyaga (s)   giving up of all duties

tzu jan (WG) *ziran* (c)   nature or naturalness

Upanisads = *Upanishads* (s)   literally 'sitting near', Indian religious texts

upadana (s)   acquisition of *karma*

upamana (s)   analogy

upaya (s)   means
upayakausalya, (s)   skill in means
Udayana   11th century Nyaya thinker

Vaibhasika = Vaibhashika   exponents of the *vibhasa* (Abhidharma commentary)
Vaisesika = Vaisheshika   atomistic approach to the analysis of how to act and the nature of the world
Vaishnava   Hindu order devoted to Krishna, and to other linked deities.
vaisya (s) = *vaishya*   the merchant caste, commoners
varna (s)   caste, class
Vasabandhu, Vasubandhu   *c.* 5th Century Buddhist thinker
Vedanta, Vedanta sutra   end of the Vedas, a variety of theoretical approaches to how to interpret the Veda
Veda (s)   the earliest Indian religious literature
vikalpa (s)   imagination, concept, doubt
vimala (s)   stage free of defilement
viparyaya (s)   making mistakes
Visistadvaita = Vishishtadvaita Vedanta   qualified non-dualism, i.e. the individual selves are parts of *brahman* but not identical with it; main thinker is Ramanuja
Vishnu   God
Vivekananda   Vedanta thinker 1863–1902
vyadha (c)   a very low class, i.e. hunters and butchers, according to Hinduism

wu (c)   non-being
wu-ming (c)   unnamable
wu-wei (c)   non-action

xie (c) *hsieh* (WG)   knights
xin (c) *hsin* (WG)   confidence
xing (c)   integrity, practice
xue (c) *hsueh* (WG)   learning
Xunzi (c) Hsun-Tzu (WG) *c.* 325–238 BCE   Confucian thinker

Yan Hui, Yen Hin   A favourite disciple of Confucius, often referred to in the *Analects*
yang (c)   bright side of the hill, active
yi (c)   change
yi (c)   rightness
yin (c)   dark side of the hill, passive
Yijing (c) *I Ching*   Book of Changes
yoga (s)   philosophical system linked with Samkhya dualism; organization of mind and body to attain enlightenment, literally 'yoking'
Yogacara (s) = Yogachara   the practice of yoga and the theory based on it; a Buddhist theory according to which only the mind exists

Yogasutra   early text of the Yoga school
yogi   someone who attains spiritual growth as a result of engaging in *yoga*
yogin (s)   a follower of yoga

Yong-woon, Han   1879–1944 (Manhae) Korean thinker
you (c) *yu* (WG)   being
you ming (c) *yu-ming* (WG)   namable

zen (j)   meditation, school of Chan Buddhism in Japan
zhen (c) *chen* (WG)   activity
zheng (c) *cheng* (WG)   correct, proper
zhi (c) *chih* (WG)   straightforwardness, knowledge, intelligence
zhong (c) *chung* (WG) the mean, middle, loyalty, centrality
Zhou, Chou   11th Century BCE Chinese dynasty, often praised by Confucius
    in the 'Analects'
Zhouyi, Chou I   'Changes of the Zhou,' i.e. 'Book of Changes'
Zhuangzi (c) Chuang Tzu (WG)   369–286 BCE Daoist thinker
Zhuangzi   Daoist text, named after its author
ziran (c) *tzu jan* (WG)   nature or naturalness
Zoroastrianism   Persian religion based on the teaching of Zarathushtra

GUIDE TO FURTHER READING

The references to the texts themselves give useful details of further reading.

Much more detailed bibliographical information about this whole area of philosophy can be found in my *Key Concepts in Eastern Philosophy*, London: Routledge, 1999 and also in Leaman, O. (forthcoming) (ed.) *Encyclopedia of Asian Philosophy* London: Routledge. This has references to each of the key concepts themselves, and general references to the whole area.

It is worth mentioning here as containing excellent reference material the following:

Carr, D. and Mahalingam, I. (eds) (1997) *Companion Encyclopedia of Asian Philosophy* London: Routledge. A collection of essays on specific areas of Asian philosophy with useful references.

The following collection of volumes has a very strong representation of philosophy from the Eastern traditions, in marked contrast to many of the other works of reference in philosophy which have recently been published and which only have token detail on this area.

Craig, E. (ed.) (1998) *Encyclopedia of Philosophy* London: Routledge.
Nasr, S. and Leaman, O. (eds) (1996) *History of Islamic Philosophy* London: Routledge. A comprehensive discussion of the area with detailed biblio-graphical material.

Two books which deal with philosophy in general with a particularly skilful orientation towards Eastern philosophy are:

Cooper, D. (1996) *World Philosophies: An Historical Introduction* Oxford: Blackwell

and

Smart, N. (1998) *World Philosophies* London: Routledge. The latter has an excellent bibliography